Contemporary
Irish Poetry
and the Pastoral
Tradition

CONTEMPORARY
Irish Poetry
AND THE PASTORAL
TRADITION

Donna L. Potts

University of Missouri Press   Columbia and London

Copyright © 2011 by
The Curators of the University of Missouri
University of Missouri Press, Columbia, Missouri 65201
Printed and bound in the United States of America
All rights reserved

5 4 3 2 1   15 14 13 12 11

Cataloging-in-Publication data available from the Library of Congress.
ISBN 978-0-8262-1943-5

∞™ This paper meets the requirements of the
American National Standard for Permanence of Paper
for Printed Library Materials, Z39.48, 1984.

Designer: Kristie Lee
Typesetter: K. Lee Design & Graphics
Printer and binder: Integrated Book Technology, Inc.
Typefaces: Galliard

For Helen L. Potts
and in memory of Ronald F. Potts

CONTENTS

PREFACE

Anthony Bradley's "Pastoral in Modern Irish Poetry" and Sidney Burris's *The Poetry of Resistance: Seamus Heaney and the Pastoral Tradition* (1990) inspired me to reconsider the relationship of Heaney and, eventually, other contemporary Irish poets to the pastoral tradition. Bradley divides Irish poets into two groups: those of the Irish literary revival who lacked direct experience of the land, much less an understanding of the people who worked on it; and those post-revivalists such as Patrick Kavanagh, whose firsthand experience of the land made them resist idealizing either the land or those who labored on it.[1] Having loved and respected Virgil's *Georgics* and the poetic tradition that grew out of it, with its emphasis on the land as the site of labor rather than of leisure, and having been raised in southwest Missouri, where my family farmed a couple of acres, I had an affinity for the georgic, or "anti-pastoral" tradition of the post-revivalists. Although I studied Yeats in college, Seamus Heaney, with his rural County Derry upbringing and his subsequently less romanticized view of country life, was the first Irish poet who really spoke to me. As I began to consider how contemporary Irish poets employed the pastoral tradition in their own work, Bradley's and Burris's postcolonial approach formed the basis for my own. Yet I could not ignore a number of other forces that have obviously contributed to and shaped contemporary Irish poets' particular versions of pastoral. Pastoral poetry since Kavanagh has served not only as postcolonial critique of British imperialism but also as a response to industrialization, modernity, the commodification of landscape, and gendered representations of Ireland and their political and social repercussions. In the latter half of the twentieth century, Irish cultural nationalism was reformulated and to some extent transformed by the environmental movement.

As Glen Love explains in *"Et in Arcadia Ego*: Pastoral Meets Ecocriticism,"
our growing awareness of profound threats to the environment has thrown
the study of pastoral open to new interpretation.[2] Terry Gifford's *Pastoral*
draws on Leo Marx's distinction between sentimental and complex pastoral
to differentiate between pastoral in which retreat is an end in itself, and pastoral in which retreat is a means to an end—one that leaves the reader "changed
and charged upon return for more informed action in the present."[3] He uses
the term "post-pastoral" to describe works in which the retreat serves to
prompt the reader to the urgent need for responsibility and action on behalf
of the environment. "Post-pastoral" moves from the anthropocentric viewpoint of pastoral, conveying "a deep sense of the immanence in all natural
things" and recognizing that our "inner human natures can be understood in
relation to external nature."[4]

Although there have been many examinations of the pastoral tradition in
contemporary American poetry, when I first began my research, I could find
no similarly extensive studies in Irish poetry. Since then, Oona Frawley's *Irish
Pastoral: Nostalgia and Twentieth-Century Irish Literature* (2005) has been
published, and while it provides an invaluable overview of representations of
nature—from early Irish poetry to the anticolonial pastoral of Yeats and the
anti-pastoral of Kavanagh—essential for a more complete understanding of
the influences on contemporary Irish poets, the only contemporary poets it
examines are Boland and Heaney. Frawley's study, by providing a framework
for my own, permitted me to devote more time to contemporary poets, as
well as explore more freely the range of uses of pastoral than I could have
otherwise.

I am grateful to the American Conference for Irish Studies, the International Association for the Study of Irish Literature, and the Association for
the Study of Literature and the Environment for providing venues as well
as inspiration and ideas for my research in its early stages. Its members provided helpful insights, opportunities to present conference papers and receive
feedback on them, as well as the means by which to meet many of the poets
in the study. At both the 1994 ACIS and the 1998 Irish Women Writers'
Conference in Dublin, I had the opportunity to hear Nuala Ní Dhomhnaill
read from her work. My thanks as well to ASLE member Richard Kerridge
and ACIS members Jody Allen-Randolph, Andrew Auge, Christine Cusick,
Joan Dean, David Gardiner, Kathryn Kirkpatrick, Jack Morgan, Jim Rogers,
Mary Ann Ryan, and Eamonn Wall for their support, advice, and, in some
cases, their research on the Irish poets in this study. At the National University of Ireland, where I spent a Fulbright year and later a sabbatical, Kevin
Barry, Nicholas Canny, Hubert McDermott, and Riana O'Dwyer were very
gracious in providing me office space and facilitating my research in whatever way they could. In my own department at Kansas State University, Lee

Behlman, Linda Brigham, Tim Dayton, Elizabeth Dodd, Michael Donnelly, Erica Hateley, George Keiser, Marcella Reekie, Larry Rodgers, Kim Smith, and Naomi Wood all took the time to answer my questions, provide insights, and/or read various sections of my book and offer useful ideas. Margaret Burton, Kyle Semmel, Kristine Kimmi, and Kimberly Carlson served as research assistants at various stages, and Burton's reading of Heaney's elegy influenced my own approach. Thanks to Mary Siegle, our department secretary, whose good cheer, helpfulness, and commitment to and interest in the research of faculty members was a constant inspiration. As I considered ways in which the poetry in this study constituted "post-pastoral," students in my spring 2009 class "Contemporary Irish Poetry and Environmentalism" asked thoughtful questions and made helpful observations that greatly contributed to my revision of the manuscript. KSU's USRG and FDA awards also permitted me to conduct more extensive research and interviews in Ireland as well as in the United States. Sean Fox, an Irishman in agricultural economics at Kansas State University, and Colin McCallum, a Scot living in Ballygawley, answered my specific questions about the landscape that inspired the poets. My thanks to Seamus Heaney, Michael Longley, Medbh McGuckian, and John Montague for their willingness to answer my questions about their work, whether by email or in person.

Early versions of parts of these chapters have appeared in the journals *Notes on Irish Literature*, *New Hibernia Review*, and *An Sionnach*, as well as in *Out of the Earth: Ecocritical Readings of Irish Texts*.[5] I'm thankful to editors like Jim Rogers, Thomas Dillon Redshaw, David Gardiner, and Cristine Cusick for their support and suggestions, as well as their commitment to helping my ideas find their way into print. I'm grateful to Dan Hornsby for his support and enthusiasm near the bitter end; he sweetened it considerably. Finally, I'm thankful to my family, Richard, Cecilia, Isabella, and especially Chuck, for believing in me and helping me find the time and motivation to complete my work.

CONTEMPORARY
Irish Poetry
AND THE PASTORAL
TRADITION

INTRODUCTION

The source of pastoral poetry can be traced to the *boukolika* ("ox-herding poems") of the mid-third-century BC poet Theocritus of Syracuse. For Theocritus, "bucolic" poetry involved the exchange of song, often in a song contest, between herders, whether of oxen, sheep, cows, or goats. Writing in response to increasing urbanization of life and the consequent longing for the simplicity of rural life, Theocritus depicted the Sicily of his carefree childhood from the perspective of the overwrought civilization of the Alexandria of Ptolemy II Philadelphus.[1]

Anthony Verity, translator of Theocritus's *Idylls* (2002), emphasizes that Theocritus's privileging of the countryside was itself derived from earlier sources: Epicureanism and Cynicism both promoted the simple life, and Plato's *Phaedrus* establishes the countryside as the site of particular aesthetic pleasures as well as of performances about love.[2] *Works and Days*, attributed to Hesiod, is also a likely predecessor, with its celebration of rural labor and the abundance of nature—from trees flowing with honey to pastures resonant with bleating flocks.

Verity contends that "the world of the bucolic poems is . . . the world which epic forgot." Whereas epic poetry is concerned with the lives of people of high social station, devoting attention to warriors' shields and weapons, pastoral poetry concerns itself with the lives of lowly herders, lavishing attention instead on the simple objects of everyday life such as wooden cups, pipes, or spinning wheels.[3] Pastoral, thus established as a form of discourse that provided the opportunity for writing about the unheroic and the everyday, also became a common outlet for poetic discourse. Humphrey Tonkin observes that Theocritus's decision to use pastoral to talk about poetry is of the utmost importance because it suggests a new way of viewing the pastoral tradition as a means of articulating a metaphor for poetic experience.[4]

1

Theocritus's great successor, Virgil, also adopted the term *bukolika* for his poems, and is generally considered more influential than Theocritus on the western tradition of pastoral poetry. Unlike any Roman poet before him, Virgil chose to imitate Theocritus, perhaps because he saw bucolic poetry as a means for coming to terms both with war and with a major cultural crisis —that of Alexandrianism. Paul Alpers' study of pastoral, *What Is Pastoral?*, observes that Virgil's *Eclogues* concern a countryside "riven by the impact of civil war."[5] Whereas Alexandrianism diminished ancient myth and heroic narration to sophisticated bookishness, Virgil's great achievement was to restore the seriousness of Greek myth to literature: "Whereas for Greek writers, gods and heroes were real and their names indicated aspects of reality, a Roman writer inevitably viewed them from a cultural and temporal distance, as signs of a noble literary tradition."[6]

After Theocritus and Virgil, bucolic poetry gradually became pastoral poetry by emphasizing certain aspects of this tradition: the relation between nature and human nature, and between the present and the mythicized past; the motif of transformation; the "pathetic fallacy"; and a rural inhabitant, who served for later poets as a substitute for the herdsman of classical pastoral.[7] Whereas pastoral has continually evolved to accommodate major cultural changes, certain common characteristics that can be traced to Virgil and Theocritus make it worthy of consideration as a distinct genre or mode. Pastoral poetry seeks to depict the human relation to the natural world, emphasizing the harmony between nature and human nature, the contrast between city and country, and the underlying tension between civilization and nature.[8] The pastoral poet selects details from rural life, enhancing and reordering them "to create a world of the imagination, invested with urban longing for an ideally simple life in nature." All pastoral implies an "awareness of two opposed worlds: country and city, simple and complex, imaginary and real."[9]

The Christianization of Europe gradually resulted in the supplanting of classical motifs with Christian. Whereas throughout the Middle Ages pastoral poetry was written primarily in Latin, the Renaissance witnessed its flowering in English. Works such as Spenser's *Shepheards Calender* (1579), Sidney's *Arcadia* (1590), Milton's "Lycidas" (1638), and Marvell's "The Garden" (1681), while perhaps the most notable and influential successors of classical pastoral, supplant many classical motifs with Christian images, resurrecting the genre as Christian pastoral by integrating the pastoral imagery of the Bible: "the Garden of Eden as a pastoral paradise; Christ as the Lamb of God, as the Good Shepherd; the humble shepherds who are the first to hear of Christ's birth; pastors, the bishop's crosier."[10] The garden, associated with Eden, and thereby with humanity's prelapsarian state, becomes an increasingly common setting for pastoral; the classical tension between rural and urban acquires a new dimension for Renaissance pastoral writers and their successors. Whereas the garden symbolizes humanity in its innocent state, movement away from the garden to the city is associated with humanity's fall from grace: "The movement from the garden to the city implicit in Christian mythology is a direct result of the Fall."[11]

Pastoral's major forms, established with Theocritus and Virgil, remained viable as well, although they too continued to evolve. From the idyll, which was originally used to describe the poems of Theocritus (from the Greek *eiyllion*, meaning "image" or "picture"), originated a whole body of short lyric poetry that idealizes nature. The elegy, a lament for the dead, a tradition that emerged from the lament for the dead herdsman Daphnis in Theocritus's first idyll, emerged as a distinct form—from Milton's "Lycidas," a personal elegy for his Cambridge friend, to Goldsmith's "The Deserted Village," a public elegy commemorating the loss of an entire people and way of life. Finally, the georgic, established as a form by Virgil's *Georgics* (Greek root, *geórgos*, meaning "farmer") provided a didactic version of pastoral in which the intention is to idealize country life but as a life of industry, not idleness, and to impart practical knowledge about agriculture.

Despite the continued appeal of all three forms, some scholars have nonetheless continued to pronounce pastoral dead, even tracing its death to as early as the eighteenth century, when Gay's mock pastoral suggested that authentic pastoral was no longer a viable form.[12] Yet pastoral poetry, albeit in altered form, continued to thrive and continued to have the potential to provide not an escape from reality but a means of confronting its complexities, in the same way it had for Theocritus and Virgil.

The pastoral tradition has long had a unique place in Ireland. As Nicholas Grene explains, "Ireland in its otherness on the edge of Europe, in its greenness and difference, has provided for the modern western world an equivalent of the ancient world's rural Arcadia."[13] Pastoral constructions of Ireland provided the means for justifying its colonization but also a critique by the Irish themselves not only of British colonialism but also its inevitable companions: modernization and industrialization. Luke Gibbons observes in his study of *The Quiet Man* that modernization—"in the form of the Enclosure Acts, market relations and agricultural improvement"—is generally considered to be the impetus for a figurative retreat to an idealized, prelapsarian world.[14] Oliver Goldsmith, born in Ireland in 1730 and leaving in 1752 to spend most of his remaining years in London, may be regarded as the first Irish poet writing in English to use pastoral as a critique of these forces (poetry in Irish deserves, and will receive, separate treatment). Anabel Patterson maintains that "the central argument of Goldsmith's *The Deserted Village* is that enclosures, by depriving the village communities of England of their widespread agricultural base, deprived their inhabitants of the decent and not too arduous work on which their welfare (and, ultimately, their right to evening and holiday leisure) depended."[15] Barrell observes that "at the centre of 'The Deserted Village' is a protest against the commodification of the rural landscape and of the human relations enacted within it." British readers, while admiring the poem's celebration of rural life, have resisted the sociological critique it simultaneously proffers, preferring to believe that Goldsmith exaggerated the effects of enclosures, clearances, and even famine-induced emigration. The poem's combination of protest and nostalgia is, for Raymond Williams, its strangest feature, but Barrell, so ready to argue for pastoral's death in England, is equally quick to dispel Williams' mystification: "In Ireland, where poets held open utopian potentials which formed constellations with blessed moments from a happier past, there would have been nothing 'strange' about it at all."[16]

Declan Kiberd, Terry Gifford, and others have likewise maintained that Goldsmith, despite his long sojourn in England, is more rewardingly read as an Irish poet describing an Irish village—specifically Lissoy, where Goldsmith was born and raised. The fact that the remainder of his life was spent in London —hardly likely to inspire any poetry set in villages—lends credence to the supposition. John Montague accepted this theory to some degree, even using an opportunity to publish in the *Dolmen Miscellany* a substantial portion of his graduate work on Oliver Goldsmith—"The Sentimental Prophecy: A Study of the Deserted Village."[17] David Gardiner observes that Montague's Goldsmith essay addresses "an author very much like Montague himself in the early sixties—an Irish writer working to be accepted in London literary society, a critic consciously reworking literary history, a poet concerned with the degradation of the countryside, and an author who, according to Montague's conclusion, 'rehearses one of the most Irish themes of all, a forecast of the downfall of Britain though imperial greed.'" Montague adds, "He [Goldsmith] produced the first anti-imperialistic poem in the period of England's greatest imperial expansion."[18] Kiberd observes that just as Virgil's *Eclogues* describes how the government rewarded triumphant soldiers with land seized from farmers, "even as a peripheral setting like Lissoy is ruined by the commercial values of the metropolis, so the metropolis itself is distorted and corrupted by the colonial mission."[19]

In Wordsworth's "Michael," the titular protagonist is a shepherd who loses his son to the dissolute city and ostensible conveniences therein. Paul Alpers describes Wordsworth's "The Ruined Cottage" as a profound rewriting of the representative situation of Virgil's poem—the contrast between the shepherd who is at home in a known world and his exiled companion.[20] Anabel Patterson's *Pastoral and Ideology* observes that Wordsworth gleaned from the *Georgics*, and perhaps also from Milton's *L'Allegro* and *Il Penseroso*, "the presence in this rustic idyll of the philosophic outsider, who distinguishes his own fully meditated happiness from the unself-conscious pleasures of the rustics."[21]

Later, John Clare was to write a version of pastoral in response to his own experience with enclosure, a process by which lands previously held in common, fostering a sense of community, were consolidated to increase their profitability at the expense of small farmers and, indeed, the ancient local customs they observed.[22] The enclosure of his parish, Helpston, destroyed the place he had known from birth, thus abolishing "the whole of his knowledge," replacing it with "a regularizing landscape of straight roads and square fields."[23] Having studied James Thomson's pastoral poem "Seasons," he went on to write his own pastoral poems, including a "Shepherd's Calendar" patterned off Spenser's calendar. In the mid-1820s, his poems recalling the landscape prior to enclosure echo classical pastoral's description of the landscape of the Golden Age as well as Christian pastoral's description of a prelapsarian Eden, emphasizing the essential freedom and innocence of the inhabitants of the pastoral landscape:

> Unbounded freedom ruled the wandering scene
> Nor fence of ownership crept in between
> To hide the prospect of the following eye
> Its only bondage was the circling sky
> Cows went and came with evening morn and night
> To the wild pasture as their common right.[24]

Clare's focus on the nonhuman aspects of the landscape led Jonathan Bate, in a recent biography of Clare, to pronounce him the forefather of environmental poetry, the first "green" poet. Indeed, Charles Martindale's observation in "Green Politics: The Eclogues"[25] that the green movement itself may be viewed as the most recent manifestation of pastoral is confirmed in the pastoral scholarship of Lawrence Buell, Greg Garrard, Terry Gifford, Glen Love, and others.

Arguably, pastoral became a more viable form than ever as the tension between nature and civilization upon which pastoral conventionally depended was given yet another source to draw from: the Industrial Revolution redefined the landscape as well as the human relationship to it, prompting new versions of pastoral from romantic poets and ultimately demanding an assessment of the place of technology in the landscape. Leo Marx's *The Machine in the Garden* examines how the pastoral retreat may be understood

> as movement away from an "artificial" world, a world identified with "art," using this word in its broadest sense to mean the disciplined habits of mind or arts developed by organized communities. . . . This impulse gives rise to a symbolic motion away from centers of civilization toward their opposite, nature, away from sophistication toward simplicity, or, to introduce the cardinal metaphor of the literary mode, away from the city toward the country.[26]

Although Marx restricts his study to American pastoral of the nineteenth and twentieth centuries, the parallels with the postindustrial western pastoral tradition as a whole are obvious.

John Barrell, in *The Penguin Book of English Pastoral Verse*, maintains that certainly by the Victorian era, "nobody could . . . believe that agriculture was anything but a highly developed industry with an unpleasant history of violent change and deep depression."[27] However, it is important to recall that pastoral never aimed to present country life as it actually was but provided instead an imaginative recreation; in response to the industrialization of farming, pastoral merely reconceptualized its purpose and approach. Barrell's complete dismissal of its relevance to contemporary culture is thus equally suspect:

> The separation of life in the town and in the country that the Pastoral demands is now almost devoid of any meaning. It is difficult to pretend that the English countryside is now anything more than an extension of the town; that the industrial and technological processes of urban production differ at all significantly from those of the "Factory-Farm"; that the function of the modern farm-manager is essentially any different from that of his urban counterpart.[28]

Charles Martindale responds to this death knell for pastoral by suggesting that paradoxically, even it may be seen as "a piece of modern pastoral, even a version of Virgil's first Eclogue, a lament for a lost harmony projected onto a past which is timeless but haunted by a sense of temporality, and for an authentic nature free from the discontents and vulgarities of the life of the modern city."[29]

Although contemporary Irish poetry is, even for skeptics like Barrell and Bull, perhaps the best proof that pastoral poetry is still a viable form, relatively few scholars have approached Irish poetry in terms of its relationship to the pastoral tradition.[30] Terry Gifford has observed that Barrell and Bull's assumption that "now and in England, the Pastoral, occasional twitches notwithstanding, is a lifeless form" is symptomatic of a pervasive tendency to view the literary ground of the archipelago of Britain and Ireland "with a cautious circumspection," and to dismiss Gaelic poetry from consideration entirely.[31] The scholars who have written about Irish pastoral are acutely aware that the pastoral tradition evolved quite differently in Ireland than in England and on the continent, and it is thus misleading to read Irish pastoral entirely according to models developed either in England or Europe. Ireland's colonization by England resulted in a different relation to the land, to language, and to industrialization, which ultimately shaped its pastoral tradition.

In colonized countries, pastoral has had special resonance, as Oona Frawley observes in *Irish Pastoral: Nostalgia and Twentieth-Century Irish Literature*:

"pastorals written under the rule of a colonial government about nature and landscape are necessarily different, and contain . . . not only idealizations of culture lost under colonial rule, but also critiques of that rule itself. Colonial pastorals are quite literally about 'homesickness'; the nostalgia contained in them is very real indeed."[32] Whereas the earliest pastoral poetry in Irish draws on classical and Christian traditions, depicting a benevolent nature as the Normans made inroads into Ireland in the twelfth and thirteenth centuries, Irish pastoral grows nostalgic as it laments the loss of nature. Medieval texts such as *Buile Suibhne* and *Acallam na Senórach* as well as Irish Bardic poetry from 1200 to 1700 grow increasingly nostalgic for a pre-Christian, pre-conquest Ireland, and representations of nature become tinged with nostalgia.[33]

Because Ireland was England's oldest colony, Irish poets' representations of its landscape have been inextricably linked to the land's literal and cultural appropriation in the course of colonization. Gaelic poets decried the felling of the woods when what they truly lamented was the fall of a native aristocracy,[34] and a later generation of poets mourned Ireland's colonization by means of portraying a woman weeping for the loss of her four green fields. Whereas the British, from Cambrensis to Spenser to the *Punch* cartoons of the early twentieth century, had represented Ireland as an untamed wilderness in order to justify British control over it, Irish writers often depicted it as a green unspoiled landscape in order to assert the Irish claim to the land and to contrast themselves favorably to industrialized England.

Furthermore, whereas England was the most rapidly and radically urbanized European country, Ireland's industrialization occurred later than that of virtually any other European country. Although Great Britain's industrialization began in the eighteenth century, Ireland's southern counties were relatively unaffected by it until World War II, when the discontinuation of the supply of English coal prompted by Ireland's neutrality necessitated reliance on peat for fuel. Ireland's relatively late industrialization meant that until quite recently it was primarily a rural and, specifically, a pastoral economy, with 69 percent of its land permanent pasture—in part because landlords found grazing a much cheaper alternative than tillage.[35] In a country that had long been defined in terms of the distinction between Celt and Saxon, Ireland and England, rural and industrial, the pastoral vision remained a viable means of establishing a national identity apart from England and of addressing the consequences of English colonization.

In the early twentieth century, members of the Irish literary revival continued to rely on the pastoral tradition to protest modernization and imperialism. The longing of Cathleen ni Houlihan, the old woman in Yeats's and Gregory's play of the same name, for the return of her "four green fields" is part of a long tradition of coded language of critique of centuries of British imperialism in Ireland. In their desire to reject English values and forms, Irish

Revivalist writers also sought models in the writers of the American Renaissance, Henry David Thoreau and Ralph Waldo Emerson, whose emphasis on the need for firsthand experience of nature was likewise a plea for independence from British cultural authority.

The pastoral of the Irish literary revival is also marked by its idealization of the Irish peasant, and its uncritical celebration of Irish peasant life would become a source of consternation for writers like Beckett and Joyce.[36] Because the revival's primary members—Yeats, Lady Gregory, and Synge (Synge's family on his father's side were landed gentry)—came from Anglo-Irish families which had owned land for centuries, deriving income from it as well as from the Irish peasants who worked on it, their understanding of the landscape was necessarily limited. Anthony Bradley's "Pastoral in Modern Irish Poetry" observes that because Yeats, and indeed most writers associated with the Irish literary revival, "was born into a particular *class* of Irish society, into a particular cultural tradition,"[37] the lack of direct experience of the land and the people who worked on it led to romanticization of rural life.

Yeats and other revivalists imbued the Irish peasant with a spirituality that they contrasted favorably with what they regarded as the gross philistinism that characterized the urban culture of materialist Victorian Britain. Watson explains the broader implications of this romanticization in terms of reconceiving Ireland: "The Irish countryman could never fall victim to the utilitarian materialism which afflicted the unfortunate Englishman, because his racial memory, imagination, even his very landscape, were saturated with the ethos of an alternative and ancient world."[38] Yeats's "The Lake Isle of Inisfree," for example, employs the simplest structure of pastoral, contrasting the basic goodness of an idealized, rural lifestyle with the dehumanized context of life in the city, specifically in terms of a contrast between the colorful, fertile island retreat of western Ireland's Inisfree with gray, dehumanized London. Yeats's contrast, reminiscent of that of Horace's comparison of his farm with the city of Rome, or with Elizabethan pastoral poetry's contrast between "a country life of delightful ease with a court life of complexity and anxiety,"[39] is no less politically motivated.

Declan Kiberd makes a similar distinction in his reading of J. M. Synge. Of the *Aran Islands*, he writes, "There are basically two kinds of pastoral. The first is that in which a leisured aristocracy plays at being poor in a spurious attempt to wish real class difference away; and the second is the more radical sort, in which a real peasantry may be depicted as having qualities thought peculiar to aristocrats. The Aran Islands fascinates because it draws simultaneously on both traditions, for its upper-class author discovers among the poor values of a lost Gaelic aristocracy."[40] Of *The Playboy of the Western World*, he writes, "Like Patrick Kavanagh's *The Great Hunger* thirty-five years later, *The Playboy* was an uncompromising exercise in antipastoral, offered at a period when some nationalists in Dublin were concocting a highly conservative version of pastoral: the timeless Irish peasant noted for his stoicism and Christian piety."[41]

Bradley's fundamentally class-based distinction between versions of pastoral informs his reading of post-revivalist poets: whereas one type is associated with "Anglo-Irish outsiders, during the period of the Literary Revival," the other was written by "native Irish insiders, in the period from the end of the Revival to the present."[42] Contending that the shared experience of most poets since Yeats, like that of most Irish people, has been "rooted in Ireland's small farms, the social organization of the rural hinterland, its folkways, pastimes, work, education, and religious faith," Bradley maintains that their closer relation to the land, as well as their closer identification with the peasants who traditionally worked on it, results in a new version of pastoral. Their world is akin to the Hardy country that Raymond Williams describes as "a border country so many of us have been living in: between custom and education, between work and ideas, between love of place and awareness of change."[43]

For Bradley and other scholars, Patrick Kavanagh, "representative of the still-emerging class with roots in the countryside but also with connections to modern urban life," clearly employs the second type of pastoral. Raised on a farm in County Monaghan and spending much of his life as a farmer, Kavanagh eventually left to launch a career in poetry in Dublin, where he had to endure the condescension of urban poets writing in the shadow of Yeats. His growing impatience with Irish poetry's idealization of the landscape resulted in a parody of pastoralism by "one who has read not only the rural landscape but William Empson too."[44] Joe Cleary writes, "For decades, Ireland had liked to think itself a wholesome rural alternative to the spiritually desiccated modern urban wasteland, but by hibernicizing and ruralizing the idiom of *The Waste Land*, Kavanagh suggested this was an illusion."[45]

Kavanagh's depiction of the peasant is a striking departure from that of the revivalists; Kiberd writes that "although the literal idea of the peasant is of a farm-labouring person, in fact a peasant is all that mass of mankind which lives below a certain level of consciousness. They live in the dark cave of the unconscious and they scream when they see the light."[46] Kavanagh's best known poem, "The Great Hunger," concerns the life of one such representative peasant, Patrick Maguire, whose plight is described by Kiberd as "at once absurd and Christian, absurd because it reflects the unexamined Christianity of a rural Ireland whose mothers tell their sons, 'Now go to Mass and pray and confess your sins / And you'll have all the luck.'"

Despite Kavanagh's critique of idealized peasant life, he nonetheless employs many of the conventions of pastoral, leading Cleary to observe that Kavanagh ultimately substitutes a pastoral for a naturalist aesthetic.[47] The first three poems he submitted for publication, to the *Irish Statesman*, are replete with pastoral conventions: his "Address to an Old Wooden Gate" apostrophizes and celebrates the everyday objects of rural life; "Ploughman" is certainly a response to poetry in the vein of Yeats's "The Song of the Happy Shepherd," depicting the landscape as the site of labor rather than of leisure. Despite the work demanded by the land, Kavanagh's persona enjoys a communion with the landscape, associating it with tranquility, simple carefree existence, and "ecstasy like a prayer." In poems such as "May," the landscape is described as a prelapsarian Eden, and in "Poplar Memory," his father's act of planting poplars figuratively transforms the world. Implicit in the poem is the notion common in pastoral—that the poet's own imagination can transform this rural world for his readers.

Kavanagh's descriptions of rural labor are thus the means for talking about literary labor. "Art McCooey," for example, originated with local lore about Art MacCumhaigh, who, while employed by a farmer to cart dung to outliers on his land, became so engrossed in composing a poem that he drove back and forth with the same load several times, "until his employer broke his reverie with a roar of complaint." In MacCumhaigh's thwarted delivery of dung to farmers, there is "an image of the artist handling a seemingly dead, even deathly tradition, but the excrement nurtures the earth back to life and allows for a celebration of rural ritual in this text written for townies."[48]

As Kavanagh's poetry suggests, Irish pastoral poets' response to colonization and commodification is to seek ways to restore Ireland, at least imaginatively, to its precolonial past. In order to do so, they have favored depictions of Ireland prior to colonization and often prior to Christianization. Contemporary Irish writers continue to rely on idealization of the landscape—a hallmark of the classical pastoral tradition—in order to reckon with their colonial past, establish a postcolonial identity apart from England, and imaginatively reclaim the land. Whereas the pastoral tradition in Ireland has drawn on classical pastoral, its Christian derivations, and its later manifestations in English romanticism and European modernism, it has also incorporated specifically Irish sources in its imaginative reclamation of the land—particularly the Celtic tradition of nature poetry. Ancient Irish nature poetry, which emphasizes the harmony between nature and human nature in the same way that classical pastoral had and was indeed influenced by the classical pastoral tradition, has arguably had a greater influence on contemporary Irish pastoral; this study addresses its impact on the tradition, considering in particular the influence of the early Irish nature poetry; the lore of place names, the *dinnseanchas*, as well as folklore and myths whose depictions of nature evoke a precolonial past.

Terry Eagleton suggests that the Irish depiction of the landscape dating back to the *dinnseanchas* is uniquely influenced by indigenous Irish culture and religion. He cites Austin Clarke's novel, *The Singing-Men at Cashel*:

"There was no hill or wood in all the land which has not been remembered in poetry. Had not those great teachers of the past taught that matter was as holy as the mind, that hill and wood were an external manifestation of the immortal regions?" Eagleton writes,

> One is tempted to detect here a relation between the Irish tradition of *dinn-seanchas*, or place-name lore, and the idealist epistemology of the greatest Irish philosopher, for whom what looks like matter is in fact rather more like what James Joyce will later call an epiphany. For Berkeley, things are at one with their presence to their perceivers, *res* and *signum* identical, the world one sublimely intricate discourse in which God enunciates himself and utters forth his darkly unfathomable substance. Berkeley's animism has a range of sources in philosophical antiquity, but as the Clarke quotation intimates, one of them may well be Gaelic" . . . in *The Demi-Gods* the Irish novelist James Stephens writes in Berkleyan style of the moon, stars and clouds as the "thoughts made visible" of the divine mind.[49]

The contemporary Irish poetry discussed in this study attests to the continued influence of classical pastoral poetry and an awareness of the western pastoral tradition that emerged from it. It seems notable that both major translations of *Georgics* in the past hundred years were undertaken by Irish poets, the first by C. Day Lewis in 1939, and the second by Peter Fallon in 2004. One passage in particular from *Georgics* underscores pastoral's continued power for Irish poets:

> Nothing surer than the time will come when, in those fields,
> a farmer plowing will unearth
> rough and rusted javelins and hear his heavy hoe
> echo on the sides of empty helmets and stare in open-eyed amazement
> at the bones of heroes he's just happened on . . .
> For right and wrong are mixed up here, there's so much warring everywhere,
> evil has so many faces, and there's no regard for the labours
> of the plow. Bereft of farmers, fields have run to a riot of weeds,
> Scythes and sickles have been hammered into weapons of war.[50]

C. Day Lewis appropriately views his 1939 translation as a response to the ravages of World War I as well as the war Hitler had begun to wage in Germany (the passage that serves as an epigraph for his translation includes a seemingly prescient reference to "hostilities in Germany").[51] Fallon's introduction to his translation observes that Virgil's poem, written in response to the ravages of civil wars that resulted in depopulated countrysides and ruined farms, is likewise a plea for restoring traditions and reestablishing the essential worth of agricultural life[52] as well as a confident prediction of "a time when weapons of war will be rusty relics in soldiers' graves, turned over by the

pointed plow."[53] Writing "in the tender aftermath of the 'Troubles,'" "while
George W Bush was rushing to war without UN backing," Fallon finds the
poem a description "of a way of life with prescriptions for a way to live": "Its
heroes earn their rewards, not for exertions and accomplishments on battlefields but for their efforts in the fields of grain and grapes, those fabled fields
of milk and honey."[54] Not surprisingly, Fallon also praises the poem for its
characters' responsiveness to the environment, and his acknowledgment of
indebtedness to the environmentally minded America poet Wendell Berry
suggests his willingness to regard *Georgics*, and indeed his own poetry, as environmental poetry that prompts a contemporary audience to its own greater
environmental awareness.

Whereas Bradley mentions many poets who might just as easily be discussed as pastoral poets, I have chosen to focus on the contemporary poets
who have written significant collections of poetry that could be considered
pastoral and whose work is in dialogue not only with their predecessors in
the pastoral tradition but also with other contemporary pastoral poets. I
have chosen to write about poets from both Ireland and Northern Ireland
because to some degree, pastoral is employed for the same purposes: their
shared history results in similar critiques of colonialism, industrialization, and
modernization, and also gives them a common literary tradition—one that is
uniquely shaped by ancient Irish literature. However, there are notable differences that also warrant attention. Ireland's partition in 1921 meant that
to some extent, pastoral traditions of North and South evolved differently.
Protestant naturalist clubs established in Northern Ireland in the nineteenth
century spawned interest in the scientific study of nature that would inspire
one of Ireland's foremost botanists, Robert Lloyd Praeger, whose influence
would be felt by contemporary Northern Irish poets like Seamus Heaney. As
mentioned previously, the North was industrialized much more rapidly and
extensively than the south, and the impact of industrialization is felt more
strongly in its pastoral tradition. Northern Ireland, as part of the United
Kingdom, experienced World War II in a way that the Republic, officially
neutral, did not, and its pastoral tradition registers the effect of war on the
landscape. Montague, Heaney, and Longley in particular incorporate their
childhood memories of World War II into their poetry, and Longley has written extensively about his father's experiences in World War I. More significantly, while in Northern Ireland, the strategic retreat of pastoral has often
been the means for contextualizing the sectarian violence of the Troubles, in
the Republic, especially in the period of economic prosperity known as the
"Celtic Tiger," the retreat is as likely to be from the forces of modernity un-
leashed by the Irish themselves.

Whatever their differences, poets from both north and south are increasingly likely to write pastoral that responds to environmental issues. Beginning

around the 1970s, the rhetoric of Irish cultural nationalism began to be employed on behalf of Ireland's environmental movement, where fears about the commodification of land and resources, the impact of globalization, and the loss of traditional ways of life all find outlets in various types of social protest involving roads, natural resources, waste management, globalization, and energy sources. Contemporary Irish pastoral, whether in Northern Ireland or the Republic, has sought a pastoral retreat from which to gain heightened sensitivity to the environmental threats to that retreat—whether they be motorways and high rises that jeopardize sacred sites; global warming, which endangers flora and fauna; or acid rain and other pollutants that permeate the ecosphere. Glen Love acknowledges that contemporary pastoral has the unfortunate potential to reflect the "same sort of anthropocentric assumptions that an ecocritical view would presume to assess,"[55] but he and critics such as Lawrence Buell and Terry Gifford contend that pastoral informed by modern ecological perspectives deserves to be read and written. Gifford cites Seamus Heaney's reputation on both sides of the Atlantic as testimony to the continuing relevance of "a pastoral poetry that returns to speak to contemporary concerns."[56] Gifford's call for "post-pastoral" that relies on pastoral conventions while demonstrating an ecological understanding of nature responsive to environmental threats is, to varying degrees, answered by all of the poets in this study.

Chapter 1, "A Lost Pastoral Rhythm: The Poetry of John Montague," examines Montague's description of the Irish landscape as "a manuscript we have lost the skill to read," discussing the way his own poetry may be conceived of as an attempt to regain that skill. In "O Riada's Farewell," Montague's preoccupation with finding "a lost pastoral rhythm" suggests the imaginative priorities of his whole oeuvre.[57] Antoinette Quinn describes John Montague as "a pastoral poet manqué, an elegist pining for the stability of lost rural rituals," observing that even the village pub in his first collection, *The Rough Field* (1972), is named "The Last Sheaf." "The Last Straw," she quips, "might have been more apt, because Montague's poetry is redolent with nostalgia for a lost world.[58]

Although Montague himself has expressed suspicion of the idealizing tendencies of pastoral, like Kavanagh he has produced pastoral poetry. Acknowledging the potential of pastoral to address wider issues, he writes of "The Deserted Village": "the pastoral clichés of eighteenth-century poetry are being used to a very definite artistic purpose, the evocation of a 'Golden Age' of rural life. Auburn is not a particular, but a universal village of the plain, a pastoral Eden evoking the essence of every Virgilian eclogue and Horatian retreat: it even has special climatic privileges."[59] He regards "The Deserted Village" as "one of the first statements of a great modern theme, the erosion of traditional values and natural rhythms in a commercial society: the fall of Auburn is the fall of a whole social order."[60]

Montague's essay maintains that the virtues that pastoral promotes are no less relevant for his own time and place: The "rural virtues," for Goldsmith, as for the Agrarians in Ireland or America, are actually the root virtues of the good society.[61] Montague's reading of Goldsmith provides a template for the way in which his own poetry employs pastoral, and arguably for much the same artistic purposes that Goldsmith had.

Yet even as early as "Hymn to the New Omagh Road" in *The Rough Field*, the threats to the pastoral retreat are more ecological than they are sociopolitical: the road construction disturbs the entire ecosystem, as wayside hedges are uprooted, streams and wells are filled in, birds' nests disappear, and "the mountain trout / turns up his pale belly to die." Montague's friendship with Gary Snyder, who would later be known as the "poet laureate of deep ecology," perhaps has some role in the ecological direction that his poetry takes. In Montague's later poetry, the threats to the rural world become more complex, as not only commercialization and commodification threaten the landscape and natural resources but environmental threats such as pollution and global warming take an increasing toll.

Chapter 2, "The God in the Tree: Seamus Heaney and the Pastoral Tradition" relies on Heaney's characterization of pre-Christian Ireland as a time when "the landscape was sacramental, instinct with signs, implying a system of reality beyond the visible realties."[62] Even early Irish Christianity maintained the belief in "the seamlessness of sacred and secular spheres" to a greater extent than other branches of the church, incorporating Ireland's holy wells, springs, and sacred mounds and hills into its ecclesiastical rituals. Heaney's pastoral differs in important respects from that of English pastoral, classical pastoral, and even the pastoral of W. B. Yeats—owing perhaps more to the Irish nature writing genre called *dinnseanchas*, defined by Heaney as "poems and tales which relate the original meanings of place names and constitute a form of mythological etymology."[63]

Heaney's review of *The Penguin Book of English Pastoral Verse* (1982) questions the editors' contention that the genre was dead, and finds evidence for the continuing vitality of pastoral in the poetry of Patrick Kavanagh and John Montague. His review sparked this writer's search for the impact of the pastoral tradition on contemporary Irish poetry. Heaney's own poetry is, of course, widely read as a continued testament to that vitality. Whereas Raymond Williams objects to the pastoralization of georgic, which, he contends, erased from cultural consciousness the facts of rural labor in works like Johnson's *To Penshurst*, Heaney maintains that the form, as written by Kavanagh, Montague, and others, acknowledges and celebrates rural labor. Heaney's own poem "Digging," significantly placed as the first poem in his first collection, states his intention to celebrate rural life, in much the same way Frost's "Invitation," likewise the first poem of his first volume, states

Frost's intention. Heaney is perhaps less willing than Montague to elegize the loss of these traditional ways of life as he is to use them as metaphors for the writer's labor.

As a contemporary Northern Irish poet, Heaney's rationale for employing the pastoral tradition—for emphasizing the harmony between nature and human nature—are much the same as they had been for Virgil, Wordsworth, and Yeats. Heaney's longing for a simpler, seemingly more innocent rural world is likewise the means for offering a critique of and response to his own social and political situation. While his reliance on Catholic terminology of the sacramental universe has sometimes been regarded as part of an Irish nationalist agenda, it is ultimately the means for conveying the immanence in nature. For Heaney, "the word that reaches into darkness is like a sacrament containing in its materiality the power to redeem life from its surface; but it is only a small step to the darkness itself becoming that sacrament."[64] The deep sense of awe that the natural world inspires in poets like Heaney is, according to Gifford, "a necessary requirement for the shift from the anthropocentric position of the pastoral to the ecocentric view of the post-pastoral."[65]

Chapter 3, "'Love poems, elegies: I am losing my place': Michael Longley's Environmental Elegies," examines Michael Longley's pastoral elegies—particularly the way in which their nostalgia for a lost pastoral world colludes with contemporary environmental concerns. Lawrence Buell, who argues for the urgency of finding better ways of imaging nature and humanity's relation to it, provides criteria for an "environmentally oriented work" that are especially applicable to Longley's poetry:

(1) relies on the nonhuman environment not merely as a framing device but as a presence that begins to suggest that human history is implicated in natural history.
(2) understands human interest to be the only legitimate interest.
(3) considers human accountability to the environment.
(4) describes the environment as a process rather than as a constant or a given.[66]

When asked about the human relationship to nature, Longley is quick to retort that humans of course *are* nature, and his poetry consistently registers an understanding of the nonhuman otherness of nature, as well as a realistic acceptance of the human position in the natural world.

Chapter 4, "Learning the Lingua Franca of a Lost Land: Eavan Boland's Suburban Pastoral," concerns Boland's novel approach to classical pastoral conventions. Beginning with her 1982 poem "The New Pastoral," Boland presents suburban Dublin as a potential site for pastoral, thereby anticipating a new direction in her poetry. Boland reacts against the Romantic tendency to represent nature as contingent on one's own consciousness, emphasizes the need for depicting a closely observed nature, and relies on the pastoral tradition to explore personal history and to accommodate women's history.

Ireland's frequent depiction as a woman—Mother Ireland, Cathleen ni Houlihan, the Hag of Beare, the Roisin Dubh, the Shan Van Vocht—has inspired an array of gendered literary approaches to the landscape, as well as responses from Irish women writers. In order to restore the "lost land," the woman poet must reject the traditional iconography employed by male poets, relying on her own portrayals in order to imaginatively restore women's real presence to the landscape.

Incidentally, the effort to restore women's presence to the landscape is a hallmark of some varieties of ecofeminism. Whereas preindustrial capitalism encouraged the view that nature (and, by association, women) was merely a commodity to be exploited, ecology's challenge to the dichotomy between humans and nature[67] is ultimately the means for reversing the subjugation of both nature and women. Carolyn Merchant contends that "we must reexamine the formation of a world view and a science that, by reconceptualizing reality as a machine rather than a living organism, sanctioned the domination of both nature and women."[68] The parallels that Boland draws between the exploitation of earth and the exploitation of women, as well as her effort, especially in *The Lost Land*, to seek figurative remediation, are characteristic of the "post-pastoral" tendency to recognize that achieving social justice for women is contingent on redressing environmental degradation.

Chapter 5, "'In My Handkerchief of a Garden: Medbh McGuckian's Minimalist Pastoral Poems," examines how McGuckian interweaves strands of the western pastoral tradition with eastern representations of nature. McGuckian's first book, *The Flower Master*, more than any of her subsequent collections of poetry, relies on the conventions associated with pastoral poetry. Just as Virgil's *Eclogues* confronts the evil of political expropriation, McGuckian registers an awareness of the conflicts in her world—both the political and social conflicts of her Northern Ireland and the conflicts that characterize gender relations in patriarchal society. The pastoral withdrawal that is central to the genre, whether made necessary by herding or by exile or accident, leads to new knowledge and is followed by a return "to fresh woods and pastures new" where endeavor will be informed by a rigorous experience.[69]

While gardens in *The Flower Master* refer to the primal garden, the Garden of Eden, the pastoral retreats in *The Flower Master* virtually always incorporate aspects of the eastern tradition, evoking in particular the small-scale, minimalist style of the Japanese tradition of gardening. Her choice of a minimalist pastoral setting—a "handkerchief of a garden"—partially reflects her urban setting in Belfast but also registers women's experience of nature, traditionally restricted to the domestic sphere, and more likely to occur in the garden than in the pastures of Theocritus and Virgil. McGuckian's pastoral retreats are thus found in gardens, flower arrangements, sun-traps, greenhouses, trees and flowers themselves, and even the female body that serves as a retreat for the developing embryo.

McGuckian's decision to incorporate eastern influences into her version of pastoral may also be viewed as the result of a long tradition for Irish as well as for modern writers: for Irish writers, the Orient offered a welcome respite from the strictures of Irish Catholicism as well as British imperialism. Modernists found in the eastern tradition possibilities for resisting modern culture. Asian minimalism seemed an essential antidote for consumerism and conspicuous consumption. McGuckian's allusions to ikebana in "The Flower Master" intersect with literary modernism's preoccupations with eastern tradition.[70] Its small-scale approach to nature, as well as its tendency to blur the distinction between nature and human nature, result in a distinctive version of pastoral. Gifford notes that for many post-pastoral ecofeminist writers, "Arcadia might be located within the body,"[71] as it is in several of McGuckian's poems.

Chapter 6, "'When Ireland was still under a spell': Miraculous Transformations in the Poetry of Nuala Ní Dhomhnaill" considers how Ní Dhomhnaill's reliance on a pastoral motif—that of shape-shifting or transformation—is amalgamated with the motif of transformation that is equally prevalent in Celtic myth. Her rendering of nature, with its emphasis on the reciprocity of landscape and self, human and animal, sacred and mundane, fantastic and realistic, may be viewed as an attempt to revive the Celtic worldview as reflected in Irish poetry that predates English colonization.

By privileging the traditional Irish worldview, Ní Dhomhnaill's poetry is an implicit challenge to the colonizer's worldview. By returning to ancient Celtic traditions—which portray a close relation between woman and land, embodied in the figure of the all-powerful earth mother—Ní Dhomhnaill simultaneously reclaims power for women; just as postcolonial writers invite their readers to look beneath the surface of the power structure, Ní Dhomhnaill continually reminds us that there is more to the feminine than meets the eye. The ancient concept of the "Great Mother" has also proven useful to ecofeminism in particular, because it suggests a means for healing the split between human and nonhuman, material and spiritual, nature and culture.[72]

Like her predecessors Montague and Heaney, Ní Dhomhnaill also values the *dinnseanchas* tradition, but her interest in them has less to do with national identity than with her appreciation for nature itself; she writes, "I believe that a renewed interest in *dinnseanchas* may enable us to share our love and admiration and wonder of the land of Ireland and can cater in an imaginative way for the need of many for a place to belong to so that we may love and cherish it rather than merely killing each other over it."[73] In her own poems about nature, Ní Dhomhnaill not only draws on rich layers of associations in the *dinnseanchas* to explain the origins of the places she encounters, but she applies the worldview reflected in them to figuratively transform her contemporary landscape: its seemingly objective features—standing stones, burial mounds, hills, springs, and bogs—thereby acquire spiritual resonance.

Finally, in "The Future of Pastoral," I rely on recent poetry by Moya Cannon, Paula Meehan, and others to anticipate the directions that pastoral will take as it flowers into various versions of post-pastoral. Inevitably, too, the pastoral impulse manifests itself in other genres, in films from *The Quiet Man* to *Dancing at Lugnasa*, plays from the Irish literary revival to McDonagh's *Leenane Trilogy*, and fiction such as Patrick McCabe's *The Butcher Boy*, Edna O'Brien's *Down by the River*, and John McGahern's *By the Lake*.

CHAPTER 1

A Lost Pastoral Rhythm

The Poetry of John Montague

Antoinette Quinn describes John Montague as "a pastoral poet manqué, an elegist pining for the stability of lost rural rituals," observing that even the village pub in his first collection, *The Rough Field* (1972), is named "The Last Sheaf." "'The Last Straw,'" she quips, "might have been more apt," because Montague's poetry is redolent with nostalgia for a lost world.[1] Although Montague himself has expressed suspicion of the idealizing tendencies of pastoral, he has acknowledged the potential of pastoral to address wider issues, most pointedly in his analysis of Goldsmith's "The Deserted Village," included in his edited collection, *The Dolmen Miscellany of Irish Writing*, where he observes that "the pastoral clichés of eighteenth-century poetry are being used to a very definite artistic purpose, the evocation of a 'Golden Age' of rural life. Auburn is not a particular, but a universal village of the plain, a pastoral Eden evoking the essence of every Virgilian eclogue and Horatian retreat: it even has special climatic privileges."[2]

Montague's discussion of Goldsmith's pastoral as a vehicle by which he makes "one of the first statements of a great modern theme, the erosion of traditional values and natural rhythms in a commercial society" provides a template for reading Montague's own pastoral poetry.[3]

Montague's essay demonstrates how the destruction of Auburn signifies the destruction of many things: "the narrator's childhood and his dreams of

escape and peaceful retirement . . . 'rural virtues,' 'all the connexions of kindred' in the family unit, 'spontaneous joys' as opposed to unnatural artifice,
virginal innocence, and, finally, poetry itself, even perhaps religion."[4] Finding
a parallel between Goldsmith's approach and that of the agrarians in Ireland
or America, Montague contends that for all of them, the "rural virtues" are
actually the root virtues of the good society, and the virtues that pastoral
promotes are no less relevant for his own time and place.[5] Montague's argument is perhaps influenced by the intersection of nationalist rhetoric with his
own personal history: his father's IRA involvement during the 1920s, which
prompted the family's move to New York, included firebranding the house of
an absentee landlord, a popular ploy of agrarians since the eighteenth century
to assert Ireland's prior claim to the land.[6] Terence Brown, in *Ireland: A
Social and Cultural History* (cited by Montague in *The Figure in the Cave*),
writes of the poets of Montague's father's era, who "celebrated a version
of Irish pastoral, where rural life was a condition of virtue in as much as it
remained an expression of an ancient civilization, uncontaminated by com-
mercialism and progress. In so doing they helped to confirm Irish society in
a belief that rural life constituted an essential element of an unchanging Irish
identity."[7] Montague describes his father as having played a part in the "Holy
War" to restore "our country," and at least in his early volumes, Montague
provides a version of pastoral that reads as a continuation of these efforts to
assert the primacy of the landscape and rural life as a means of restoring that
which was lost in the process of colonization.

Montague's contention that "the fall of Auburn is the fall of a whole
social order"[8] illuminates his descriptions in his first collection, *The Rough
Field* (1972), of the country village where he was raised, Garvaghey. The
word comes from the Gaelic *Garbh acaidh,* which translates as "the rough
field," thereby evoking not only the terrain but the rough, uncertain political history of Montague's Northern Ireland. Garvaghey's name is a particularly apt reminder of the Troubles because of the Protestant Orange Order's
insistence on following the old line of its annual march down the mainly
nationalist Garvaghy Road to commemorate William of Orange's victory
over Irish Catholics at the Battle of the Boyne, which has in turn annually
provoked Catholic resistance. Just as Goldsmith's descriptions of the land's
dispossession in "The Deserted Village," invite comparison with Virgil, so
do Montague's. Writing against the specific backdrop of the Irish civil war
and the troubles that followed, Montague alludes to ancient struggles over
land, nevertheless attuned to the consolation to be found in it.

He opens the collection with an epigraph from the Afghan that relies on a
farming metaphor to respond to the sorrow of war:

> I had never known sorrow,
> Now it is a field I have inherited, and I till it.

Like Ireland, Afghanistan was occupied for years by the British (who were finally defeated there in 1921), endured a period of civil war as a result of ethnic and religious conflict, and ultimately lost much of its population as a result of territorial conflict when the country of Pakistan was formed.

Following the "Afghan" passage is an epigraph from the Greek poet George Sephiris, who witnessed Turkish takeover of his birthplace, Smyrna:

> The Greeks say it was the Turks who burned down
> Smyrna. The Turks say it was the Greeks.
> Who will
> discover the truth?
> The wrong has been committed.
> The important thing is who will redeem it?

The seemingly endless territorial conflicts of Turks and Greeks parallel the conflicts between Protestants and Catholics in Montague's Northern Ireland: both conflicts began centuries ago, the Greco-Turkish conflict originating with the arrival of Turkish nomads in the Byzantine empire in the eleventh century, and the Northern Irish with the arrival of the Normans in the twelfth century but intensifying with the settlement of the Ulster Plantation. Both have their roots in religion, the Greco-Turkish stemming from conflicts between Muslims and Christians; the Northern Irish, between Protestants and Catholics. The burning of Smyrna to which the passage refers occurred in 1922, the same year that the Irish civil war began.[9] Finally, Montague quotes a passage that locates the heart of the conflict in a specific town, much as Montague locates his own chronicle in the village of Garvaghey thereby registering the repercussions of a series of violent upheavals in Northern Ireland. Like the poetry originating from the Greco-Turkish conflict, Montague's poetry represents a quest to "discover the truth," rejecting the impulse to perpetuate the conflict in favor of seeking redemption through art. The convention of proffering rural labor as a panacea for war and a metaphor for poetic composition dates back to classical pastoral poetry: Virgil's *Georgics* depicts the farmer's sickle ultimately prevailing over the weapons of war it uncovers, and the poem's figurative labor presumably accomplishes the same goal.

Montague's preface to the book recalls the time in the early 1960s when he received a prize for a poem he had written, "Like Dolmens Round My Childhood," which he describes reading in the assembly rooms of the Presbyterian church in Belfast, "a drab Victorian building in the heart of the city." "Presbyterian" and "Victorian" represent obvious contrasts with Montague's own Irish Catholic nationalist identity: the largest denomination in Ulster, traditionally anti-Catholic Presbyterians formed their first Northern Irish presbytery with chaplains of a Scottish army that had arrived to crush the rising of 1641[10] and continue to be largely Unionist. The sound of "the rumble of drums" outside as Orangemen prepared for their annual parade on July 12, a date recalling the final defeat of the Catholics at the Boyne in 1690, contrasts with the rhythm and harmony of the poem he reads. His reading of the poem in this setting rife with conflict leads him to consider the broader implications of the conflict he had been born into:

> Bumping down towards Tyrone a few days later by bus, I had a kind of vision, in the medieval sense, of my home area, the unhappiness of its historical destiny. . . . Although as the Ulster crisis broke [in 1969], I felt as if I had been stirring a witch's cauldron, I never thought of the poem as tethered to any particular set of events. . . . Experience of agitations in Paris [1968] and Berkeley [1965] taught me that the violence of disputing factions is more than a local phenomenon. But one must start from home—so the poem begins where I began myself, with a Catholic family in Garvaghey, in the county of Tyrone, in the province of Ulster.

Montague's "vision, in the medieval sense" might well allude to the Irish *aisling,* or vision poem, a form that originated in the Middle Ages and became a popular means of addressing Ireland's political destiny. Yet it also recalls the medieval Piers Plowman, whose May Day vision on Malvern Hill of a "fair field full of folk" is a metaphor for the fate of the world, a vision presumably permitted by his rural occupation and simple, humble persona much as, in the Gospels, shepherds were the first to learn of the birth of Christ. Montague's sense of his own region's historical destiny likewise seems contingent on his capacity for empathy with rural ways. Piers and his pilgrims must plough the field in order to arrive at truth, and Montague's vicarious redemption of the land via poetic composition requires the figurative act of ploughing through a rough field.

Montague's description of Belfast, by contrast, is heavy with urban, industrial imagery of iron and brick:

> *Catching a bus at Victoria Station,*
> Symbol of Belfast in its iron bleakness. . . .
> Brood over a wilderness of cinemas and shops
> Victorian red-brick villas, framed with aerials. . . .

Throughout the passage are legacies of the colonial enterprise: a station, and indeed an era, named for the English queen who reigned at the height of British imperial domination; the iron bleakness of Belfast, the British industrial city and northern capital, which was to be cut off from the agrarian republic as a result of the Irish civil war; the "wilderness" of cinemas, shops, and Victorian villas framed by aerials—a modern cityscape that evokes the postlapsarian wilderness into which Eve and Adam must wander.

Only upon his departure from Belfast does he get a glimpse of landscape seemingly untouched by the forces of modernity, the "dour, despoiled inheritance" that recalls that of fallen humanity banished from Eden:

> A fringe of trees affords some ease at last
> From all this dour, despoiled inheritance . . .

Interspersed in Montague's account of homecoming is a chronicle of the Northern Irish Troubles, beginning with the arrival of Lord Mountjoy in Omagh, whose victory at Kinsale, County Cork, in 1601 led to the conquest of Ireland by English forces. Hugh O'Neill, whose clan had established a fortress in Omagh and ruled the ancient province of Ulster until the seventeenth century, was Lord Mountjoy's next target. Rather than invading Ulster to destroy O'Neill, the English strengthened their forces and began raiding Ulster to destroy crops, hoping to starve O'Neill into submission or a premature attack. Although O'Neill attacked again, he was finally defeated by Lord Mountjoy in Omagh in 1602. O'Neill signed the Mellifont treaty against his will in 1603, effectively permitting him to keep his land while adopting English law and shedding his Irish title, marking defeat for Gaelic Northern Ireland.[11]

Even today a townland near Omagh is called Mountjoy, and Montague is well aware of the landscape's association with defeat. Significantly, in his travels across Ireland, Montague finds a friendly face only upon reaching the end of the Pale—the region in and around Dublin over which the English traditionally had jurisdiction:

> End of a Pale, beginning of O'Neill—
> Before a stranger turned a friendly face. . . .

Yet his refusal to romanticize it, to reduce it to a series of abstractions, is indicated by his rejection of either the Romantic sublime or easy allegory in favor of particular details of the landscape itself:

> No Wordsworthian dream enchants me here
> With glint of glacial corrie, totemic mountain,
> But merging low hills and gravel streams,
> Oozy blackness of bog-banks, tough upland grass;
> Rough Field in the Gaelic and rightly named
> As setting for a mode of life that passes on:
> Harsh landscape that haunts me,
> Well and stone, in the bleak moors of dream,
> With all my circling a failure to return.

His recollections of childhood in Garvaghey, where his "first mornings" were "fresh as Eden . . . like first kiss," are grounded in the Edenic imagery of the Christian pastoral tradition.

In this rural world, he is able to "assume old ways," to make a figurative return to childhood and innocence.

Delving further into the past, he looks at a silvered daguerreotype of his grandfather, country lawyer, hedge schoolmaster, rustic gentleman. When, sixty years later, his succession was broken and his descendants scattered to Australia and the United States, the house in Ireland fell into decay and registered the changes wrought by modernity: "the wide hearth with its cauldron shrank to a coal-fired stove / And tiled stone." The cauldron, which Montague had mentioned in his preface (referring to his own poems as stirring a witch's cauldron), is associated in Irish mythology with plenty and the powers of resuscitation—rather like the cornucopia of classical tradition. Dagda's cauldron, brought from the north to Ireland by the Tuatha Dé Danaan, "was reputedly always full of broth, and no one ever went from it unsatisfied."[12] Given the cauldron's association with wisdom, inspiration, rebirth, and the power to raise the dead, its shrinkage to a coal stove symbolizes the demise of indigenous Celtic culture and its imaginative and religious traditions in exchange for dependence on England, as well as on its industrial products, emblematized by the coal stove. Hence, Montague associates the loss of this childhood world with the loss of the old religion, as well as with the loss of traditional values. Dagda's cauldron, from which nobody went away unsatisfied, has been replaced by a coal stove that continually must be replenished by a people who are thereby continually reminded of their lack of self-sufficiency and their inability to be satisfied with what they have.

The next stanza, "The Country Fiddler," describes Montague's uncle, who played the fiddle at barn and crossroads dances until he left for the New World, when he left his fiddle in the rafters, never again to play it. Montague's description of the end of the music—"a rural art stilled in the discord of Brooklyn"—implicates urbanization and immigration as culprits responsible for silencing the music and thereby suppressing a culture. As young Montague witnesses the gradual deterioration of the fiddle, his country relatives ask if he "also had music," but "the fiddle was in pieces / And the rafters remade" before he discovered his craft. Meanwhile, Irish priests, in deference to the 1935 Dance Hall Act, forbade the centuries-old tradition of dancing at the crossroads and in homes, invalidating the fiddle's original purpose.[13] The "broken tradition" of Irish culture is a recurring metaphor—succession broken by emigration, Celtic custom riven by colonization and Christianisation. He ends the poem, "So succession passes, through strangest hands," and Montague is indeed the successor of his uncle, although his music is poetry.

"Like Dolmens Round My Childhood, the Old People" recalls a world now lost—and Montague, in a characteristically pastoral gesture, connects the present with the mythical past, conflating the ancient world of myth and legend with the Ireland of his childhood. The "dolmens" of his title refer to the standing stones found throughout England and Ireland, occasionally in a circular pattern and thought to mark tombs. In this poem, the country people of Montague's childhood form a protective circle around him, and their loss signifies the loss of traditional values to the modern world.

Jamie MacCrystal, who had always been generous with his money and his possessions—tipping Montague a penny every pension day, feeding "kindly crusts to winter birds," a transferred epithet that signifies his harmonious relationship with the natural world—is, upon his death, robbed of everything, only his corpse left undisturbed. His generosity is immediately eclipsed by a world of modern acquisitiveness, in which getting and spending have become the ultimate goals, rendering the human expendable.

Maggie Owens, surrounded by animals—"even in her bedroom a she-goat cried"—recalls a vanished Ireland in which people once shared their habitations with their animals, a custom to which their English colonizers responded with ridicule and reaffirmations of their own sense of superiority, as the *Punch* cartoons of the late nineteenth century reveal. "Fanged chronicler of a whole countryside," Owens is reputed a witch, and is reminiscent of the Irish *cailleach*, literally translated as "old woman," but actually a powerful Irish sovereignty figure who passes through at least seven periods of youth, so that each husband passes from her to death of old age (MacKillop 62). Traditionally depicted standing at the crossroads, symbol of the bridge between death and rebirth, the hag in Montague's poem also bridges recent and remote history, Irish and English languages, as well as Celtic and Christian beliefs.[14] The crone is usually depicted as hideous in appearance, sometimes with the head of a snake, hence "fanged," yet Montague again depicts her close relationship with the natural world as a source of piercing spiritual insight.

The Nialls, who "lived along a mountain lane / Where heather bells bloomed, clumps of foxglove," symbolize the direct contact with nature that the poet associates with ancient Ireland, as does Mary Moore, subject of the next stanza, who "tramped the fields / Driving lean cattle from a miry stable." Their death is metonymic for that of ancient Ireland:

> Curate and doctor trudged to attend them,
> Through knee-deep snow, through summer heat,
> From main road to lane to broken path,
> Gulping the mountain air with painful breath.

Whereas an isolated mountain existence had been simply a familiar way of life for the old people (Edna O'Brien's "Irish Revel" and *Country Girls Trilogy* also feature a "mountainy girl" emblematic of traditional Ireland), the curate and doctor, symbols of modernity, must struggle to reach them, fighting the obstacles of unpaved roads and nature's climatic extremes as though against an alien force.

The Irish countryside of Montague's past is depicted as the repository of the myths and legends of ancient Ireland:

> Ancient Ireland, indeed! I was reared by her bedside,
> The rune and the chant, evil eye and averted head,
> Fomorian fierceness of family and local feud.

"Fomorian" refers to one of a group of Celtic sea demons associated with the destructive power of nature (MacKillop 211–12), yet Montague recognizes it as a source of strength to which proper deference is due. Montague struggles with the dilemma expressed by Frost—"what to make of a diminished thing"—because the successors of these old people lack their courage and tenacity: their natures, as well as the natural world he knew, are gone.

Thus, whereas "curate and doctor," symbols of modernized, Christianized Ireland, must "gulp the mountain air with painful breath," representing their disharmony with the natural world, the old people form a protective circle around him, sheltering him from outside forces of modernity and providing a sense of connection with the personal, familial, and communal past. Whereas Montague's own nuclear family and sense of place had been broken up by the Irish Civil War, the family's displacement to New York, and his mother's abandonment of him in Ireland, he maintains a sense of continuity, thanks to the aunts who raised him as well as the village's old people who supported and influenced him. The old people serve as reminders not only of the recent past of Montague's childhood but of the distant past of Ireland, whose Celtic culture is symbolized by the dolmens, standing stones that with their "dark permanence" symbolize immortality, the sacredness of life, continuity with the lost generations of Ireland as well as its mythic past.

In "The Leaping Fire," Montague begins with a reminiscence of his aunt Brigid, who kept the hearth fire alive, sifting through the ashes each morning. The hearth fire, necessary for warmth, light, and sustenance, was a symbol of life and of family continuity. Montague's readers know that the hearth fire will eventually be replaced by a coal stove. St. Brigid, his aunt's namesake, was "patroness of the hearth, the fire, and the forge,"[15] and Quinn observes that his aunt's role is to figuratively "fan the flames of the poet's inspiration."[16] Thus, Brigid's simple rural task takes on profound personal and literary significance as a source of life and inspiration: "I draw on that fire."

This sequence poem begins with "The Little Flower's Disciple" in which he chronicles his aunt's religious devotion, equal only to her devotion to the young John and to the survival of the family farm. "The Little Flower" refers to St. Therese, so determined to enter a convent at the age of fifteen that she sought permission from the pope himself. St. Therese's fragile constitution was purportedly destroyed by the harsh convent regimen, resulting in her untimely death at the age of twenty-three.[17] Like St. Therese, Montague's aunt's devotion forces her to bear a "harness of humiliation" until

> the hiss of milk into the pail
> became as lonely a prayer as
> your vigil at the altar rail.

His tribute to his aunt associates her simple life of faith, her sweetness, with "that of the meek and the selfless, / who should be comforted," an allusion to Christ's beatitudes as well as to the classical pastoral virtues. Just as St. Therese had a vision of her father's death years before it occurred, Montague's aunt had reputedly once heard the banshee wail, an omen of death. As she lies dying, he is in Paris, where he hears a low, constant crying that he imagines to be a banshee's wail, "over the indifferent roofs of Paris," "among autobuses / & taxis, / the shrill paraphernalia of a swollen city."

> I crossed myself
> From rusty habit
> Before I realised
> why I had done it.

The indifference and shrillness of the city, where an ostensible banshee's wail is lost amid, or indistinguishable from, the sound of traffic, contrasts with the rural world he left behind, and which Brigid represents, where religious belief—whether Celtic or Christian—does not seem anachronistic.

"Christmas Morning," although set in rural Ireland, simultaneously evokes a rural world reminiscent of biblical accounts of Christ's nativity and the English literary tradition's evocation of classical pastoral imagery in its depictions of the nativity (perhaps most famously, "Milton's "On the Morning of Christ's Nativity," with its shepherds who "sate simply chatting in a rustic row," unaware "that the mighty Pan [Christ]/ was kindly come to live with them below"):

> Lights outline a hill
> As silently the people,
> Like shepherd and angel
> On that first morning,
> March from Altcloghfin,
> Beltany, Rarogan,
> Under rimed hawthorn,
> Gothic evergreen,

Grouped in the warmth
& cloud of their breath,
Along cattle paths
Crusted with ice . . .

God's choice of shepherds to be the first to hear of the birth of the Christ child has long been educed as proof of God's privileging of a simple, rural lifestyle; pastoral poetic tradition had likewise privileged the lifestyle of shepherds, who were also, of course, a feature of Montague's childhood world. The rustic cattle paths they travel lead to the lighted crib much as the star led to the Christ child in the biblical account. By juxtaposing shepherds with angels in the poem, Montague likewise pays homage to them as a source of illumination.

"The Bread God," mentioned shortly thereafter, refers to Protestant propaganda accusing Catholics of idolatry—of worshiping the "Bread God"—which stems from the Catholic belief in the doctrine of transubstantiation. Protestant propaganda is interspersed with idyllic scenes of life in rural Ulster. "Penal Rock: Altamuskin" describes the Mass Rock, whose lesson may be learned by leaving one's car and descending the steps to recall "poor Tagues . . . people of our name" who sheltered in the glen for years. Although a visit to the Mass Rock is a token of religious devotion for the Irish, Montague notes that its lesson requires leaving the car—figuratively turning one's back on modernity—as well as descending—humbling oneself and acknowledging one's connection to the "poor Tagues" (the source, incidentally, of Montague's own name)—in order to appreciate its power.

The last stanza, "An Ulster Prophecy," is based on an Irish folkloric tradition known as the "Song of Lies," which involves listing a series of impossible events in order to hint at the impossibility of a particular event. Liam Ó Dochartaigh's "*Ceol na mBréag:* Gaelic Themes in *The Rough Field*" observes that Montague directly adapts John B. Arthurs' (Sean Mac Airt) examples of oral tradition from *Ulster Folklife*,[18] essentially adding ecclesiastical and sectarian elements. The revised text of his *Collected Poems* (1995) highlights these elements even more. The first line, "I saw the Pope breaking stones on Friday," foreshadows Catholic Ireland's subservience to England, when starving famine victims were forced to do hard physical labor—breaking stones and building roads—as though they deserved punishment for their plight. The fourth, which envisions "Roaring Meg firing rosary beads for cannonballs," alludes to "the monster cannon given to the city of Derry in 1642 by the Fishmongers' Company and used with great effect in the defence of 'London's Derry' against James II during the siege of 1689." Ó Dochartaigh contends that the rosary beads of prayer, highly improbable fodder for a cannon, represent "an alternative impossibility: that the cannon balls of the ward have been replaced with rosary beads of prayer," leading to peaceful resolution of conflict and a United Ireland.[19] However, given the context of the rest of the poem, in which religion in Northern Ireland has been reduced to little more than a justification for violence and bloodshed, rosary beads as cannon fodder are just as likely be a metaphor for the sectarianism at the root of the Troubles.

"A mill and a forge on the back of a cuckoo" juxtaposes two symbols of industrialization with a natural symbol, the cuckoo, reputed to bring good luck as well as good weather. A mill and forge would certainly crush a cuckoo, foreshadowing the fate of the industrialized North, which, as Montague himself observes, "had more tractors than the rest of Ireland" at the end of World War II. Furthermore, he expresses skepticism about the increase in factory farming as a measure of "progress": "we once used nature, now we're *abusing* it."[20] The final line, which envisions the "curlew in flight / surveying / a United Ireland," is similarly ominous. Curlews, whose whistles portend rain as well as bad luck for anyone who hears them at night, are allegedly particularly bad omens for sailors who see one in flight. Hence, his "Ulster Prophecy" for a "United Ireland" seems tantamount to suggesting that it will be united only when hell freezes over, consistent with the spirit of the "Song of Lies."

Montague's reference to "a severed head speaking with a grafted tongue" comes from an old Gaelic poem quoted in section 4 of the poem "A Severed Head": "Who ever heard / Such a sight unsung / As a severed head / With a grafted tongue." In early Celtic society, the head was a prized trophy in battle and symbolized divine power, the essence of being, the seat of the soul. It had powers of prophecy, healing, fertility, speech, independent movement, and incorruptible life. Ross concludes that "the cult of the human head then constitutes a persistent theme throughout all aspects of Celtic life, spiritual, and temporal, and the symbol of the severed head may be regarded as the most typical and universal of their religious attitudes."[21] The severing of the head from the body, its preservation, its association with wells and sacred water, and its powers of speech and prophecy are all recurring features in Celtic tradition and belief.[22] For Montague, the image of the severed head evokes a culture severed from the body of its traditions and forced to speak the "grafted tongue" of English, expressing the dilemma not only of the Irish people but of the Irish poet resigned to representing the culture in the language of the oppressor.

In section 1, "The Road's End," he takes the mountain road, "driving cattle / to the upland fields," enjoying all the traditional benefits of pastoral:

> No need to rush to head off
> The cattle from sinking soft
> Muzzles into leaf-smelling
> Spring water.

Yet during his leisurely stroll down the mountain road, he observes the alterations in the landscape, which likewise register the impact of modernization:

> Now there is a kitchen extension
> With radio aerial, rough outhouses
> For coal and tractor.

Montague's meticulous description of the landscape, "so light in wash it must be learnt / Day by day, in shifting detail," implicitly conveys the value of learning the landscape in all of its subtle and ever-changing beauty in order to appreciate it and to restore it to its premodern value.

Montague's simile for the slopes strewn with deserted cabins—"like shards of a lost culture"—is reminiscent of Joyce's in *Portrait of the Artist*, in which Irish literature is described as "the cracked looking glass of a servant," his pithy assessment of the impact of colonization on Irish culture. Yet Montague's word choice reminds us that not only the culture but the landscape itself is in shards as a result of colonization. The challenge for the artist is to restore, through the power of memory and imagination, that which has been lost.

> Only the shed remains
> In use for calves, although fuschia
> Bleeds by the wall, and someone has
> Propped a yellow cartwheel against the door.

In the farm's demise, the fuchsia "bleeds," conveying the violent impact of modernity as a wound that needs to heal.

In section 2, "A Lost Tradition," Montague's ancestral homeland in Country Tyrone is depicted on a map studded with place-names derived from an Irish that has been dead in that area for generations. In an ancient Gaelic manuscript that no contemporary reader can understand, Montague finds an image of his own geography of disinheritance.[23] The poem echoes the conventions of the Irish *dinnseanchas*, in which the places named had significance that resonated beyond their literal meaning, acquiring layers of meaning from the folklore and mythology associated with them. Montague has acknowledged their personal and literary significance:

> There is an old Irish poetical form, *dinnseanchas* or place wisdom. It was part of traditional bardic training, a sense of the historical layers and legends which give character to an area, a local piety deeper than the topographical . . . One of the exercises that fanatical priest had given us was to collect place-names; so I learnt that I was brought up in the Rough Field, and was going to school in the Glen of the Hazels. Like a stream driven underground, Irish still ran under the speech and names of my childhood.[24]

Montague's insistence on using the Irish place-names, as well as providing translations for them, is his way of reminding the reader of the significance of these places in Irish culture, and thus the means by which he figuratively restores to life that which has been lost.

Hence, "The Glen of the Hazels" where the poet attended school recalls a time when the hazel tree was venerated and associated with holy wells. James MacKillop observes that whereas the ash and birch reputedly had powers to resist fairy magic, the hazel was considered so favored by the fairies that it was often burned (MacKillop 179). A tradition in the prose *dinnseanchas* connects a venerated well with hazel trees. Connla's Well was reputedly located under the sea, a traditional site of the Irish otherworld. The hazels of wisdom grew at the well and fell into the water, where they would be eaten by the sacred salmon that thereby acquire their supernatural wisdom. Anne Ross concludes that "the nuts of this tree seem to have been accredited with singular powers and qualities by the Celts, and their presence in this extraordinarily complex Belgic well can be taken to have a deeper significance than . . . would otherwise be appreciated."[25]

Montague recalls that "Close by / Was the bishopric of the Golden Stone," a reference to the bishop's see of Clogher, which was named for one of these stones, covered with gold (*clogher,* or *cloch oir,* translates as "golden stone"), which was the chief idol of pagan Ireland (MacKillop 100). Montague's place-name is an amalgamation of its ancient Celtic and its contemporary Christian significance, reinforcing his portrait of an Ireland in which ancient pagan and Christian attitudes toward nature coexisted (the stone was reputedly still there long after Christianization) and indeed may continue to coexist.

His reference to "the Rapparee, Shane Barnagh," a seventeenth-century Irish plunderer who watched his brother die and is remembered in the place-name "Brish-mo-cree," "breaks my heart," likewise recalls Ireland's turbulent religious history. Rapparees were Irish guerrillas who fought for the Jacobites during the 1690s Williamite war in Ireland. The source of the heartbreak for Montague thus arises presumably not only from the death of a man but from the death of a whole tradition and the language through which the tradition was conveyed.

In section 4, "The Flight of the Earls," the fiddler plays "as by some forest campfire / listeners draw near, to honour / a communal loss." The music of the fiddler is replaced with "burnt houses, pillaged farms, / a province in flames." The passage recalls the fiddle that Montague found in the rafters—an example of how personal loss resonates into familial, communal, and national loss, as colonization, war, and the inevitable incursion of modernity destroy the landscape.

Section 5, "A Grafted Tongue," recalls the earlier imagery of the severed head, developing it not only as a symbol for speakers of Irish who were forced to speak English but for Northern Irish poets negotiating between two cultures and, particularly, for Montague himself as poet. Montague's reference to "a severed head" that now "chokes to speak another tongue" is also a reference to his own stammering, traced to the time in his childhood when he was called on to speak Irish in front of a group of students, although Quinn observes that it first occurred a year after his mother's abandonment of him.26 Montague's own displacement as the child of Irish parents—transplanted to America and then back to Ireland—required him to learn a new language—Irish—and adapt to a new culture. His personal experience thus serves as a synecdoche of Ireland as a whole, whose language, once outlawed under British colonization, was restored with Irish independence. The schoolmasters who had once punished children for their failure to speak English now punished them for their failure to speak Irish—ironic given that Irish children were punished in the name of Irish nationalism.

In "A Grafted Tongue," losing the language is tantamount to going home to

> find
> the turf-cured width
> of your parent's hearth
> growing slowly alien.

Once again, "hearth" carries great symbolic weight: not only a language is lost but a way of life: a family, a community, a landscape, and a source of inspiration, because in "cabin and field" they still speak the old tongue.

Although section 6, "Even English," resists easy idealization of the landscape—"a high, stony place . . . bogstreams, / Not milk and honey—but our own," it nonetheless depicts precolonial Ireland as a promised land whose conquest represents a much more pervasive loss than the colonizer's commodifying can comprehend:

> I assert
> a civilisation died here;
> it trembles
> underfoot where I walk these
> small sad hills.

At the town pub, "The Last Sheaf," which is on the verge of going out of business, the boss has begun to "diminish his own stock," which refers to his liquor supply but also to the diminishing supply of (live)stock associated with the decline of the pastoral economy and rural communities as a result of modernity and urbanization. According to E. Estyn Evans's *Irish Folk Ways,* "the last sheaf" is also known as the *cailleach* or hag;27 therefore, the pub's closure marks not only the end of a rural lifestyle but a view of the world in which myth played a central role. The regulars respond by singing "the songs / That survive in this sparse soil" and reminiscing about childhood and its losses.

He recalls a time when, as a boy, he found a swallow's nest and showed it to another boy, who broke the swallow's eggs, one by one, "against a sunlit stone." The threat to the eggs, and indeed to this precarious pastoral retreat under a bridge, is clearly symbolic of the more comprehensive threat of modernity, as the "traffic drumming overhead" and the poem's conclusion suggest:

> To worship or destroy beauty—
> That double edge of impulse
> I recognize, by which we live;
> But also the bitter paradox
> Of betraying love to harm,
> Then lungeing, too late,
> With fists, to its defence.

The poet who perhaps sees his own purpose as figuratively lunging to the defense of this dying world is likewise well aware that he is too late, doomed only to elegize what has been lost, not to restore it.

Section 3, "Salutation," seems to be his farewell not only to the place but to a simpler way of life: "the flat, helpless way Henry's milk / Horse fell, as we raced to school" is contrasted with the way "a white Catalina / From the Erne base (an old pupil) Rose out of a hole in the hedge, / Sudden as a flying swan, to circle / Over the school in salutation / And fold into cloud again." Catalinas, American- and Canadian-built flying boats first flown in 1935 and phased out after World War II, are inevitably associated with the incursion of modernity, and, in particular, modern warfare's heightened potential for mass destruction of people and land, which ultimately brings to a close any hope of a rural life of peace and simplicity. The airboat reminds the poet of a swan, so often a symbol of beauty and transformation in Irish folklore and poetry, but here, an omen of the imminent destruction of rural life. Northern Ireland, as part of the United Kingdom, experienced warfare in a way that the Republic, officially neutral, did not, and its pastoral tradition registers the effect on the landscape.

Section 4, "The Source," describes climbing the mountain in whose stream "legend declared a monstrous trout lived," conflating literal present with mythic past: "Was that / The ancient trout of wisdom / I meant to catch?" He recalls when he and Old Danaghy's son

> robbed a
> Bee's nest, kicking the combs
> Free; our boots smelt sweetly

> For days afterwards. Snowdrop
> In March, primrose in April,
> Whitethorn in May, cardinal's
> Fingers of foxglove dangling
> All summer: every crevice held
> A secret sweetness. Remembering,
> I seem to smell wild honey
> On my face.

His homage to the land, with its lingering scent of honey and its comforting, predictable succession of flowers, indeed depicts it as a kind of promised land, a pastoral retreat.

"Hymn to the New Omagh Road" charts the destruction of the land for the sake of progress:

> *As the bulldozer bites into the tree-ringed hillfort*
> *Its grapnel jaws lift the mouse, the flower,*
> *With equal attention, and the plaited twigs*
> *And clay of the bird's nest, shaken by the traffic,*
> *Fall from a crevice under the bridge*
> *Into the slow-flowing mud-choked stream*
> *Below the quarry, where the mountain trout*
> *Turns up its pale belly to die.*

Hillforts, small enclosures that were probably dwellings, folds for animals, or places of occasional refuge, were also thought to be sacred enclosures associated with fairies and the old religion. The fairies ostensibly preferred to live underground, especially under a hill, and the "tree-ringed hillfort" recalls the ancient Celtic worship of trees (MacKillop 177). The bulldozer, destructive symbol of modernity, devours the hillfort, the symbol of ancient Celtic culture, along with the symbols of nature, the mouse and the flower "with equal attention." The upheaval wrought by technology and modernity leaves the bird's nest "shaken by traffic," as the mountain trout "turns up its pale belly to die."

Here, the threat to the pastoral retreat is ecological, as the road construction results in the disruption of a complex ecosystem. The title of section 1, "Balance Sheet," alludes to the bureaucratic process involved in the road's construction. Whereas balance sheets, by their very impersonality and perfunctoriness, would seem to downplay the significance of the natural world lost in the process of road building, Montague's balance sheet lovingly catalogues the losses of flora, fauna, and their habitats in such detail that the reader cannot fail to feel their significance: the barn, home of pigeons and swallows; stone-lined paths and all the flowers—"crocuses, overhanging lilac or laburnum / sweet pea climbing the fence"; "all signs of wild life, wren's or robin's nest, / a rabbit nibbling a coltsfoot leaf, / a stray squirrel or water rat." Naturally occurring flora and fauna suddenly face criminalization as they are deemed unlawful under the all-consuming dictates of modern "progress": "the uprooting of wayside hedges with their accomplices . . . an unlawful assembly of thistles." Montague's ironic contrasts underscore the profound nature of the upheaval that occurs, in which all that had grown naturally is destroyed to make way for the man-made. Ultimately, all vestiges of the old religion, which had been dependent on the close connection with the natural world, are banished as well for the sake of progress:

> The removal of all hillocks
> and humps, superstition styled fairy forts
> and long barrows, now legally to be regarded
> as obstacles masking a driver's view.

In other words, all that had once been regarded as essential for humans to enter the otherworld and achieve immortality is reduced to nothing more than obstacles to progress. A subsequent section, "Gains," makes it clear that although the new road will provide jobs for people, it is the local merchants, and ultimately, international capitalists, who will be the real benefactors.

Montague's recognition of the significance of the nonhuman losses to the pastoral retreat is characteristic of the environmentally aware tradition of post-pastoral. Although Liam Leonard's *The Environmental Movement in Ireland* traces Irish environmentalism to the late 1970s Woodquay protests, Montague's considerably earlier remonstrance against road construction and other incursions of modernity on the landscape anticipates some of the major concerns of Irish environmentalism: "the excessive use of nitrogen and other fertilisers of industrialised forms of agriculture; the pollution of inland waterways from agricultural, industrial and domestic sources; the loss of biodiversity and habitats . . . patterns of land use and urban and suburban development which each year decrease green spaces; to the congestion and pollution associated with an explosion of privatised car transport."[28]

Environmentalism would take many years longer to reach Montague's rural Northern Ireland: while the economic dependency of the Republic of Ireland shifted from a reliance on Britain to a policy of attracting U.S. multinationals, Northern Ireland had made no such transition, remaining "subservient" to the wider U.K. economic circle.[29] Northern Ireland's economy went into decline in the 1970s and 1980s as an apathetic distant government remained slow to invest in the strife-torn province. The political conflict and poverty of Northern Ireland in the 1960s certainly forestalled any consideration of it in environmental terms. Although America's Environmental Protection Agency was created in 1970, the Northern Irish equivalent, the

Department of Environment, was not created until 1999, and whereas the first Earth Day was held in America in 1970, drawing national attention to the ecology movement (Gaylord Nelson was inspired by the teach-ins protesting the Vietnam War), even as recently as April 16, 2010, one forlorn blogger in Belfast reported that no events for Earth Day had been scheduled.[30] Montague's prodigious sensitivity to and abiding preoccupation with environmental issues is evidence of the early impact of Gary Snyder, "the poet laureate of deep ecology," whom Montague befriended while at Berkeley in the mid-1960s. Perhaps more broadly, the shift in American attitudes toward the environment that occurred in the years immediately prior to publication may be detected as well.

"Glencull Waterside" elegizes these losses, interspersing lines from local poet Patrick Farrell's (1856–1938) poem by the same title about a landmark on the Omagh Road, which, although sentimental, allows for the simultaneous existence of the natural and the supernatural, the literal and the imaginative: "Like walking though enchanted land where fairies used to dwell."[31] Montague has commented that with the loss of the old religion and the death of the earth goddess theme in Irish poetry, "the feminine, fertile land was identified with a national cause, [and] Irish poetry began to grow sentimental."[32] In fact, the feminization of the native population and the depiction of Ireland as a woman strongly connected with the natural world (with flowing hair and robes, bare feet, and garlands of shamrocks) was initially the colonial oppressors' rationale for conquest of both people and land. Although Montague relies on ironic juxtaposition of sentimental vision with contemporary reality, it effectively conveys his horror that a living landscape has been reduced to nothing but a dead commodity, justifying its destruction. As the "crustacean claws of the excavator" devour and regurgitate the land, as the topsoil is lifted from the earth "like a scalp," as all of the secret places resume new life as building material, "a brown stain" remains, suggesting the culpability of the builders as well as the acquisitive society complicit in the destruction of the landscape.

Section 5, "Patriotic Suite," remembers the "herdsmen aristocrats" who constituted the ancient tribes of Ireland and, under pressure from a new order, "merged into hills, / The ultimate rocks where seals converse," signifying their close relationship with nature while also merging past and present, history and legend. Northern Irish "selkie" or "roan" stories feature seals who can shed their skins and take human form, in some legends presumably providing explanations for the ancestry of the indigenous inhabitants. By blurring the distinction between humans and animals, Montague recalls a distant past that did not define itself by the modern dichotomy between nature and human nature, while at the same time anticipating environmentalism's more recent challenge to the same dichotomy. Relying on the imagery common to pastoral poetry, he recreates the pastoral existence of these tribes:

> There they supped rain-water, ate sparse
> Berries and (grouped around slow fires
> At evening) comforted themselves
> With runics of verse.

The "herdsman aristocrats" comfort themselves with verse, and in classical pastoral, poetry presumably arose as naturally as bird song from the shepherds living in harmony with the land. Montague notes that only with the revolution were these "herdsmen aristocrats" remembered and ancient pastoral traditions evoked.

In the sixth section of "Patriotic Suite," "The Enterprise," it is clear that the enterprise of road building and modernization has pushed organic life aside, whereas the mechanical prevails: no sign of life except the crane tilting into emptiness, smoke drifting from cottages, cars crawling like ants. Montague mourns the loss of precolonial, preindustrial Ireland through his reference to "Hy Brasil," a mythical mysterious island, an earthly paradise, once believed to lie at the same latitude as Ireland but far out to sea (MacKillop 237). The existence of this precolonial paradise is perpetually threatened by technological innovations, symbolized by the "self-drive car" with which Montague concludes the poem, as once again the organic is eliminated in favor of the mechanical.[33] Epitomizing the final, devastating effect of road building, a brown stain seeps away, discoloring the grass and thickening the stream's current; earth itself is depicted as a body that bleeds.

Throughout his poetry, Montague often relies on the traditional Irish figure of the cailleach, and one purpose would seem to be to provide a precolonial figure closely identified with the natural world in order to reestablish the ancient connection to it, no less essential to an ecological worldview. In "The Wild Dog Rose," Montague describes the old woman who had once haunted his childhood as a cailleach—yet because the hag of Irish mythology is closely connected with the natural world, integral to the life cycle, as well as a symbol for Ireland itself, Montague's metaphor allows him to interweave personal, national, and environmental concerns:

> "The wild rose
> is the only rose without thorns,"
> she says, holding a wet blossom
> for a second, in a hand knotted
> as the knob of her stick.

She is herself the wild rose—ultimately harmless, possessing the beauty of roses, perpetually serving as a reminder of the natural world with which she lives in close relation as well as the necessity of avoiding hyper-civilizing forces in Ireland. Later poems such as "The Sean Bhean Bhocht" rely on the figure to represent the transition from Celtic religion to Christianity: the old woman is a repository of Christian and Celtic stories, of a hill where the fairies of Ireland and the fairies of Scotland fought all night, where the dead queen was buried, where St. Patrick passed by and left his footprint.

> . . . secret spirals of the burial stone . . .
> But beneath the whorls of the guardian stone
> What fairy queen lay dust?

Montague's reference to the "fairy queen" alludes to Spenser's Christian allegory as well as to the many Celtic myths of fairy queens symbolically buried with the introduction of Christianity. Implicit in these myths is the ancient concept of the "Great Mother" or sovereignty goddess embodied in the land—a concept that has proven useful to ecology because it suggests a means for healing the split between human and nonhuman, material and spiritual, nature and culture.[34] Many of Montague's later poems, including "Seskilgreen" (260), "For the Hillmother" (261), and "Saga Queens" (269) continue to rely on the figure of the Irish sovereignty goddess in order to suggest a relationship between nature and human nature that neither pits humans against nature nor sets them above it.

Montague's epilogue describes "floating above a childhood village / remote but friendly as Goldsmith's uburn," "our finally lost dream of man at home / in a rural setting." The harsh landscape that haunts him is "going, going, GONE," auctioned off to the forces of modernity. Terry Gifford's *Pastoral* draws on Leo Marx's distinction between sentimental and complex pastoral to differentiate between pastoral in which retreat is merely an end in itself, and pastoral in which retreat is a means to an end—one that leaves the reader "changed and charged upon return for more informed action in the present."[35] Montague acknowledges that "only a sentimentalist would want to return to this world," yet he insists on the importance of a figurative return, as had his most important poetic predecessors from Goldsmith to Clare to Kavanagh. Recovery from the "colonial mentality," which Margaret Atwood has defined as "the belief that the great good place is always somewhere else,"[36] would seem to necessitate a figurative retreat to the precolonial. Pastoral elegy is the means for reasserting the value of what has been lost in the process of colonization and of figuratively recreating it, thereby serving as a source of healing for the culture. Yet Montague's pastoral is also complex in the sense that it brings the reader to a deeper appreciation of nature while simultaneously confronting the ultimate consequences of environmental degradation.

Montague's future volumes, although they continue to rely on the imagery of pastoral, are more appropriately described as pastoral elegies, written with an increasingly heightened awareness that the rural world is vanishing. *A Slow Dance* (1975) opens with the poem "Sweeney" and relies on the image of the legendary northern Irish king who retreated from the noise of battle into the wilderness and took on the characteristics of a bird. Sweeney's transformation becomes for Montague the means for portraying the integral relationship of nature and human nature, and because Sweeney is himself a poet, the need for the poet to recognize his own role as the embodiment of this relationship. Earlier, in "Roseland" *(The Rough Field)*, Montague had written, "Seemsh no escape. Poet and object / must conshumate,"[37] resorting to stage Irish pronunciations that in turn are based on Irish Gaelic pronunciations, reaching back to a precolonial past to figuratively restore a precolonial relationship between nature and self.

A Slow Dance continues to anthropomorphize nature, portraying it as a healing power for which "the sounds and sights of Ireland—fuchsias, whins, boglands, winds, snails, wrens, cattle, streams, squirrels embody a sense of beatitude and timelessness."[38] In "Errigal Road," a poem reminiscent of Frost's "Mending Wall," the narrator walks down the lane with his Protestant neighbor, discussing their adjoining property and the local landmarks celebrated in myth. These landmarks that predate Christianity compel them to put aside their own religious differences and transcend the sectarianism that has consumed many of their compatriots: Fairy Thorn Height, for example, is the site of a tumulus that "open[s] perspectives beyond our Christian myth." Similarly, Knockmany Hill, topped by a large passage grave with stones incised with swirling patterns similar to those at Newgrange, is traditionally considered to be the burial site of the mythological mother goddess Aine, loved by the warrior Finn McCool.[39] While they imagine "men / plotting against the wind" at Whiskey Hollow, and are well aware that men elsewhere plot against one another (and there seems to be an oblique allusion to "Mending Wall," in which the narrator's neighbor is actively engaged in building a wall to shut him out), peace prevails in their vicinity, leading his neighbor to exhort him to "tell them down South that old neighbours / can still speak to each other around here."

Yet even in this relatively isolated region, nature has come under siege so often that its healing power is limited: Foxhole Brae, which used to team with foxes, now has hardly any: only one "red quarry slinks through the heather." Ironically, the "little red fox" *(an maidrin rua)* immortalized in so many Irish language poem—and evolving into a symbol of the Irish peasant and, more generally, Irish resourcefulness under colonization—has been virtually eradicated by its own people.[40] Foxes, like other mammals, face higher mortality rates from traffic or disease as the human population increases.[41] Not coincidentally, the impact of warfare has become increasingly inescapable:

> last week, a gun battle outside Aughnacloy,
> machine-gun fire splintering the wet thorns,
> two men beaten up near dark Altamuskin,
> an attempt to blow up Omagh Courthouse.

While Montague's poetry continues to insist on some design or harmony in nature, as in "Windharp," he has increasing difficulty locating it; his own heightened awareness of seemingly irresolvable political conflict and the growing environmental crisis account for poetry that can more accurately be described as post-pastoral, except on those occasions when the landscape can be glimpsed through other more innocent eyes, such as those of his daughters, the subjects of several poems in *Mount Eagle* (1979). His brief excursions into their pastoral retreats—whether gardens, forests, or fields—are not enough to erase his awareness of "this strange age of shrinking space" in which he is doomed to live.

The Great Cloak (1978)[42] is less concerned with rural landscapes than with love and its demise, and when pastoral imagery is employed, it is done so in the service of representing romantic love. A lover's name, for example, is described as "Eden-like," but the landscape is not necessarily, unless inhabited by the lovers and seen through their eyes. One poem at the intersection of love poetry and pastoral is "Pastourelle," which refers to a poetic genre popular throughout France in the twelfth and thirteenth centuries. William D. Paden defines *pastourelle* as a poem in the pastoral mode, commonly featuring a country setting and a shepherdess protagonist and her lover. Told from the man's point of view, with narrative interspersed with dialogue, the plot comprises a discovery and an attempted seduction. This turns the song of courtly love on its head, by having as the object of desire not a noble lady where social constraints dictate events, but a commoner, with the less-refined associations that would be drawn by the listener.[43] A hawk carries the human away as he would a mouse or mole, symbolizing the way death will ultimately take its human prey.

The Dead Kingdom (1984)[44] continues to explore "Goldsmithian simplicities," depicting Montague's childhood home as a pastoral retreat, from "the hidden sweetness / of a whitewashed well," to Abbeylara Garden, where "it was always summer" but also always threatened by change:

> only the earth and sky
> unchanging in change,
> everything else fragile
> as a wild bird's wing;

bulldozer and butterfly,
dogrose and snowflake
climb the unending stair
into God's golden eye.

The elegiac tone extends beyond the inhabitants of the landscape to the landscape itself, a gesture that anticipates the direction of contemporary environmental elegy, which seeks to move from an anthropocentric view of nature to a more comprehensive sense of its worth: "So sing a song for / things that are gone, / minute and great, celebrated, unknown."

The world of myth and legend, which exists side by side with the visible world and is as alive for him as it had been for poets in the classical pastoral tradition, is destroyed by the forces of modernity: in later volumes, Montague's concerns move beyond road construction to other ecological threats that have had particularly deleterious effects on Ireland. Montague's future volumes, although they continue to rely on the imagery of pastoral, are more appropriately described as pastoral elegies, written with an increasingly heightened awareness that the rural world is vanishing. In *The Dead Kingdom* (1984), he seeks to return to "Goldsmithian simplicities,"[45] while in "Gone," he simultaneously acknowledges the cultural and ecological losses that prompted Goldsmith's pastoral nostalgia as well as his own: "Like the Great Forests / of Ireland, hacked down / to uphold the Jacobean / houses of London."[46] In *Irish Folk Ways* (1957), E. Estyn Evans observes that Ireland relied more than the rest of Europe on whins for fuel because of its deforestation in the sixteenth and seventeenth centuries.

Northern Ireland has likewise relied on peat (12 percent of land area in Northern Ireland is peat) as opposed to English coal, which is simply peat at a much later stage. With the demise of native woodlands, peat became the major source of fuel in Ireland during the seventeenth and eighteenth centuries. Traditionally peat was cut by hand using a special turf spade known as a *sleán* or *slane* until World War II, when peat became a vital domestic fuel source again as the supplies of coal from Great Britain almost ceased. Mechanized peat extraction is much more destructive to the landscape than manual extraction: it requires more extensive drainage, inhibiting the presence and actions of microorganisms; destroys the surface vegetation, which can erode and destabilize the entire surface of the bog; decreases the height and biomass of the vegetation, which rapidly reduces the invertebrate populations and ultimately endangers animals further up the food chain such as birds and mammals, as there is less food and cover for nesting. Montague's "Bog Royal" considers the long-term effects of this extraction, referring to peat as "our land's wet matrix."

"Come back, Paddy Reilly"
to your changed world;
pyramids of turf stored
under glistening polythene;
chalk white power stations,
cleaned swathes of bog,
a carpet sucked clean!
Here the yellow machines
churned roots of bog-oak
like lopped antlers,
the sunken remnants
of the Great Forests
of Ireland, hoarse-hunt—ing horn of the Fianna,
the encumbered elk
crashing through branches,
a houndpack in full cry.[47]

Just as the bog-oak roots are chewed and devoured by modern machinery, the Irish elk, thought to be purely mythical until skeletons were found in Irish bogs, emblematic of a time when myth and history were regarded as inseparable, is figuratively devoured for the sake of ostensible progress.

As he had done in *The Rough Field,* Montague relies on precolonial Irish figures to convey the integral relationship between nature and human nature. "The Gruagach"[48] refers to the solitary fairy of Irish and Scots Gaelic traditions, sometimes depicted as an ogre or giant. Because his hair is characteristically long, he is linked to the *woodwose* or wild man of the woods. In Scotland, a gruagach may also refer "to a fairy woman dressed in green or to a slender, handsome man" (MacKillop 230). In Montague's poem, the gruagach is merged with the landscape as its curves become those of the mountains, its ribs "bleached ribs of rock. The gruagach's embodiment in the landscape intimates the integral human relationship with the landscape, and Montague suggests that for the herdsmen who encounter the gruagach, it is a reflection of their own "dirty and misshapen selves."[49]

What, for Montague, began as a protest against the destruction of the countryside where he grew up has since become, by his own definition and that of others, environmental poetry. In Montague's later poetry, the threats to the rural world become more complex as not only commercialization and commodification threaten the landscape and natural resources but as environmental threats such as pollution and global warming take an increasing toll. In "The Errigal Road,"[50] the narrator walks with his Protestant neighbor along the road, discussing the significance of the landmarks they encounter. "Foxhole Brae" is notable because although it used to be "crawling" with foxes, there is now evidence only of one. Fairythorn Height's very name is a reminder of pre-Christian Ireland, as is Knockmany Hill, "its brooding tumulus / opening perspectives beyond our Christian myth."[51] Montague implies here and elsewhere that a figurative return to pre-Christian Ireland is a means for quelling sectarian conflict, but in this poem, the neighbors' shared appreciation for the threatened landscape itself is of greater import than anything wrought by the Northern Irish Troubles: "Soon all our shared landscape will be effaced. / a quick stubble of pine recovering most."

"The Water Carrier" recalls the childhood task of carrying water in buckets "not as return or refuge, but some pure thing, / Some living source, half-imagined and half-real, / Pulses in the fictive water that I feel." The poem, resonant with all of the traditional mythical associations of water in Celtic culture, suggests that by returning to the rural world of his childhood, the poet likewise returns to a "living source," of emotional sustenance as well as poetic inspiration.

"Soliloquy on a Southern Strand" is written from the perspective of a priest recalling his boyhood in rural Ireland.

> When I was young, it was much simpler;
> I saw God standing on a local hill,
> His eyes were gentle and soft birds
> Sang in chorus to his voice until
> My body trembled, ardent in submission.

While he depicts the farm of his youth as a friendly place where he can live in harmony with a God who is not merely an abstraction but a living presence, and the priest tells him "each hair is counted," at college he must contend with darkness, uncertainty, anonymity, and shame, silently listening to town boys laugh in the dark "at things that made me burn with shame." "Dirge of the Mad Priest" echoes the nostalgic tone, suggesting that the source of the priest's madness is the changes wrought by modernity. He observes that in spring now, although more people come to mass and are better dressed, the peace is increasingly disturbed by the crack of guns as the Irish Troubles continue. As the renewal traditionally promised by spring is replaced by violence, Montague's subjects increasingly retreat to the rural world of their childhoods:

> Only those hold my affection
> who, stolid as weights,
> rested in the rushy
> meadows of my childhood . . .

In an interview with Dennis O'Driscoll, Montague was asked about his apparently "very strong feelings about the destruction of our environment" that his poem "Springs," with its reference to "our foul disgrace," manifests. Montague replies, "Anyone would have if they had ever known, as I did briefly but very strongly in Garvaghey, the old pastoral rhythms and seen the earth cultivated in a natural way." He goes on to explain that "Springs" "is an environmental poem . . . based on the sight of a dying salmon which had UDN. I would think of that poem as a kind of charm. Charms and spells are aspects of poetry. Shakespeare is full of them."[52] In Irish mythology, and throughout Montague's poetry, salmon is considered a sacred fish—a repository of otherworldly wisdom—but in "Springs," he shifts his focus to the environmental plight of the salmon. UDN (ulcerative dermal necrosis) is a chronic dermatological disease that causes lesions that become quickly infected with overgrowths of a fungus that make the fish look as though they're covered in slimy white pustules. Although many sources claim there is no known cause for it, articles at least since 2000 point to global warming as a likely culprit.

Hence, where once Montague initially set out to capture the "old pastoral rhythms" for the sake of restoring some sense of national identity, his most recent concerns have been ecological. Montague's theme has not changed; it has merely evolved. Observing the four best long poems by Irishmen since the late eighteenth century (among which are *Lawrence Bloomfield* and *The Great Hunger*), Montague concludes that they "are all variations on the same rural theme," and thus the message of "The Deserted Village" still applies to Ireland, particularly its ending, which "seems especially relevant, now that we are part of the European Economic Community."[53]

"Richness and narrowness, the world and our province; we must have both. Or rather we must have them all."[54] Whether with local, national, or global appeal, Montague's pastoral poems, like Goldsmith's, remain as charms to restore that which is lost—so that the voices "which haunt our land . . . should be made to blend, as a symphony contains its dissonances, structures of healing,"[55] reflecting a view of poetry that has informed the pastoral tradition since its inception.

CHAPTER 2

"The God in the Tree"

Seamus Heaney and the Pastoral Tradition

Seamus Heaney's 1975 review of *The Penguin Book of English Pastoral Verse* observes that its selections come primarily from the seventeenth and eighteenth centuries, and include only three poets who could be considered modern—Hardy, Hopkins, and Yeats—suggesting that the editors regard pastoral as a dying tradition. Heaney questions this assumption, contending that poems by more recent poets such as Edward Thomas, Hugh MacDiarmid, David Jones, and others should be considered versions of pastoral: "surely the potent dreaming of a Golden Age or the counter-cultural celebration of simpler lifestyles or the nostalgic projection of the garden on childhood are still occasionally continuous with the tradition as it is presented here."[1] Furthermore, while acknowledging that Irish writing was outside the editors' scope, Heaney maintains that great Irish pastoral poetry like Kavanagh's *The Great Hunger* and Montague's *The Rough Field* deserve to be regarded as more than "occasional twitches" of a dying tradition.[2] While Heaney's review likely serves as mild reproof for the editors' decision to include primarily English writers, it more importantly establishes what Heaney regards as essential criteria for pastoral poetry and implies that whatever demise it has suffered in English poetry, Irish writers have chosen to sustain it.

Heaney challenges the editors' contention that "the pastoral vision is, at base, a false vision, positing a simplistic, unhistorical relationship between the ruling landowning class—the poet's patrons and often the poet himself—and the workers of the land; as such its function is to mystify and to obscure the harshness of actual social and economic organization," likening its attitude to that of Raymond Williams' Marxist critique of the pastoral tradition in *The Country and the City.* Implying the short-sightedness of interpreting pastoral poetry solely in terms of its rendering of class relations, Heaney responds that "the Marxist broom sweeps the poetic enterprise clean of those somewhat hedonistic impulses towards the satisfactions of aural and formal play out of which poems arise, whether they aspire to delineate or to obfuscate 'things as they are.'"[3] Heaney has celebrated poetry's origin in aural and formal play by citing Yeats's analogy between singing and poetry to emphasize that poetry, like music, should have many social functions besides that of social critique: it may also be used for celebration, for commemoration, and for reconciliation of opposites. In his introduction to "The Singer's House," Heaney states that simply because suffering is all around us is no reason to regard music—or poetry—as any affront to suffering. In fact, the greater the burden of our suffering, the greater our need for the freedom that poetry can offer. His sense that pastoral is a viable means of finding this freedom governs his own poetic approach to the pastoral tradition. He has referred to the landscape around the family farm where he grew up as "a version of pastoral,"[4] considers influential other poets whose work he classifies as pastoral, and been designated by many scholars as a pastoral poet.[5]

The most sustained examination of Heaney as pastoral poet, Sidney Burris's *The Poetry of Resistance: Seamus Heaney and the Pastoral Tradition,* considers the way in which Heaney appropriates the language of pastoral as the means for imaginatively reclaiming his country's colonized land.[6] Burris cites Heaney's early poem "Anahorish" as one example:

> Heaney imagines that the name itself possesses ineffable powers of cultural sovereignty. Irish place-names in the United Kingdom become for Heaney subversive incantations that both glorify his Celtic lineage and establish its integrity in British Northern Ireland. The poem dexterously appropriates a landscape politically British in its legal demarcation but linguistically Irish in its nomenclature.[7]

Yet in addition to establishing cultural sovereignty is Heaney's persistent need to transcend, at least imaginatively, the conflict altogether. Heaney's lecture "Place and Displacement: Recent Poetry of Northern Ireland," which he delivered at Dove Cottage in 1984, provides perhaps the clearest statement about the direction of his poetry. Referring to the political situation in Northern Ireland, Heaney suggests that in the face of such an intolerable reality, "the poet's artistic drive . . . is to move to a higher level of consciousness and resolve the conflict symbolically in art . . . The contemporary poet in Ireland is compelled to 'outstrip' the unbearable political reality of Ulster, to transcend it in highly formal lyrics, to enter the linguistic mode of play' that momentarily intensifies him and detaches him from his predatory circumstances." For Heaney, "the poetic transcendence is not an evasion of sympathy with national conditions but rather a transposition of that sympathy into symbol."[8] In his essay on lyric poetry, Theodore Adorno discusses the poet's role in transcending material reality: "protesting against these conditions, the poem proclaims the dream of a world in which things would be different."[9] In his own version of complex pastoral, Heaney's dream of a Golden Age represents not only resistance to the order that has been but an imaginative establishment of a new order that transcends the dichotomies of the old ones.

Burris and others have acknowledged Ted Hughes's influence on Heaney's use of pastoral as class critique. Burris observes that Heaney perceived Hughes's stylistic project as a type of "rebellion" against the middle-class culture of England, suggesting a similar sensibility in Heaney's own "rough diction."[10] According to Blake Morrison, Heaney's first two books are generally regarded "as examples of post-1945 nature poetry—an imprecisely defined genre, but one presided over by Ted Hughes and reputed to be in opposition to 'idealized' Georgian treatments of nature because of its emphasis on the harsh, actual, predatory and corruptible." Morrison notes the readiness with which early reviews of Heaney assimilated him into this genre: "there was talk of his 'fidelity to his rural experience,' of his poetry's being 'loud with the slap of the spade and sour with the stink of turned earth,' and of how 'his words give us the soil-reek of Ireland, the colourful violence of his childhood on a farm in Derry.'"[11]

Yet Heaney scholars have been equally ready to dismiss an arguably more important influence on Heaney's pastoral—Robert Frost—because Frost's poetry ostensibly fails to address social and political issues considered to be obligatory territory for the Northern Irish writer. Despite Heaney's contention that Frost was "the first poet who ever spoke to him,"[12] Burris states in his introduction to *Poetry of Resistance* that he doesn't intend to consider the influence of Frost because "the historical awareness of the poets seemed in important ways to have little in common—their pastorals are conceived to accomplish radically different goals."[13] Critics have often misconstrued Frost's ostensible neglect of political issues in poetry, deciding that this omission indicates his political obtuseness, or worse, apathy. Yet Frost was attuned to these issues, as Tyler Hoffman's book *Robert Frost and the Politics of Poetry* eloquently demonstrates. Hoffman maintains that Frost's pastoral was actually the means for stating his opposition to unconstrained capitalism, which he considered a major threat to the small farmer.[14] Yet Frost believed in taking an indirect approach to politics in poetry—one that he felt would ultimately enable him to achieve a more comprehensive perspective on political issues.

Rachel Buxton observes in *Robert Frost and Northern Irish Poetry* that both Frost and Heaney chose to translate Virgil's *Eclogues* 1 and 9—the ones most clearly animated by contemporary political injustice. Buxton cites the need for "strategic retreat" as a motivation for American writers from Thoreau to Frost, quoting Richard Wakefield: "More than merely choosing isolated individuals as their subject matter, American writers have themselves often lived and worked in isolation; Thoreau . . . to the comparative wilderness of Walden pond, and Dickinson . . . to an upstairs bedroom in Amherst. Their best writing was from and often about these places of retreat."[15] She concludes that strategic retreat is equally important for Heaney, exemplified in works such as *Sweeney Astray* and *Sweeney Redivivus:* "In the same way that Sweeney is exiled from Irish society while remaining on Irish soil, Heaney, in this period, appears to be trying to sever the more binding of those emotional ties to the North while still remaining sufficiently close to observe and reflect."[16]

Frost's own oblique approach to politics is perhaps best delineated in his essay, "The Poetry of E. A. Robinson," which originally served as the introduction to Robinson's collection of poetry, *King Jasper.* Frost's essay expresses admiration for what he calls poets of "grief" rather than simply of "grievances" in order to convey the necessity not only of addressing the timely factors that directly provoke conflict but of imaginatively transcending them in order to present them from within the context of the timeless problems of human existence.

> The latest proposed experiment of the experimentalists is to use poetry as a vehicle of grievances against the un-Utopian state . . . "art can be considered good only if it prompts to action" . . . But for me, I don't like grievances. I find I gently let them alone wherever published. What I like is griefs and I like them Robinsonianly profound. I suppose there is no use in asking, but I should think we might be indulged to the extent of having grievances restricted to prose if prose will accept the imposition, and leaving poetry free to go its way in tears.[17]

Frost obviously overstates his case here, because in his own poetry, he does indeed address issues that might be considered grievances. Yet to be merely a poet of grievances—to regard grievances as ends in themselves—is to fail to acknowledge the complexities of political conflict, poetry, and indeed of life itself. Frost's conception of the poet's role illuminates Heaney's conception of his own role:[18] approaching through indirection—by transcending the immediate problem—thereby permits an ultimately more resonant response. Even Burris, although choosing to focus on Heaney's direct and particular engagement within the political arena, acknowledges Heaney's concurrent predilection for transcending its confines.[19]

Heaney's need to transcend the immediate sociopolitical situation is reflected in his frequent reliance on the conventions of early Irish nature poetry, which he describes as having been composed in a time when the landscape was "sacramental, instinct with signs, implying a system of reality beyond the visible realties,"[20] and thereby capable of reflecting inner and outer worlds simultaneously. His assessment of the role of poetry suggests the way in which his own poetry seeks to replicate and restore this system of reality:

> Poetry of any power is always deeper than its declared meaning. The secret between the words, the binding element, is often a psychic force that is elusive, archaic and only half-apprehended by maker and audience . . . this early poetry is sustained by a deep unconscious affiliation to the old mysteries of the grove, even while ardently proclaiming its fidelity to the new religion.[21]

Heaney implicitly reminds the reader that his pastoral is not by any means solely the product of English pastoral, but also of the body of early Irish nature poetry that is the cultural inheritance of the indigenous Irish. In his essay "The God in the Tree," he compares early Irish nature poetry with a pointedly different literary tradition—Japanese *haiku*—"in its precision and suggestiveness," and he distinguishes it from English and classical pastoral poems:

> It almost seems that since the Norman Conquest, the temperature of the English language has been subtly raised by a warm front coming up from the Mediterranean. But the Irish language did not undergo the same Romance influences and indeed early Irish nature poetry registers certain sensations and makes a springwater music out of certain feelings in a way unmatched in any other European language.[22]

Heaney's statement of his preference for this kind of precision—as opposed to what he considers the vague Romantic descriptions proffered in English poetry—is likewise his means for rejecting in his own poetry a solely English language and literary tradition in favor of one that incorporates strands of the two dominant cultures in Northern Ireland:

> In the syllables of my home I see a metaphor of the split culture of Ulster . . . Certainly the secret of being a poet, Irish or otherwise, lies in the summoning of the energies of words. But my quest for definition, while it may lead backward, is conducted in the living speech of the landscape I was born into. If you like, I began as a poet when my roots were crossed with my reading. I think of the personal and Irish pieties as vowels, and the literary awarenesses nourished on English as consonants. My hope is that the poems will be vocables adequate to my whole experience.[23]

Heaney refers to John Montague's description of the Irish landscape as "a manuscript which we have lost the skill to read," yet elsewhere he indicates that relearning this skill is possible and even essential for Irish writers. Heaney's use of the term "country of mind" also appears in his discussions of Wordsworth and Yeats, both of whom, Heaney believed, succeeded at rising above the local conflict that they witnessed, thereby imposing their own visions upon place rather than simply accepting visions from it. Like the ancient Irish poetry Heaney describes, and like his predecessor John Montague's poetry, Heaney's poetry reaches both literally and figuratively for a common ground. His use of Irish words and place-names not only allows him to look beyond the political and religious discord in Ireland, it grants him considerable poetic freedom to render the invisible by means of the visible.

In particular, Heaney's reliance on the *dinnseanchas,* "poems and tales which relate the original meanings of place names and constitute a form of mythological etymology," enables him to acknowledge the importance of place while simultaneously transcending it. By relying on the same premise as the *dinnseanchas,* which had incorporated both the literal and the figurative significance of the places they named, Heaney pays homage to his literary heritage while at the same time reaching beyond the Irish Troubles to the timeless dilemmas that underlie them. To convey the power of the ancient Irish poetry of place-names, Heaney draws analogies from the sites that have relatively recently acquired special literary significance, such as Yeats's Ben Bulben, Drumcliff, and Innisfree, leading him to conclude,

> All of these places now live in the imagination, all of them stir us to responses other than the merely visual, all of them are instinct with the spirit of a poet and his poetry. Irrespective of our creed or politics, irrespective of what culture or subculture may have coloured our individual sensibilities, our imaginations assent to the stimulus of names; our sense of the place is enhanced, our sense of ourselves as inhabitants not just of a geographical country but of a country of mind is cemented.[24]

While Heaney acknowledges that Yeats shares in the "love of place and lamentation against exile" that characterizes the Celtic sensibility,[25] Heaney's pastoral differs substantially from that of Yeats. Anthony Bradley notes that Yeats, as a member of the class more likely to own the land than labor on it, tends to employ "the simplest structure of pastoral," which idealizes the Irish countryside and its people. Heaney, however, raised in an Irish-Catholic family on a farm, could hardly view the shepherd's (or, more generally, the farmer's) place in society as elevated, and his eye-level description of rural life is therefore more realistic and attentive to regional detail. His pastoral might in fact be more accurately described as anti-pastoral,[26] in that it responds to the classical pastoral tradition's tendency to idealize nature by offering realistic, particularized descriptions of the countryside as the site and object of labor.[27] Heaney has discussed the way in which pastoral "beget[s] anti-pastoral, just as the Genesis story had given shape to the "persistent dream of paradise" while simultaneously acknowledging the world of "sweat and pain and deprivation" outside Eden.[28]

Whereas Yeats's model for pastoral seems to be Virgil's idealizing *Eclogues,* writers like Heaney, Kavanagh, and Montague have tended to find their precedent in the more realistic, labor-oriented *Georgics,* the counterpart to the *Eclogues.* The Irish poet Peter Fallon's 2004 translation of Virgil's *Georgics* is further testament of this continued preference, and his introduction to the translation implies the significance of the *Georgics* for Irish poetry: "Tracing the legacy of civil wars—depopulated countrysides, farms in ruins—. . . in contrast with the idealization of *The Eclogues,* this glorification of peasant life and its responsibilities displays a deeper level of compassion and a broader comprehension of sickness, disease, time's passing, and death."[29] Whereas Burris places Yeats' pastoral in the tradition of Alexander Pope, who emphasized pastoral's power to idealize while ignoring its power to critique a sharply divided society, Heaney's pastoral more closely resembles that of the rural working-class poet John Clare in its consciousness of the tensions between rural and urban worlds.[30] Burris explains Clare's appeal to poets like Heaney: "Poetry that addressed country affairs was often seen during Clare's time as deriving its strength from the peasantry's quaint cadences, not from its vision of Virgilian mythology."[31] For Heaney, the strength of relying on "quaint cadences" hearkens back to an early goal of pastoral poetry to "insinuate and glance at greater matters" through "homely persons" and "rude speeches";[32] it is also a declaration of personal and cultural independence from imperializing forces. When he describes, for example, his mother's diction in "Clearances," a poem dedicated to her, her resistance to sacrificing her regional dialect in order to conform to standard pronunciation and grammar is viewed not as a weakness but as a strength—it symbolizes her refusal to turn her back on her own identity as manifested through her speech patterns.

Heaney's first collected poem, "Digging," is at once an eloquent tribute to Heaney's father, his ancestry, his family's way of life, and his country. Ireland was long an agrarian, single-crop economy, dependent on potatoes for sustenance and on peat for fuel. While pastoral poetry—the poetry of shepherds—has long been regarded as an evasion of reality, for Heaney, it proves the most appropriate way of confronting reality; one could even argue that pastoral is the most realistic way to render a country where, even today, only about 17 percent of rural land is cultivated while the rest is pasture, and, in fact, until relatively recently, sheep rather than cows were the primary livestock.[33]

Heaney immortalizes the simple rural task of digging—for potatoes in his father's day and for turf in his grandfather's day—finally making it analogous to the writing process.

He reveals the tension between Ireland past and present, and thereby between rural and urban, traditional and modern, by acknowledging his inadequacy to these earlier generations: whereas his grandfather's turf digging is precise and neat, Heaney recalls himself as a boy, carrying milk to him "corked sloppily," and concludes, "But I've no spade to follow men like them." The product of an industrialized Northern Ireland for which higher education, after the 1947 Education Act, was a more viable option for the Catholic population,[34] Heaney is alienated from the land as well as from his forefather's rural world, and thus must rely on a pen for digging through figurative "living roots" of his ancestry and nation. Yet his metaphor echoes the adage "the pen is mightier than the sword," as well as the passage in Virgil's *Georgics* quoted in the introduction in which the farmer's digging, as well as the poet's figurative act of digging, turns up the dead soldiers' weapons, suggesting war's transience when compared to the eternal act of seeking sustenance in the land, as well as the poet's potentially more lasting literary labor of celebrating the land. Thus, like his pastoral predecessor, Heaney also addresses the essential role of poetry in transmitting cultural values that provide alternatives to violent conflict.

Heaney's characteristic refusal to idealize nature is perhaps nowhere more evident than in his depiction of the overwhelming, even threatening fecundity of nature. Traditional English pastoral tends to portray a perpetual springtime in which nature provides in exact proportion to human needs and wants. For example, one of the most familiar English pastoral lyrics, "The Passionate Shepherd to His Love," implies that nature will supply the nymph's every desire, from "beds of roses" to "shepherds' swains" who "shall dance and sing / For thy delight each May morning." Poets have been compelled ever since to contest this too-easy harmony. For many Irish poets (as for anyone in a country where the indigenous population has been conquered and dispossessed), the landscape has historically been not only a site of labor but a symbol of the dispossession and oppression carried out by the colonizers; any realistic rendering of it is itself a political act.

Thus, in Heaney's poetry, nature is just as likely to literally make him sick as tend to his every need. In one of his earliest poems, "Death of a Naturalist," nature is depicted as a terrifying, engulfing force rather than personified, as Wordsworth and others have, as gentle teacher or mother. Heaney's title initially seems to suggest that he has decided to abandon "nature poetry" because of the experience he describes in the poem. Rather, Heaney is merely conceding that this experience has taught him that he can no longer approach nature merely as "naturalist"—one who studies nature in the same impersonal, objective sense that one might study other subjects. Emerson's exhortation, "Study Nature. Know Thyself," resembles Heaney's newly discovered approach to nature. Studying nature cannot be undertaken without deep involvement of the self because of course the self is part of nature.

When the poem begins, Heaney is a schoolboy hearing his polite, reserved schoolteacher's explanation of the mating habits of frogs:

> Miss Walls would tell us how
> The daddy frog was called a bullfrog
> And how he croaked and how the mammy frog
> Laid hundreds of little eggs and this was
> Frogspawn. You could tell the weather by frogs too
> For they were yellow in the sun and brown
> In rain.

Heaney loads her lecture with dramatic irony, and in his recording of the poem at Harvard, there is mild mockery in his voice as he reads these lines. He questions her tactful evasion of "the facts of life," as when she implies that the daddy frog merely *croaks* to set everything into motion. Furthermore, he questions the presumption that nature serves as teacher: these frogs don't tell humans anything about the weather that they couldn't have discerned on their own. The remainder of the poem undermines the teacher's concept of a benevolent nature—portraying it instead as a terrifying force in its own right. His critique of his teacher's lecture is a tacit critique of the whole idealizing tradition of nature writing. Significantly, only through a private, personal encounter with nature can Heaney begin to grasp how inadequate her explanation, and thereby the tradition of nature writing, is:

> Then one hot day when fields were rank
> With cowdung in the grass the angry frogs
> Invaded the flax-dam; I ducked through hedges
> To a coarse croaking that I had not heard
> Before. The air was thick with a bass chorus.
> Right down the dam gross-bellied frogs were cocked
> On sods; their loose necks pulsed like sails. Some hopped:
> The slap and plop were obscene threats. Some sat
> Poised like mud grenades, their blunt heads farting.
> I sickened, turned, and ran. The great slime kings
> Were gathered there for vengeance and I knew
> That if I dipped my hand the spawn would clutch it.

When Heaney encounters the frogs on his own, his teacher's sanitized lecture proves completely inadequate, accounting neither for the sheer number, energy, and vitality of the frogs nor for their threat to the human world. Most important, it does not account for their effect on him personally—the way in which the very experience makes him see everything in his life differently—including himself and his own instincts. Something of their unstoppable lust and vitality he suddenly recognizes in himself. Forced to confront his own guilt over taking the frog spawn, he consequently must acknowledge that he participates in a world of vice; all that disgusts him about their world he finds reflected in himself. In poem after poem, when Heaney attempts to confront dark forces within himself, he turns to the natural world for analogies and explanations. Yet in so doing, he renders the traditional relation between nature and human nature with the specificity, precision, and complexity of vision that sentimental pastoral often lacks.

Door into the Dark (1969), whose title and central metaphor recall Frost's "Door in the Dark," is replete with the stock pastoral figures of horses, cattle, and herdsmen common to the pastoral tradition as well as more specifically Northern Irish images such as whin burning, salmon fishing, and roof thatching. In *Irish Folk Ways* (1957), E. Estyn Evans observes that Ireland relied more than the rest of Europe on whins for fuel because of its deforestation in the sixteenth and seventeenth centuries. Greater poverty in Ireland resulted in longer and more extensive reliance on primitive tools and techniques; consequently, even as late as the mid-twentieth century, thatched roofs had only recently become rarities there.[35] As in classical pastoral, Heaney's poems that describe rural activities—from hacking stalks with billhooks to forging iron—likewise provide analogies for the writing process.

Heaney's subsequent shift in setting from rural Derry to Scandinavian bogs, anticipated in "Bogland" (*Door into the Dark*) and "Tollund Man" (*Wintering Out*, 1972) and culminating in his collection *North* (1975), would superficially seem to represent a discontinuation in his interest in the pastoral tradition. His shift in setting, which coincides with his 1972 decision to move from Belfast south to a cottage in County Wicklow, has invited many scholars to perceive a concurrent shift away from pastoral. However, although he seems to have been compelled to find a setting more conducive to imaginative transcendence of the Northern Irish troubles, he nonetheless continues to address their ramifications. Growing out of his desire to raise his children in a rural area reminiscent of the one in which he grew up, his move to Wicklow incidentally permitted him the vantage point from which to continue to explore "the pastoral myth of a childhood Eden threatened by sundry afflictions."[36] Yet the bog poems may be read as darkly ironic versions of pastoral, in that they also recall a time when earth was sacramentalized and deified, albeit with destructive consequences for some of its human worshipers, as well as to render the harmony between nature and human nature, albeit strange and unsettling to a contemporary audience.

P. V. Glob's *The Bog People,* which describes northern European victims of ritual murder sacrificed to the goddess Nerthus roughly two thousand years ago, and since recovered from bogs throughout northern Europe, provides Heaney with a metaphor for the violence that pervades his own North.[37] Heaney's personification of the bogs into which victims were thrown revives the earth's ancient role as deity, recalling a time when it was regarded as holy ground and victims were ritually sacrificed to it, as in "Tollund Man," who becomes "bridegroom to the goddess." Likewise, as in classical pastoral poetry, nature and human nature merge, as bog victims are rendered inseparable from earth and its harvest: the Tollund man, for example, has a "peat-brown" head, "mild pods" for eyelids, and seeds in his stomach that await germination. Classical pastoral elegies parallel the death and anticipated rebirth of the deceased with that of the land's vegetation, and another poem about a bog victim, "Strange Fruit," makes the parallel even more explicit with its allusion to the American blues song in which the "strange fruit" on the trees are the lynched bodies of African Americans. The subject of "Punishment" is "a barked sapling," with a shaved head "like a stubble of corn"; the Grauballe man, with the grain of his wrists like bog oak, the ball of his heel like a basalt egg, "seems to weep the black river of himself." These victims, both through their literal preservation in the earth as well as the poet's figurative rendering of them, are perennial reminders of the quintessential human relationship with the landscape.

Furthermore, the unique preservative properties of the peat in which the bodies were found in northern Europe provides a metaphor for contemporary Northern Irish bogs as a "memory bank" retaining the evidence of past cultures and civilizations, thus enabling Heaney to place the Troubles in a broader context. Heaney says, "I tried, not explicitly, to make a connection between the sacrificial, religious elements in the violence of contemporary Ireland and this terrible religious thing in *The Bog People.*"[38] Thomas Docherty in "Postmodernism, Landscape, Seamus Heaney" discusses how Heaney attempts to forge a history by "confronting the bog as 'the memory of a landscape'; the palimpsest record of history which is now conceived as 'a manuscript which we have lost the skill to read.'"[39] The verse form he employs imitates the bog, its lines like layers of history, its structure an attempt to keep the past alive. In the bog poems, earth itself acts as a remarkable preservative, granting a kind of immortality to its victims and testifying, as pastoral poetry does, to that time when the landscape was "sacramental, instinct with signs." As Heaney anticipates going to Aarhus in "Tollund Man," he imagines "watching the pointing hands / Of country people, / Not knowing their tongue." Although he speaks of northern Europe, his description simultaneously recalls that of the indigenous Irish upon the arrival of the English; the "man-killing parishes" of Jutland are just as much his own.

In "Exposure," the concluding poem in *North*, the characteristic descriptions of the bog people are extended to Heaney himself, who claims to "tak[e] protective colouring from bole and bark, feeling every wind that blows." While he suggests that he might have missed "the once-in-a-lifetime portent, / The comet's pulsing rose," he elects instead the role of "inner emigre . . . wood-kerne." But just as the word "wood-kerne" has definite political overtones (wood-kernes were the shadowy Gaelic outlaws who resisted Ireland's colonization), so *North* as conceived by Heaney was an ambitious historical myth with a definite political mission—"the book all books were leading to," as he once described it.[40] His decision to associate himself not with heaven and light but with earth and shadow suggests an acquiescence to obliqueness and ambiguity in assessing a political situation usually viewed polemically. His last poem also demonstrates his continued interest in pastoral as a means of reaching this perspective: Burris contends that "ultimately the sense of what Clare termed 'rurality' pervades this poem, endowing the countryside with the maternal, sustaining qualities that describe the traditional pastoral refuge, the retreat from the hustle and bustle of daily life that encourages philosophical detachment."[41] Yet once again the countryside is not so much a retreat from reality as another means of confronting it.

Although the topography of *Field Work* (1979) is much more restricted than that of *North* (ordnance-survey scale), and the time scale drastically diminished (four years instead of two thousand), the book continues in the elegiac mode of the bog poems while also continuing to explore new venues for the pastoral tradition. Blake Morrison speaks of the way in which *Field Work* "teasingly confront[s] what he calls the 'simple-minded' belief that poems with rural or archaic images . . . aren't engaging with the modern world" by placing at the center of the collection ten highly wrought sonnets about life in Glanmore, "with its mists and wet hedges, its ploughs and tractors, its cuckoos and corncrakes, its rats and deer, its rowans and elderberries, and so on."[42] Heaney implicitly compares himself with other famous figures who retreated into the sanctuary of rural life: Horace enjoyed a "leafy privacy" far from Rome, and Heaney's friend Ann Saddlemeyer's loan of the Wicklow gate lodge is reminiscent of Maecenas' gift of the Sabine farm.[43] Notably, Horace's "retreat" served as an oblique declaration of his unhappiness with civil war, just as Heaney's has been considered a response to the civil strife in his own country.

Likewise, whereas the idyllic scenes in "Glanmore Sonnets" may seem to erase evidence of violence, they ultimately bring the Irish Troubles into sharper relief: the first few poems in *Field Work* establish a backdrop of violence on which the pastoral vision of "Glanmore Sonnets" will unfold. Burris notes that Clare's poetry involves confrontations between landowners and peasants,[44] which corresponds, in Heaney's poetry, to the tension between

British soldiers and Irish farmers. Thus, in an early poem in *Field Work,* "The Toome Road," a farmer who encounters British soldiers approaching down his roads "as if they owned them," responds,

> I had the rights-of-way, fields, cattle in my keeping,
> Tractors hitched to buckrakes in open sheds,
> Silos, chill gates, wet slates, the greens and reds
> of outhouse roofs.

Congenial relations between the farmer and the owner of the land are implausible because traditionally the farmer is Irish and the landowner, English.

In "The Strand at Lough Beg," widely regarded as the most traditional of Heaney's pastoral elegies, spent cartridges that litter the path Colum McCartney takes across the strand to fetch the cows seem doubly ominous against the peaceful backdrop of rural County Derry. Margaret Burton has examined the way in which Heaney fuses the images of a spent metal gun cartridge and ejaculated penis to portray an English colonial culture "of wasted and wasting power" that disrupts an Irish pastoral world represented by Colum's simple task of fetching the cows:

> In contrast to the genital, ejected cartridges of the second stanza and the cold-nosed guns of the first, the synecdoche which, in figuring the shooters and attackers, synthesizes body parts with machinery, the cattle are whole, living, sentient creatures [who] graze "up to their bellies in an early mist / And now they turn their unbewildered gaze / To where we work our way through squeaking sedge / Drowning in dew."[45]

Despite the violent disruptions, McCartney's death prompts the hope of regeneration traditionally promised in pastoral elegy, here represented through the greening of the landscape and the plaiting of the scapulars "with rushes that shoot green again." Heaney will later question this too-easy harmony in *Station Island,* when the ghost of Heaney's cousin returns to accuse him of using nature to evade pressing political issues—a scene that Gifford cites as "the most breathtaking accusation of pastoralization by a poet against himself in literature."[46]

Heaney's poem "Casualty" also incorporates many elements of traditional pastoral elegy, deviating from classical pastoral in certain respects in order to create a "radical pastoral" comparable to that delineated by Declan Kiberd in his analysis of the pastoral poetry of Goldsmith and Kavanagh. The poem commemorates a Catholic man who was a regular at his father-in-law's pub in Derry, but as a result of the curfews imposed on Catholic neighborhoods in the aftermath of Bloody Sunday, he fatally chooses to drink at a Protestant pub that is bombed during his visit. Heaney shapes pastoral conventions to elegize the subject while also commenting on the troubles in Northern Ireland as well as on the role of poetry under such conditions.

Heaney's subject, an alcoholic fisherman, is described warmly as "a dole-kept breadwinner, but a natural for work." Whereas pastoral elegy evolved in such a way as to exclude people of no social importance, it originally featured the lowest on the social ladder: the first *Idyll* of Theocritus is in fact a song about the death of a neatherd, Daphnis, and it also incidentally mentions an old fisherman. Only in later poetry did Daphnis come to represent Julius Caesar.[47] Whereas pastoral broadened long ago its concerns beyond that of shepherds per se, Heaney still establishes the tension between rural and urban life through his description of this man's roughness, his relative lack of education, and his unstable (especially since the advent of corporate fishing) seasonal occupation as fisherman. Indeed, one strand of pastoral—"piscatory pastoral"—was devoted to exploring the lives of fishermen. Of course the life of Christ provides perhaps the greatest example of piscatory pastoral: Christ chose fishermen as his disciples and promised to make them "fishers of men." The fisherman's apparent lack of social status ironically heightens his personal power over the narrator, and the poem highlights the broader issue in Northern Ireland of class conflict disguised as a religious conflict.

Traditionally, the pastoral elegy begins with a statement of the reason for the grief: Heaney's poem deftly demonstrates how this seemingly socially insignificant character proves a worthy subject of elegy. Despite being "dole-kept," the fisherman possesses traditionally rural virtues, described not only as hard-working—a "natural for work"—but comfortable with solitude, honest, direct, independent, wise, and even preternaturally perceptive. The poem's young narrator, not having made peace with the civilizing influences upon him, finds the man worthy of adulation, stating "I loved his whole manner," because he possesses the finesse and self-confidence that the narrator lacks: the older man can order a drink without having to raise his voice, nor even say a word (albeit the result of an alcoholism that the poem acknowledges is beyond his control). The man also possesses the "fisherman's quick eye," and even, ostensibly, the magical ability to see as though with eyes in the back of his head, thus Heaney's oxymoronic reference to "his turned, observant back."

Because the narrator is from a similar rural background, he has not yet grown comfortable with his "other life" as an educated man and a writer of poetry, and is reluctant to discuss his feelings about the subject about which this older man obviously feels comfortable enough to ask. When the older man mentions poetry, the narrator attempts to change the subject "to eels / Or lore of the horse and cart / Or the Provisionals." His suggested topics of conversation recall a motif in classical pastoral—digressions on topical, frequently satirical, issues. Yet these topics prove on closer inspection to be not really digressions but integral to the fabric of the poem. Heaney conflates appropriate pastoral topics—evidence of the simple, rural life, such as the man's fishing and the lore of the "horse and cart"—with the harshest reminders of the drawbacks of civilized life—namely the presence of war, manifested here in the reference to the provisionals, as well as, of course, the aftermath of Bloody Sunday. Virgil had written his pastoral in the midst of the ravages of civil war, and war and violence are inevitably perversions of pastoral peace and content, highlighting the contrast between nature and civilization. The narrator's insistence on changing the subject from poetry to Northern Irish politics, as well as his refusal to acknowledge the potential connection between the two, is the poet's critique of his own failure to address the Irish Troubles.

Heaney's description of this man who "drank like a fish," and was willing to go "miles away" from his home for the sake of a drink, conveys the enormity of his addiction, invoking the popular stereotype of the drunk Irishman. Yet his extended comparison certainly transforms the stereotype into loving recollection through its beautiful, alliterative metaphor: "Swimming towards the lure / Of warm lit-up places." Although the man's alcoholism drove him to ignore the curfew "others obeyed," which was to some extent a betrayal of his Catholic community (and Heaney acknowledges in his introduction to the recording of the poem that this might be considered a kind of faithlessness), Heaney depicts it here as an admirable defiance, consistent not only with his solitary drinking but with his presumable decision to avoid the funeral of the thirteen killed on Bloody Sunday. Immediately following the description of the "common funeral," Heaney writes, "But he would not be held / At home by his own crowd," referring to the fisherman's decision to ignore the curfew but suggesting his defiance of any and all communal expressions of grief, inspiring Heaney's own avoidance of the man's funeral. Heaney depicts the cloying sense of camaraderie of the funeral attenders, their bourgeois conformity and respectability, their "sideways" talking implicitly contrasted with the fisherman's refreshing directness and honesty:

> Those quiet walkers
> and sideways talkers
> Shoaling out of his lane
> To the respectable
> Purring of the hearse.

Heaney might also be offering a quiet counterargument for his own heretofore conventional poetic response: rather than conforming to the rest of the "tribe" (emphasized by the exact rhyme of "walkers" and "talkers"), talking "sideways" rather than straightforwardly, shoaling like a school of fish to the sound of the hearse, Heaney opts finally to venture out on his own to respond to the death and express his grief on his own terms.

While Heaney's poem is on one level an elegy for the fisherman whose life was lost, its description of the funeral for the victims of Bloody Sunday allows it to serve as a group elegy as well as a personal one. Goldsmith's "The Deserted Village" eulogized the anonymous many who died, as opposed to the heroic individual usually deemed a worthier subject of elegy. Instead of depicting the conventional adornment of graves with flowers, Heaney depicts the dead ones themselves as flowers. Similarly, Heaney writes,

> rained-on, flower-laden
> Coffin after coffin
> Seemed to float from the door
> Like blossoms on slow water.

Classical pastoral featured floral tributes for the deceased, and post-Renaissance poetry often includes elaborate passages in which flowers appear to deck the hearse or grave, with various flowers having symbolic meaning appropriate to the scene. Here, the coffins are flower-laden but also blossom-like. The coffins themselves, rather than the lost lives within them, are the floral tributes—hollow tributes to the culture of death in Northern Ireland.

In celebrating the death of the herdsman Daphnis, Theocritus relies on the folk tradition of associating it with the annual death of Nature itself;[48] the convention of the "pathetic fallacy," Ruskin's term for the depiction of Nature as sharing human sorrow, was integral to the pastoral tradition from its very origin.[49] Reaching its culmination in Milton's great pastoral elegy "Lycidas" (which includes an entire chorus of mourners, from animals—wolves, jackals, lions—to trees, flowers, rivers, caves, and mountains), the lament of nature is manifested in "Casualty" through the interminable rain during the funeral. Given the unusually high rainfall in Northern Ireland, rainfall might seem more a plausible occurrence than an artificial convention, but Heaney's selective description enables him to achieve the effect of the best pastoral elegy.[50] In the intervening centuries since "Lycidas," the poet's use of pathetic fallacy has come under attack for anthropomorphizing nature; however, recent ecocritical theorists contend that the form must be reconsidered given that the human disconnection from nature is precisely the cause of our current ecological crisis.[51] In *Pathetic Fallacy in the Nineteenth Century,* Josephine Miles argues that "the attribution of feeling to things . . . is more than a device mentioned in rhetoric books; it is a way of seeing the world and expressing that view."[52] Helena Feder's ecocritical reassessment of Romantic poetry concurs, stating that "it is through the assumption of reciprocity that the 'fallacy' attributes 'human' qualities to the 'inanimate' and/or natural world."53

Heaney's use of water imagery, which continues in his description of the fisherman's own funeral, echoes "Lycidas" in another important way; whereas the earlier poem's water imagery is an acknowledgment of Milton's protagonist's death by drowning, Heaney's is just as surely homage to his subject's occupation, which, however humble in the eyes of the community, allows for an intimacy with the natural world that evades the city dwellers.

In the final section of the poem, Heaney strives in several respects to emulate the old fisherman: just as the fisherman had chosen to miss the funerals of the victims of Bloody Sunday, and to "break our tribe's complicity" by ignoring the curfew others obeyed, Heaney chooses to miss his funeral. In refusing to attend, Heaney not only violates the conventions of the funeral elegy, he also violates those of this culture of death. Like the fisherman, Heaney intuits the ineffectuality of communal grief, choosing to eschew conformity and respectability—"the slow consolation of a dawdling engine"—in favor of the freedom that comes with solitude:

> I tasted freedom with him.
> To get out early, haul
> Steadily off the bottom,
> Dispraise the catch, and smile
> As you find a rhythm
> Working you, slow mile by mile,
> Into your proper haunt
> Somewhere, well out, beyond.

The implication is that the fisherman finds his "proper haunt," not necessarily immortality in any conventional sense. Heaney's reference to "proper haunt" is also metaphoric of his own poetic practice, which seeks to find a rhythm through which to convey a personal response to the troubles in Northern Ireland, to avoid tribal complicity in his poetry as well as in his life.

Heaney's use of rhetorical questions throughout the poem as a means of coming to terms with grief and loss is typical of the elegiac tradition, yet in this poem they echo beyond the fisherman's death, interrogating the narrator not only about the fisherman's life but about his own. The memory of his refusal to answer the man's questions is tinged with remorse and resonates beyond the poem's immediate context: "now you're supposed to be an educated man. Puzzle me the right answer to that one." While the fisherman's question obviously compels the narrator to consider the injustice of the deaths that have occurred, it likewise interrogates the use the narrator has made of his own education, his failure to seek and find answers to matters of life and death. The poet then poses an unanswered and indeed unanswerable question: "How culpable was he / That last night when he broke / Our tribe's complicity?" One function of elegiac questioning is to release the energy locked in grief or rage and to channel it in the form of a question that is not an indication of ignorance but an expression of protest.

In the final lines, Heaney pleads hopelessly for more questions: "Dawn-sniffing revenant, / Plodder through midnight rain, / Question me again." Haunted by this man whose unanswered questions acquire great resonance after his death, the narrator regrets that the fisherman is no longer there to ask his questions and that when he was alive, the narrator had no answers for him, nor indeed for any of the victims of the Troubles.

The poet protests not only the senseless death of the fisherman but all of the deaths of victims of sectarian violence. Whereas Sacks suggests that "asking a question of someone else may be designed to deflect guilt,"[54] Heaney's elegy asks the dead subject to question him again, thus forcing Heaney to share the burden of guilt. The poem's abrupt transition to second person, likewise a convention in pastoral elegy, reinforces his acceptance of the burden of guilt, reminding the reader that the elegy responds to the human condition but also to individual loss.[55]

A basic assumption of pastoral is that "a complete consideration of simple people" enables one to "say everything about complex people."[56] Through this apparently simple fisherman, Heaney explores the ironies and complexities of the troubles in Northern Ireland as well as the possibilities for poetic responses to them.

Heaney's "Glanmore Sonnets" speaks of landing "in the hedge-school of Glanmore," at once a reminder of the legacy of British colonization, which resigned Irish children to seeking education in hedge schools, but also a suggestion that Heaney and his family's sojourn in Glanmore involves a figurative return to Heaney's own rural childhood. Heaney describes "each verse returning like the plough turned round," alluding to the ancient Greek writing style, boustrophedon, with lines alternately written left to right and right to left, as well as to the ancient Greek pastoral motif of rural labor as an analogy for poetic labor. In Sonnet 3, the cuckoo and corncrake are pastoral motifs; the corncrake in particular is a frequent feature of Irish pastoral—its harsh cry more appropriate to anti-pastoral. Jonathan Allison's "Seamus Heaney's Anti-Transcendental Corncrake" examines the corncrake's associations in Irish poetry with an idyllic, preindustrial pastoral landscape. Heaney's choice of the cuckoo is particularly appropriate: the bird's now threatened extinction, its association with prewar Ulster and the tradition of mowing with a scythe rather than a combine harvester, and its harsh cry symbolizing the "guttural muse" of the Irish language enrich Heaney's postcolonial, ecological version of pastoral.[57]

The already implicit comparison to Wordsworth's pastoral—evident in both the form and the content of the sonnet sequence—is made explicit here as well, as the narrator compares himself and his wife to "Dorothy and William," who likewise sought refuge in a cottage retreat. In Sonnet 4, the reminiscences about childhood begin, and in 5, the childhood memory of a boor-tree, "our bower as children," a miniature rural retreat. Death and violence are nonetheless present here, symbolized in Sonnet 9 by the black rat, chaff, and the blood on the pitchfork. The bay tree at the gate recalls Daphnis, the shepherd who was the mythical founder of pastoral poetry, and whose name means "laurel" or "bay tree." Longus's third-century pastoral romance *Daphnis and Chloë* describes two children found by shepherds and raised together, becoming shepherds and eventually lovers. They spend their later life in pastoral retreat, thus providing another parallel to the story of Dorothy and William Wordsworth as well as to the poet and his wife. In 10, Heaney compares the couple with other pairs of lovers who flee conflict and escape to the countryside: Lorenzo and Jessica, who, in Shakespeare's *Merchant of Venice,* elope to Belmont, an idyllic site on a hilltop on the coast of the Ionian Sea, where they are finally free to pursue a relationship; and Diarmuid and Grainne, Irish lovers who flee Grainne's jealous husband and find refuge first in a bower and then throughout the countryside.

Perhaps no single period in Heaney's poetry more adequately emblematizes his use of the pastoral tradition than his translation of the legend of Mad King Sweeney. Heaney's original translation describes how, when Ronan, king of Dal-Arie, marked out a church in Sweeney's territory, Sweeney grabbed his psalter in anger and threw it in the lake, after which he was summoned to battle at Moira. After a day and a night had passed, an otter rose out of the lake with the psalter and brought it, completely unharmed, to Ronan, who cursed Sweeney. Although Sweeney clearly provokes the battle that follows, he flees from it, turning into a bird that then roams the countryside. In his preface to *Sweeney Astray,* Heaney writes that "insofar as Sweeney is also a figure of the artist, displaced, guilty, assuaging himself by his utterance, it is possible to read the work as an aspect of the quarrel between free creative imagination and the constraints of religious, political, and domestic obligation."[58] Heaney gradually shapes the Sweeney legend in such a way that it provides not only justification for the artistic life but for his own retreat into rural life as well as a specifically Irish version of the classical pastoral retreat.

In *Sweeney's Flight,* Heaney's revision of his original translation, he chooses sections of the poem that will stand by themselves as lyric poems—sections that also, incidentally, emphasize the pastoral qualities of the original, portraying

Sweeney's flight from battle as more a pastoral gesture than an act of disrespect toward a holy man: only one line alludes to Ronan's curse, merely referring to Sweeney as "Ronan's victim," suggesting that Ronan, as the representative of the established church, and not Sweeney, the representative of pre-Christian Ireland, is the aggressor. Like classical pastoral, the poem features an idyllic landscape that also seems charged with divinity: "Sainted cliff at Alternan, / nut grove, hazel wood!" Its protagonist also comes to exist in harmony with nature, initially resenting the curse upon him that requires him to roam the countryside but gradually finding peace and identifying more with birds than with humans: "I saw great swans and heard their calls / sweetly rebuking wars and battles." A sharp contrast is drawn between the civilization that has exiled him and the peace and harmony of the natural world:

> Woods and forests and wild deer—
> things like these delight you more
> than sleeping in your eastern dun
> on a bed of feather-down.

Nature provides the solace that the human world lacks:

> The alder is my darling,
> all thornless in the gap,
> some milk of human kindness
> coursing in its sap.

The "milk of human kindness" alludes to Lady Macbeth's description of her husband: she fears he has too much "milk," but he proves himself to be devoid of it as he murders one character after another.

Civilization is depicted as an incursion on this peaceful, natural setting:

> But what disturbs me most
> in the leafy wood
> is the to and fro and to and fro
> of an oak rod
> I prefer the scurry
> and song of blackbirds
> to the usual blather
> of men and women.

Set against the freedom of the "leafy wood," the carved oak rod, a product of civilization, is a symbol of human punitive measures ("spare the rod and spoil the child"), and, more generally, social strictures that run counter to nature's course. The "blather of men and women" offers no music to his ears, merely an unwelcome form of social control. He opts instead for the simple, uncultivated activities of birds, shunning the warmongering of the world he left behind:

> let us forage, nest and hide
> in ivy in the brown-floored wood
> and hear behind the late birds' song
> sounds of water in Glen Bolcain.

By merging his voice with that of Sweeney's, the poet imaginatively recreates Sweeney's vision to produce a version of Irish pastoral. "The King of the Ditchbacks," which evolved from the experience of translating *Sweeney Astray*, is the most consummate expression of this vision:

> so my vision was a bird's
> at the heart of a thicket
> and I spoke as I moved
> like a voice from a shaking bush . . .
> a rich young man
> leaving everything he had
> for a migrant solitude.

Heaney's literary career has been described as a series of leaps from "gritty pastoralism" to a "meditative style that countered traditional Catholic meditations with secular alternatives," and finally, "to a linguistic poetry whose characters and plots derived from little-known words." These ostensible "leaps" have left many critics baffled, leading one anonymous reviewer in the *Times Literary Supplement* to complain that *Wintering Out* (1972) skirted around themes that Heaney was hesitant to tackle head on and that "no one was plucking up" cobbles "to throw them at anyone." Henry Hart, author of *Seamus Heaney: Poet of Contrary Progressions*, mocks the whole notion "that Heaney has to be poetry's Sam Peckinpah to be taken seriously."[59]

Heaney's "leap" in his volume *Seeing Things* (1991),[60] although seeming to signify his penchant for greater and greater abstraction, nonetheless reflects his continued interest in the pastoral tradition. His continued reliance on pastoral suggests not only his reluctance to tackle themes head on but his predilection for the themes that both engage in and transcend particular conflicts—a rendering of reality as sacramental that ultimately serves to place the Northern Irish troubles into context. "Seeing things" is colloquial for hallucinating, which might suggest that Heaney's sights and insights are nothing but illusions. Skeptics might benefit from Shaw's preface to *Saint Joan*, in which he defines illusions as "the unconsciously reasoned conclusions of genius."⁶¹ Throughout the book, Heaney incorporates the imagery of optical and auditory illusions as if to suggest that acknowledging the illusory—thereby challenging sensorially or rationally derived experience—is essential to the process of "seeing things." Nothing is what it appears to be, but everything ultimately is more than it appears to be; it shimmers and echoes beyond the usual physical limitations imposed by the senses.

Heaney's need to *see things* in this more comprehensive sense seems to justify his decision to continue to explore the subjects of earlier volumes—the fields and hedges of the Irish landscape—in spite of critics who claim that the pastoral tradition is depleted and that Heaney employs bucolic imagery simply to evade pressing political issues. By narrowing his field of vision, he does not necessarily reduce his capacity for the visionary: the regional and the universal, long regarded as antithetical concerns for the Irish writer, are related. *Seeing Things* carefully balances the "marvelous," or supernatural, with the earthly, or natural, in the same way that classical pastoral did: the conventional setting for pastoral, Arcadia, was thought to be the abode of supernatural entities.

In *Seeing Things,* the visual equivalent of this psychic force is an optical illusion, and its auditory equivalent is the kind of elaborate echo that a seashell produces. The literary precedent for Heaney's technique seems to be Celtic vision poetry, a form that apparently developed independent of English vision literature such as the *Vision of Piers Plowman,* with its May Day morning on Malvern Hill, which took four or five centuries to reach Ireland. Heaney's use of this genre, in keeping with his practice of relying on Irish rather than English forms whenever possible, also enables him to suggest that the genre's worldview holds true for his poems: given the context, of course one is supposed to regard these visions as true—only a modern mind would discount them as hallucination.

The poem "Field of Vision" may be read as an illustration of Heaney's technique. It describes a woman who sat for years in a wheelchair staring at the same scene. Her ostensible limitations of space and of movement result, ironically, in her expansive vision. Confronting her provides a kind of education for the narrator, a perspective

> where you could see
> Deeper into the country than you expected
> And discovered that the field behind the hedge
> Grew more distinctly strange as you kept standing
> Focused and drawn in by what barred the way.

Heaney's technique corresponds to the metaphor that unifies the book: crossing the threshold between life and death to see his father "face to face."

The book opens with a passage from the *Aeneid* which describes Aeneas's effort to see his father face-to-face. In order to see him, Aeneas must first consult the sibyl, who

> chanted fearful equivocal words and made the cave echo
> With sayings where clear truths and mysteries
> Were inextricably
> twined.

On a personal level, Heaney confronts the same kind of ambiguity while trying to see his own father, a world full of echoes and resonances that make "clear truth" impossible to discern. While Aeneas is instructed to pluck the golden bough, which he must hand to Persephone before entering the underworld, Heaney's equivalent task is to wield "the silver bough," an allusion to the *Voyage of Bran,* which begins, "I bring you a branch of Evin's apple tree, / With silver twigs and crystal buds and blossoms."[62] In the *Voyage of Bran,* while Bran is with his warriors at the royal fort, they see a woman who sings quatrains to them about the Isles of the Happy—the branch refers to her poetry and to the promise of these isles. The metaphor for this ancient poem in turn applies to the book that Heaney offers to his readers, and on a literal level, to his father's walking stick, which is passed on to him upon his father's death.

Just as the walking stick symbolizes the wealth of wisdom passed down from parent to child—our very being a legacy from our parents—seemingly insignificant objects, gestures, and events throughout *Seeing Things* resound in such a way as to transcend their times and places. In his poem "The Ash Plant," Heaney associates the ash stick with the role of judge and of poet— "Or wield a stick like a silver bough and come / Walking again among us: the quoted judge"—and also with the preservation of life; in Irish folklore, the ash was a charm against drowning, carried by emigrants to America after the potato famine.

In the title poem, "Seeing Things," the simple memories of a Sunday morning trip to Inishbofin resonate through time and space. In the façade of a cathedral, which depicts the baptism of Christ, Heaney sees "in that utter invisibility / The stone's alive with what's invisible," and the air wavers "like the zig-zag hieroglyph for life itself." Common elements—water, stone, and air—are transformed through the Sunday morning ritual and the ritual of baptism. The name Inishbofin means "island of the white cow," and legends have arisen concerning enchanted white cows that appear out of the water as a symbol of regeneration or fertility;[63] islands themselves seem to rise up out of the water. During this brief incident he glimpses his destiny:

> As we went sailing evenly across
> The deep, still, seeable-down-into water,
> It was as if I looked from another boat
> Sailing through air, far up, and could see
> How riskily we fared into the morning,
> And loved in vain our bare, bowed, numbered heads.

In the final section of the poem, Heaney succeeds in seeing his father "face to face"; like the legendary island, his father miraculously rises up out of the water: "And there was nothing between us there / That might not still be happily ever after."

Appropriately, the central metaphor of crossing the threshold between life and death is reiterated in poems about crossings and balancings of all sorts. In "Casting and Gathering," two contrary states of mind are defined in terms of contrasting places—the left and right banks of a river—and actions—casting and gathering fishing line. The first two stanzas are alternately euphonious and cacophonous, underscoring this contrast:

> On the left bank, a green silk tapered cast
> Went whispering through the air, saying hush
> And lush, entirely free, no matter whether
> It swished above the hayfield or the river.
>
> On the right bank, like a speeded-up corncrake,
> A sharp ratcheting went on and on
> Cutting across the stillness as another
> Fisherman gathered line-lengths off his reel.

The third stanza balances two ways of seeing oneself and the world, both of which prove equally essential:

> One sound is saying, "You are not worth tuppence,
> But neither is anybody. Watch it! Be severe."
> The other says, "Go with it! Give and swerve.
> You are everything you feel beside the river."

The breadth of Heaney's poetic diction becomes a way of embodying the manifold nature of reality, as well as acknowledging the polyglossic nature of the linguistic situation within Northern Ireland. Heaney's diction represents a fusion not only of literal and figurative but of Irish, Scots, and English. While in earlier books Heaney depicts a struggle between the "guttural muse" of Gaelic and the alliteration of English, *Seeing Things* demonstrates the productiveness of linguistic fusion. By using a blend of Irish, Scottish, and Anglo-Saxon words, Heaney aptly captures and places in context the clash of cultures that shaped his native Northern Ireland. Local conflict is both subsumed by and reflected in elemental and semantic conflict.

Heaney also melds English and Irish poetic traditions, balancing the dark and heavy imagery that characterizes *North* with the sunnier imagery of classical poetry, a technique he had relied on in previous poetry—one that enables him to meld ancient Irish poetry with parallel classical sources. "It almost seems that since the Norman Conquest, the temperature of the English language has been subtly raised by a warm front coming up from the Mediterranean."[64] In the poem "The Skylight," Heaney describes himself as a person who by nature prefers the "low and closed . . . claustrophobic, nest-up-in-the-roof effect," but, when the slates are removed at his wife's insistence, he is nonetheless transfixed by the "extravagant sky."

As in classical pastoral, rural pastimes often provide metaphors for the poet's role, yet here they also express the book's central motif and theme: strivings that reach beyond the visible. In "The Pitchfork," Heaney describes what he claims was his only mark of distinction in the farming community where he grew up: his ability to throw a pitchfork. While throwing it, he experiments with traditional roles, playing "warrior or athlete." The pitchfork is made of ash, as spears traditionally were. As he had in earlier books, Heaney finds his favorite analogies for the writing process within the field of agriculture, not only because the terms imply a directness, a concreteness that we often fail to associate with mental activities, but also because pastoral poets celebrated the simple life by associating their own craft with it. One uses a pen as one would use a farm implement—to dig with, to aim for, to shape, or to build. The last lines, therefore, suggest the transcendence that Heaney seeks in poetry:

> And then when he thought of probes that reached the farthest,
> He would see the shaft of a pitchfork sailing past
> Evenly, imperturbably through space,
> Its prongs starlit and absolutely soundless—
> But has learned at last to follow that simple lead
> Past its own aim, out to an other side
> Where perfection—or nearness to it—is imagined
> Not in the aiming but the opening hand.

His choice to follow "that simple lead / past its own end" is itself political; while Heaney initially recognizes the pitchfork's potential as a weapon, and therefore a tangible source of power, he ultimately refuses to regard it as such, thereby acknowledging his preference for the open hand to that of the aiming hand—peaceful resolution of conflict rather than violence.

In *Seeing Things,* Heaney refers to the fossil poetry of "hob and slate," an allusion to Emerson's description of words as "fossil poems," which intimates that he shares Emerson's view of language. This same view led the linguist Richard Trench to write that "many a single word . . . is itself a concentrated poem, having stores of poetical thought and imagery laid up in it."[65] Heaney's reference to "hob and slate" reminds us that writing originally involved cutting into something, and his poems reflect that action—cutting, changing, shaping the surface of reality rather than passively recording it as a journalist or realist might. In his poems about writing, he suggests that the Old English "scop"—shaper or creator—best describes his own role as a poet. Thus, what may seem like pointless word play serves to illuminate layers of meaning in order to render reality as sacramental. He describes earth itself as "ocarina earth," resonant for those who seek to know it.

In the final section of "Squarings," Heaney writes,

> In famous poems by the sage, Han Shan,
> Cold Mountain is a place that can also mean
> A state of mind. Or different states of mind
> At different times.

Likewise, Heaney's descriptions of the landscape have distinct parallels with human mental states—heights that bring temptation; dampness that reminds him of his servitude to the body, "that earth house I inherited"; river currents that recall "the very currents memory is composed of." He writes,

> I can't remember never having known
> A land of *glar* and *glit* and floods at
> *Dailigone.* My silting hope.
> My lowlands of the mind.

He thus links the conditions of the land with his own mental state. In another poem in *Seeing Things,* Heaney asks, "Where does spirit live? Inside or outside?" His decision to leave this question open is itself a way of *seeing things.* His inner life is deeply connected the outer world of nature; answering any questions about his own identity therefore involves looking outward on the landscape.

The Spirit Level (1996) marks Heaney's return to the pastoral world of Glanmore and *Sweeney Astray,* its simple pastoral activities—plaiting a Brigid's girdle, cutting wild mint, plowing—again serving as metaphors for poetic composition: "the poem as ploughshare that turns time." "Astray in home truths out of Horace," Heaney describes the sharpening stone that was to be a gift to his father:

So set the drawer on freshets of thaw water
And place the unused sharping stone inside it:
To be found next summer on a riverbank
Where scythes once hung all night in alder trees
And mowers played dawn scherzos on the blades.

Marvell's "Mower" poems had substituted a mower for a shepherd, with Death the final mower. So Heaney elegizes his father as well as the pastoral landscape associated with him.

Electric Light (2001)[66] is even more attentive to the history of the genre of pastoral than Heaney's earlier works. Meg Tyler's *A Singing Contest: Conventions of Sound in the Poetry of Seamus Heaney,* which devotes a chapter to Heaney's pastoral, focuses on his use of eclogue, observing that three poems in the volume are given the title of eclogue. Rather than viewing Virgil's *Eclogues* as escapist, Tyler emphasizes "darker forces . . . at work" in their composition: "In Virgil's day, the mid-30s B.C.E., civil war had been tearing Italy apart for years. Such turmoil shaped Virgil's poetry implicitly and explicitly, just as internecine warfare has affected Heaney's verse."[67] "Bann Valley Eclogue" views the Bann Valley "through the refractive lens of Virgil's Fourth Eclogue," from its invocation of the muses to its tribute to Virgil as a "hedge-schoolmaster." Hedge schools, the Irish Catholic response to British laws that prohibited Catholics from being educated, were held in secret by schoolmasters who moved from place to place.[68] Because classical languages were taught in hedge schools (Latin was still the language of the church) in which both teachers and students had undergone various kinds of dispossession, "Bann Valley Eclogue" seems in several ways a direct descendent of Virgil's pastoral. As the persona anticipates the birth of a child, the personification of the Bann Valley parallels the birth process—from the Bann River waters that break, to the earth's "birthmark," to the cows sluicing with milk at the poem's conclusion.[69] Virgil, too, had represented his hope for civil peace and a new world order by means of an anticipated birth. Heaney, however, reimagines the classical pastoral setting in Northern Ireland, replacing Virgil's flowers that pour forth from the cradle with "big dog daisies [that] will get fanked up in the spokes" of the baby's pram, she-goats with cows, ivy spray with shamrocks on St. Patrick's mornings. Finally, the peace that Virgil anticipates is given a specifically Northern Irish twist: "Let her never hear close gunfire or explosions."

Although "Virgil: Eclogue IX"[70] is a translation of rather than a tribute to Virgil, the translation of "old green hedge" for the "green foliage" that serves as a site for singing recalls the earlier allusion to Irish hedge schools. When an outsider arrives to claim rights to Moeris's "bit of ground," Moeris responds with, "All's changed," echoing Yeats' "Easter 1916" and suggesting a parallel between the territorial conflict and civil war of Virgil's day and the civil war following the Easter 1916 uprising. In both cases, the ensuing social upheaval reverberates beyond the dispossession of a single landowner.

"Glanmore Eclogue" revisits issues of land and ownership, recalling Ireland's own history more than Virgil's, with "Land Commissions making tenants owners, empire taking note at last too late" while in late twentieth-century Ireland, "Outsiders own the country nowadays . . . [as] small farmers . . . are priced out of the market." The poem concludes with a specifically Irish version of the medieval "cuckoo" song, the oldest printed song in the English language, but this time adapted to an Irish setting, featuring bog cotton, yellow-blossoming whins, and bog banks that "shine like ravens' wings."

"Sonnets from Hellas," inspired by Heaney's trip to Greece, juxtaposes the terrain of ancient Greece with contemporary Northern Ireland. Heaney's travelogue is a kind of Odyssey that opens with "Into Arcadia" in which he crosses Argos into Arcadia, the site of Virgil's eclogues. Arcadia has been immortalized not only as the consummate pastoral setting but as the setting of Nicolas Poussin's painting of Arcadian shepherds, which features a tombstone with the phrase, "Et in Arcadia ego," interpreted either as a reminder that death is ever present even in Arcadia or that the deceased, too, once enjoyed life's pleasures. Either way, Heaney's sonnet sequence is a reflection on mortality as well as a reminder to the reader of the continued significance of classical pastoral on contemporary culture. Heaney imbues the setting with a sense of continuity between ancient and contemporary worlds: from the irrigation system made of reeds to the goatherd with his goats at the filling station, "subsisting beyond eclogue and translation."

Section 4, "Augean Stables," occurs at the legendary site of the fifth labor of Heracles, which was to clean out the stables of King Augeus. He managed the task by rerouting the courses of the Alpheus and Peneus rivers. There in Olympia, among green willows and river shallows, they hear of the murder of Sean Brown, GAA official murdered by loyalists in Derry in 1997. Heaney ironically counterpoints the legendary rush of the rivers' water and the idyllic setting of the stables with "the hose-water smashing hard back off the asphalt" to wash away the blood of the murder victim.

Section 5, "Castalian Spring," is set on the slope of Mount Parnassus, sacred to the muses, and also the site of the Oracle of Delphi. Because a shepherd was reputedly the first to observe the apparently magical properties of the landscape, the pastoral privileging of the shepherd's perspective gained momentum. As the home of the Muses, Parnassus became known as the home of poetry, music, and learning. Heaney and his companions imagine Gaelicized new names for Mount Parnassus, "Poetry Hill," that imply the connection with his own poetic tradition. He concludes the section with the word "boustrophedon," a writing style described earlier in the chapter, whose alternating direction saves the reader from the need to return to the left margin with each new line. It means "like an ox while ploughing" and thus is another of Heaney's many analogies between writing and rural labor.

District and Circle (2006) marks a literal return to Anahorish, the site of Heaney's earliest pastoral poems, as well as a figurative return to the metaphors that the setting supplied. The cover, the photograph of a young man in early twentieth-century rural Ireland standing beside an "agitator"—an early washing machine—advertises this return and embodies the tension between traditional and modern, rural and urban, so characteristic of pastoral. As in Heaney's earlier collections, rural labor provides metaphors for life as well as for literary labor: swinging sledges, haying, killing pigs, tying sheaves, forging iron in an eighteenth-century blacksmith shop (in a translation of an eighteenth-century Irish poem), crafting harrow pins, and making *súgán* (straw rope used for tethering animals and for making chairs, baskets, and other woven goods). In "Súgán," the poet recognizes that he holds within his hands the power to "bind and loose"—a power that clearly resonates beyond the immediate setting to poetry and to life. "The Turnip-Snedder," a device for cutting heads off turnips "in an age of bare hands and cast iron," employs rhythm imitative of the snedder, finding in the turnip cycle a metaphor for the cycle of human life.

Heaney also pays homage to his pastoral lineage. The characters in "Anahorish 1944" are killing pigs when the Americans arrive, and the graphic details recall the first influence on Heaney's version of anti-pastoral: Ted Hughes's "View of a Pig." Heaney has described how the poem suddenly made "the matter of contemporary poetry . . . the material of [his] own life,"[71] and Gifford describes how Hughes' ironic pastoralisms lead to "post-pastoral" in their use of myth to reconnect humans to the nature in themselves.[72] Another poem, "Stern," is dedicated to the memory of Hughes. In "Edward Thomas on the Lagans Road," Heaney pays homage to yet another pastoral predecessor, whose contrast with Heaney's own poetry corresponds to the contrast between the idyllic landscape of pre-World War II Ireland with the modern, postwar world.

"Tollund Man in Springtime" resurrects the Tollund man, the subject of one of Heaney's earlier bog poems, whose death as the result of ritualistic violence had been employed as a metaphor for victims to the violence in Northern Ireland. At the time he composed "The Tollund Man," he had considered blasphemy—"consecrat[ing] the cauldron bog / Our holy ground and pray[ing] / Him to make germinate." In his twenty-first-century return to the subject, his prayer seems to have been answered: the Tollund man reawakens from his pastoral burial ground to traffic and transatlantic flights and airport screening machines. Like Montague, Heaney shifts his emphasis from national to international affairs, yet pastoral continues to provide a unifying theme. The Tollund man finds the contemporary world overwhelming and unlearnable, longing for what he has come to regard as the true source of learning—the simple sight of cattle out in rain. For Heaney as well, pastoral remains the only way to make sense of the contemporary world as he recalls the sites of his earlier pastoral—Moyulla, Glanmore, Anahorish—carrying Tollund rushes with him.

Heaney writes in *Station Island,*

> Be adept and be dialect,
> tell of this wind coming past the zinc hut,
>
> call me sweetbriar after the rain
> or snowberries cooled in the fog.

Denis Donoghue paraphrases the lines thus: "trust in what you know, but go beyond it, make your poetry a pastoral above the indefeasible divisions which in any case you can't avoid."[73] Heaney's later poetry represents a continuation of his efforts both to address these divisions and to imaginatively transcend them by means of the pastoral tradition. Whereas Heaney writes a complex pastoral attuned to contemporary sociopolitical concerns, his forays into post-pastoral—with its direct engagement with environmental issues—are less frequent than Montague's. The kind of sustained attention to the environment that characterizes post-pastoral is more fully realized by Michael Longley.

CHAPTER 3

"Love Poems, Elegies: I am losing my place"

Michael Longley's Environmental Elegies

In an interview with Fran Brearton, then a student at the University of Durham, Michael Longley was asked to discuss the closing lines of his book *The Ghost Orchid:* "Love poems, elegies: I am losing my place. / Elegies come between you and my face." Longley quips that while Fran is at the stage in her life for going to weddings, he has arrived at the stage for going to funerals, and thus he is writing more and more elegies.[1] Yet even Longley's first collected poem, "Epithalamion," is richly elegiac, suffused with the awareness that everything is dying: in the midst of this wedding song, Longley reminds his bride that even the darkness is

> growing elderly, the flowers are withering . . . the stars dissolved,
> Amalgamated in a glare,
> which last night were revolved
> Discreetly round us.[2]

The poem demonstrates how quickly life moves from aubade to elegy—from the lovers' arrogant certainty that the stars, and even the sun itself, orbit around them, to the awareness that all—including the lovers themselves—will die. The couple that had been "rendered royal" by the moths seeking light in their room will someday be gone, and he hopes that at least all these dying things will "when we rise, be seen with dawn / As remnant yet part raiment still, / Like flags that linger on the sky when king and queen are gone."

While a classics student at Trinity College, Longley was particularly interested in the Roman love elegists,[3] and his early poetry is influenced by Latin elegy, especially Catullus and Sextus Propertius.[4] Longley's first collected poem is also self-consciously pastoral in its rendering of the tension between rural and urban worlds: the silence and tranquility of the couple's garden, with its folded flowers, contrasts with the "loudly reprobate" train, which "shoots from silence into silence." Pastoral and elegy have long been complementary literary forms,[5] and Longley's employment of them has been regarded as the means by which he conveys his attitude toward violence in Northern Ireland, which grows out of his philosophy of life in general—epitomized in his poem "According to Pythagoras" as "the fundamental interconnectedness of all things."[6]

Elmer Kennedy-Andrews suggests that Longley's entire aesthetic has been specifically designed to manifest this idea of interconnectedness:

> In a context of social conflict and violence, this Whitmanesque idea of the unity of all creation can have a powerfully steadying and reassuring effect. As a tenet of faith it can help ensure against demoralization and defeat, as it can against dogmatism and partisanship. . . . In . . . "According to Pythagoras," a free working of a passage from Ovid's *Metamorphoses*, the theme is the flux of life. The idea of "the fundamental interconnectedness of all things" is presented in biological and physical terms, as a basic fact of life: life is generated out of the putrefaction of death, the shore-crab's claw grows into a scorpion, worms into butterflies, germs into grogs, larvae into bees, eggs into birds, rotting spines into snakes; hyenas change sex, chameleons change colour, lynxes' urine becomes stones. Formally, the notion of universal interconnectedness is acted out in the links that Longley establishes with Pythagoras and Ovid, in the fusion of classical and contemporary worlds.[7]

While Longley's emphasis on interconnectedness obviously suggests an alternative to Northern Ireland's legacy of sectarian violence, his frequent references to biological interconnectedness suggest that along with his need to traverse social, cultural, and political boundaries is the need to challenge the boundaries traditionally posited between the self and nature. In an interview with Jody Allen-Randolph, Longley has stated that "the most urgent political problems are ecological: how we share the planet with the plants and the other animals. My nature writing is my most political."[8] Asked in the same interview to describe the distance between the poet and nature, Longley confidently replies, "None. The poet is part of nature. Language is part of nature."[9]

Notably, the science of ecology is also grounded in the interconnectedness of all things. Robyn Eckersley's *Environmentalism and Political Theory* explains that in the ecological model of the living world, "there are no absolutely discrete entities and no absolute dividing lines between the living and the nonliving, the animate and the inanimate, or the human and the nonhuman."[10] Jonathan Bate's *Song of the Earth* maintains that ecology builds a model that demonstrates the wholeness of the living globe: "the extreme intricacy and precision of its interconnected working parts—winds, currents, rocks, plants, animals, weathers, in all their swarming and law-abiding variety." It simultaneously demonstrates "the extreme smallness" of the earth, "its finiteness and frailty." In so doing, the ecologist "puts the whole globe into our hands, as something now absolutely in our care."[11]

Thus, the poet's traditional quest to create a microcosm for the reader has the potential to merge with the ecologist's vision, and, according to Lawrence Buell in *The Environmental Imagination* and other works, the "environmentally oriented work" accomplishes precisely this fusion of visions. Buell's description of the "environmentally oriented work" applies particularly well to the poetry that Longley writes:

(1) it relies on the nonhuman environment not merely as a framing device but as a presence that begins to suggest that human history is implicated in natural history;

(2) it understands that human interest is not the only legitimate interest;

(3) it considers human accountability to the environment;

(4) it describes the environment as a process rather than as a constant or a given.[12]

Longley's poetry consistently registers an awareness of the nonhuman otherness of nature, as well as a realistic acceptance of the human position in the natural world. Thus while Longley elegizes the lives lost to violence in the North, the true source of his elegiac lament ultimately lies in the environment from which those lives arose in the first place. His fear of "losing [his] place" arises not merely from a personal sense of loss but from a complex consideration of the ramifications of losing *place* in comprehensive terms. Jonathan Bate's speculation, in *The Song of the Earth,* on the role of poets in the next millennium certainly applies to the renewed sense of purpose that Longley's most recent collections in particular have manifested: "Could it be to remind the next few generations that it is we who have the power to determine whether the earth will sing or be silent?"[13]

In "Revaluing Nature: Toward an Ecological Criticism," Glen Love calls for a redefinition of pastoral "in terms of a new and more complex understanding of nature . . . a more radical awareness of its primal energy and stability, and a more acute questioning of the values of the supposedly sophisticated society to which we are bound."[14] Although Love anticipates that this redefinition will be undertaken by American poets, Longley's abiding conviction that the human relationship with the natural world and with the plants and animals is the major issue right now has blossomed into an environmental elegy that radically revisions its pastoral prototype.

Even more than Montague, Longley has a naturalist's understanding of the complexity of the ecosystem and the ramifications of environmental degradation. Elegies, traditionally the poet's means of commemorating the dead, establishing the value of what had been lost and figuratively restoring to life, are Longley's means for seeking to restore an environment riddled by loss—through pollution, erosion, extinction, global warming, overfishing, and farming. Pastoral elegy in particular has the greatest potential for conveying the devastations of environmental loss. Bate writes, "The myth of the natural life which exposes the ills of our own condition is as old as Eden and Arcadia, as new as Larkin's 'Going, Going' and the latest Hollywood adaptation of Austen or Hardy. Its endurance is a sign of its importance. Perhaps we need to remember what is 'going, going' as a survival mechanism, as a check upon our instinct for self-advancement."[15]

"Elegy" had referred in classical poetry to any poem written in elegiac meter (alternating hexameter and pentameter lines) but gradually came to mean any poem dealing with subjects common to the early Greco-Roman elegies—complaints about love, sustained formal lamentation, or somber meditations. The definition that gradually gained currency, especially after the sixteenth century, was that of "a poem of mortal loss and consolation."[16] Elegies have typically been marked by several conventions: an invocation of muses; allusions to classical mythology; elegiac lists of the dead; and a poet persona who speaks in the first person, questioning justice, fate, or providence within the context of his or her own time and place and finally moving from private emotion to a higher level of understanding, arriving at consolation and renewal by rendering the figurative transformation of the deceased. In Christian elegies, the lyric reversal often moves from despair and grief to joy when the poet reconceptualizes death as entry into the bliss of eternity.

Pastoral elegies feature several other conventions: the elegized friend is represented as if he were a shepherd; the mourner charges with negligence the nymphs or guardians of the shepherd who failed to preserve him from death; appropriate mourners appear to lament the shepherd's death; flowers are used to deck the hearse or grave, with various flowers having contextually appropriate symbolic meaning; effects of the death upon nature (disruptions in climate, and so on) convey a personified Nature's grief and sympathy; and ultimately, the poet accepts the inevitability of death and hopes for immortality.[17] Many of the most famous pastoral elegies in English, including Milton's "Lycidas" (1637), Shelley's "Adonais" (1821), and Arnold's "Thyrsis" (1867), participate in this tradition, which dates back to Greek Moschus's "Lament for Bion" and the first idyll of Theocritus by way of Virgil's *Eclogue* 5, which elegizes the shepherd Daphnis. Although throughout most of the eighteenth century the prejudice against pastoral elegy (and elegy in general) persisted except for poems like Dryden's "To the Memory of Mr. Oldham" and Gray's "Elegy,"[18] nineteenth-century Romantic and Victorian poets such as Shelley and Arnold continued to write them. Industrialization, which led to mass migration from the countryside to the city, resulted in rural nostalgia as well as a renewed preoccupation with defining culture specifically in terms of the tension between urban and rural—a tension out of which pastoral poetry grew.

Ireland's colonial status influenced the evolution of its pastoral tradition but also its elegiac tradition. Jahan Ramazani observes that although elegy in its traditional form has been abandoned by modern and contemporary poets in Europe and the United States, it survives in Ireland, where "more of the traditional funeral rites and mourning practices have survived than they have elsewhere in the dominant cultures of the West."[19]

Thus, whereas Sacks contends that World War I rendered the pastoral elegy obsolete, citing Yeats's pastoral elegy for Robert Gregory, "Shepherd and Goatherd," as one of the last pure pastoral elegies of the twentieth century, pastoral elegiac conventions were appropriated to offer a critique of colonization —as well as the industrialization and modernization that accompanied it. Particularly in Northern Ireland, the division between country and city— rural and industrial—has also to some degree emblematized the tension between Catholics and Protestants, with Catholics asserting their claim to "four green fields"—a precolonial, agrarian Ireland—as Protestants maintained a relative stronghold in the industrialized North. Whereas pastoral has been dismissed as a conservative mode through which the upper class might establish its claims on the land, the tension between country and city thus proves generative once again as Protestant poet Longley reconceives it as a way of contextualizing sectarian conflict: his pastoral elegy reminds the reader of the necessity of the environment for the survival of the human species to the mutual benefit of Catholic and Protestant. While Montague acknowledges the interconnection between social structure and ecosystem, Longley seamlessly integrates them. Furthermore, his recent poetry has increasingly forgone pastoral's anthropocentric worldview, proposing an even more radical reordering of cultural values.

While one can certainly argue that is impossible for anyone, particularly a lyric poet, to relinquish the human perspective, it is possible to transfer preference to the interests of the ecosystem, including its human members, as opposed to those of humanity as a separate and exclusive group, just as it is possible to be male without being sexist. Robyn Eckersley argues that we should not confuse ecocentrism—and the attempt to critique and move away from anthropocentrism—with the idea of attempting to see from an other-than-human viewpoint. Eckersley writes,

> One common criticism is that it is impossible to perceive the world *other* than from an anthropocentric perspective since we are, after all, *human* subjects. This criticism, however, entirely misses the point of the critique of anthropocentrism by conflating the identity of the perceiving subject with the content of what is perceived and valued, a conflation that Fox has called the "anthropocentric fallacy."[20]

Transformation, a popular motif used in classical pastoral and pastoral elegy to convey the relation between self and nature, as well as in Christian pastoral elegy to offer hope for transformation by anticipating immortality for the dead subject, is adapted in Longley's poetry to a post-Christian contemporary worldview. In Longley's version of pastoral elegy, transformation is simply part of nature's course; consolation lies in the fact that death signifies a return to nature, and immortality is achieved by attaining oneness with the natural world that has sustained our earthly lives. Longley's environmentally oriented poetry appropriately focuses less on the transformation of human subject than on the transformation of natural object, as in "The White Butterfly," an elegy based on a Blasket Island tale in which a cabbage white is transformed into the soul of the deceased. In "Spring Tide," the overview of traditional memorials to the deceased—burial mounds, pyramids, graveyards—culminates in a reminder that the landscape on which these memorials rest is first and foremost a meadow into which the spring tide flows: "It [the tide] behaves like a preservative / And erases neither the cattle's / and the sheep's nor my own footprints." The landscape is itself a memorial to lost lives, commemorating not only human lives, traditionally named in elegiac lists for the dead, but all life forms carried by the tide:

> The spring tide has ferried jellyfish
> To the end of the lane, pinks, purples,
> Wee flowers beside the floating cow-pats.
> The zig-zags I make take me among
> White cresses and brookweed, lousewort,
> Water plantain and grass of parnassus
> With engraved capillaries, ivory sheen:
> By a dry-stone wall in the dune slack
> The greenish sepals, the hidden blush
> And a lip's red veins and yellow spots—
> Marsh helleborine waiting for me
> To come and go with the spring tide.

Instead of Charon, the ferryman who traditionally carries souls across the river to the underworld, it is the tide itself that carries them—and it carries not only human souls but all life forms, including the flowers, which obliquely allude to the flowers that "blush unseen" in Gray's "Elegy in a Country Churchyard," symbols for country people destined for anonymity. Nature is thus depicted not merely as metaphoric of human nature but as worthy of consideration in and of itself. Instead of the traditional Christian consolation of the afterlife, the consolation is that the poet, too, will come and go with the spring tide, achieving a kind of immortality through his oneness with the natural world.

Arguably, Longley's approach even during this period represents a continuation of a lifelong interest in nature for its own sake, an interest that perhaps allows him to put the Troubles in perspective. Violence, whether in nature or society, has long been one of Longley's central themes, and from the perspective of post-pastoral, there is no distinction between the two: nature *is* culture. In Longley's first volume, *No Continuing City*, "Persephone" incarnates violence in the predatory figures of the ferret, the weasel, the stoat, and fox that cross the winter landscape. Longley identifies the basic duality in nature: silent predators associated with winter are nonetheless graceful, beautiful creatures, and Persephone, the corn goddess, ends winter's domain with her annual return from the underworld to restore the land's fertility.[21]

Longley's attempt to locate and render balance in nature by means of his depictions of animals who "learn to adapt to altered circumstances in order to survive" is integral to his effort to comprehend the turmoil of the Troubles. Thus, Brian John concludes,

> It would be a serious misreading to confuse Longley's elegant diction and strict forms, his County Mayo landscapes and acute observations of flora and fauna, with indifference towards or evasion of twentieth-century horrors. Like other poets from the North he has been expected to write about the violent conflict in his society, to comment, take sides, condemn. But he refused in 1971 to be "some sort of super-journalist" and, in the manner of Wilfred Owen, saw his duty rather as "to warn."[22]

Tracing Longley's use of elegy, Ruth Ling cites "Wounds" in *An Exploded View* (1972), Longley's first elegy for specified victims of the Troubles, as well as "a tentative and measured enquiry into the appropriateness of elegy as a form."[23] Yet in the same volume is a pastoral elegy called "Casualty," which, unlike Heaney's famous poem by the same name, does not elegize a victim of the Troubles but rather an animal that dies and decays. "Ghost Town," with its "sad cottages, scythes rusting in the thatch," is reminiscent of Goldsmith's pastoral elegy "The Deserted Village," although this village's demise signifies not so much a surrender to cultural upheaval as to nature's changing and all-consuming course, represented by the enfolding bog. Rather than speaking mournfully, as Goldsmith did, of those who had abandoned the village for the sake of trade, Longley writes as one who seeks to be the town's last denizen, "the local eccentric," as it reverts to wilderness. His opening line "I have located it, my ghost town," recalls the traditional setting of pastoral poetry, the *locus amoenus,* subverting the reader's expectations for it by submerging his privileged human perspective in the bog.

Significantly, *No Continuing City* also includes "Journey out of Essex," which refers to John Clare's escape from a madhouse and his four-day walk to his childhood home in rural Helpston. Longley's almost verbatim quotations from Clare emphasize the way in which the escape is undertaken not so much for his own sake but for that of the flora and fauna of the countryside: "that they may recuperate / Alongside the stunned mouse, / The hedgehog rolled in leaves." Jonathan Bate's biography of Clare convincingly portrays him as our first environmental poet: "More than any of his predecessors, Clare has a *relationship* with nature, and it is a relationship between equals. Nature is an interlocutor, not just subject matter. . . . This ethic . . . is what separates Clare from his Romantic contemporaries."[24] Fran Brearton observes that Longley's pastoral is influenced by the precision of observation and ecological consciousness of poets like Clare. While Brearton traces Longley's pastoral strain to a later collection, *An Exploded View* (1972),[25] poems in *No Continuing City* suggest that the pastoral strain runs throughout Longley's oeuvre, with Clare's poetry providing a likely model for Longley's own approach to nature: "Landscape," for example, describes the landscape not by means of a "quasiromantic projection of the self into nature, but of an incursion of the natural world into the stable, self-recognizing perspective of identity."[26]

In "Edward Thomas's War Diary," Longley consciously writes out of the English pastoral tradition associated with Thomas. Thomas, who wrote pastoral poetry and died in action during World War I, describes his dream while in the trenches, that he was "at home and couldn't stay to tea . . . then woke where shell holes / Filled with bloodstained water." Longley's poem provides a grim parody of the tea ceremony: instead of comforting domestic ritual, Thomas encounters death; instead of delicate teacups filled with tea, he gets shell holes filled with blood-stained water; and instead of the beautiful countryside where, in good weather, tea would often be taken, he gets a landscape destroyed by war; a place that should be teeming with birds, flourishing with trees, is now bereft of them. Longley's depiction of nature's remarkable capacity to renew itself—in the green feathers of yarrow, the singing larks—recalls that of Thomas's, who "skirted the danger zone / to draw panoramas" and comes to life in Longley's poem.

"Company," undoubtedly inspired by the contrast between Longley's Belfast home and the Mayo cottage that serves as his summer retreat, begins in the midst of the towers in Belfast, surrounded by vigilantes, customs officials, border guards, and victims of violence. As if in response to all of this divisiveness, he introduces his own division in the poem, providing a second section that expresses his longing for peace in the countryside—a simple life in a cottage with a thatched roof, cattle, tall grasses, the simple rural ritual of going to the well. Longley might be alluding to Yeats, who retreats to a Norman tower that becomes a symbol for the life of the mind but also for the isolationist Protestant response to Irish independence. He opts not merely for symbol but for a genuine pastoral retreat, complete with all the sensory experiences that the setting provides, including direct exposure to the elements—"the rain leaning against the half-door."

In *The Echo Gate* (1979), Longley's grandmother's gift of "second sight" in the poem of the same name enables her to figuratively "carry flowers out of smoke"—to find redemption in nature even in the midst of destruction—which might serve equally well as a metaphor for Longley's own gift. The book's often pastoral settings are interspersed among elegiac laments for victims of violence—whether of colonial Ireland ("Oliver Plunkett") or of the Northern Irish Troubles ("Wreaths"). "Home Ground," dedicated to "S.H." (Seamus Heaney), imagines a childhood in the country as a pastoral paradise in which nature renders culture superfluous: rurality necessitates that "gentians, fairy flax, wild strawberries" serve as art, a grass blade as music. In "Ash Keys," the narrator talks to himself as the ash keys scatter and he stands in the middle of a field redolent with loss—of his youth, his community, a way of life (herding cattle), and an environment inevitably altered by the changes wrought by modernity.

Despite its primarily urban setting, Longley's "Wreaths," three poems that elegize victims of the Troubles, is based on one of pastoral elegy's primary metaphors: the elegizing poet figuratively strews the grave of the deceased with flowers. Sacks traces the ancient origin of the practice to the rituals related to the death and rebirth of vegetation gods, observing that "bouquets" of elegies were pinned or thrown on Sir Philip Sidney's hearse: "elegies have found ways to 'strew the laureate hearse,' if only figuratively with showers or rather fictions designed to 'interpose a little ease.'" The poet's "weaving a consolation" has long been a metaphor for the act of weaving the burial shroud,[27] and Longley's three interwoven elegies are themselves "wreaths" that commemorate the dead.[28]

In "Greengrocer," which describes the murder of the Longleys' greengrocer, the tragic irony of his death is that it occurs while he sells Christmas wreaths to the "deathdealers"; thus his wreaths and fir trees of evergreen, ancient symbols of eternal life, are replaced by funeral wreaths of death. The third poem, "The Linen Workers," approaches the Troubles through the memory of Longley's father who had fought and been wounded on the

Somme in 1916, and whose "old wounds woke / as cancer" when Longley was twenty.[29] In the poem, the murders of ten linen workers (a massacre that took place in January 1976, when masked men from the Provisional IRA stopped a van of linen workers and killed all of them except the lone Catholic in the group)[30] are juxtaposed with that of Christ and of Longley's father. Following the first stanza, which imagines Christ's teeth ascending with him into heaven, Longley describes the deaths of the linen workers, when "there fell on the road beside them spectacles, / Wallets, small change, and a set of dentures / Blood, food particles, the bread, the wine."

The final stanza anticipates Longley's father's reburial, reminiscent of a pagan burial ritual to prepare the deceased for the afterlife, when Longley will balance spectacles on his father's nose, fill his pockets with money, and slip his dentures into his dead mouth. Ruth Ling suggests that "Longley is reluctant to 'bury' through elegy until he can find a 'balance' as taut and paradoxical as that between resurrection and suffering such as Christ . . . is seen to undergo in the first stanza."[31] By sacramentalizing the small, intimate personal belongings of the deceased and vicariously returning them to their owners, Longley suggests hope for transformation. Elmer Kennedy-Andrews observes that because Longley's references to spectacles, money, and false teeth also recall the concentration camps, his elegy effectively embraces all victims of violence,[32] invoking the power of memory, love, and poetry to redeem loss and suffering, figuratively resurrecting the dead.

Longley's "Bog Cotton," which Fran Brearton describes as a "healing pastoral" though conceding it "makes no such grandiose claims for itself,"[33] reimagines battlefields as habitats not only for the poppies worn by the English to commemorate World War I but for the bog cotton that thrives in the peat of Northern Ireland. Bog cotton, which was traditionally believed to have magical healing properties for the sheep who ate it, was also used as dressing for wounds during World War I. More broadly, the peatlands themselves, traditionally a source of a fuel alternative to coal, might be said to have healing properties, serving as a preservative for the humans and the archaeology deposited in them, protecting biodiversity by providing a habitat for a variety of flora and fauna, and providing storage for carbon and water, thereby offsetting the global warming that would increase threats to biodiversity.[34]

Thus, unlike traditional Christian pastoral elegists, Longley finds his "balance" not in Christ's suffering and resurrection but in the ecosystem. The cool, wet climate of Ireland is ideal for producing peat (12 percent of land area in Northern Ireland is peat). Deprived of English coal and forced to turn to its own fuel sources during World War II, Ireland came to rely exclusively on peat, which thus inevitably evokes a distinctively Irish botany, landscape, history, and national consciousness. By combining elements from both English and Irish traditions, proposing a new commemorative emblem of Northern Irish war dead, Longley at least figuratively re-creates the means for reconciliation between Northern Protestants and Catholics. Elmer Kennedy-Andrews notes that Longley's choice of bog cotton is probably influenced by Heaney's use of the bog as a distinctively Irish symbol of Irish culture[35]—a symbol that conveniently allows both poets to circumvent the sectarian associations of Christian symbols.

Whereas victims of sectarian violence in the north were often disposed of in bogs, thus the term "bog jobs," Longley's celebration of bog cotton suggests that the selfsame landscape might yield a life-affirming alternative. The imagery of Irish bog cotton, which Longley associates with the stanching of wounds, also contrasts starkly with the poppy's bloody and divisive associations.[36] In Longley's note to the poem, he acknowledges two World War I poems, Keith Douglas's "Desert Flowers" and Isaac Rosenberg's "Break of Day in the Trenches," both of which rely on the poppy's red color as a symbol for wartime bloodshed. By contrast, Longley's bog cotton is metaphoric of peace, imagined as a pillow for the head of a wounded soldier, rags used to staunch wounds, or to tie to bushes around holy wells, representing the prayers for healing offered by pilgrims in the distinctly Irish Catholic practice of frequenting holy wells for cures. Under Cardinal Cullen's regime, Irish priests sought to replace folk practices—holy wells, local pilgrimages, and stations (worship held in cottages rather than churches)—with modernized Roman worship.[37] Yet precisely because their suppression coincided with that of Irish nationalism, these distinctively Irish folk practices came to symbolize Irish national identity. Whereas Catholic Ireland has discouraged the wearing of the poppy because of its Unionist associations (Irish Catholics who fought in the wars did so on behalf of Britain and at the expense of their own ongoing war of independence), Longley suggests bog cotton as a symbol that promises reconciliation and healing of the religious breach.

Longley's pastoral nostalgia, coupled with the elegiac mode, culminates in the twenty-first century in a series of environmental elegies. But in the 1970s, when Longley discovered and translated the pastoral love elegist Tibullus, the Northern Irish Troubles were considered to be a more immediate and pressing impetus. In his discussion of Longley's poem "Peace," Peacock speculates that when Longley was asked by the Peace People of Belfast to write a poem for their paper, Tibullus 1, 10 caught his eye because it is an antiwar poem written by a love elegist.[38] Peacock emphasizes that although in Augustan Rome, war and military service were accepted as necessities of life in an empire, poets such as Propertius, Tibullus, and Ovid claimed their preference for love affairs rather than military service "within the rather Bohemian ethos of the love elegy."[39] By proffering an intentional upending of cultural norms, privileging love rather than war, to a Northern Irish audience in the

1970s, Longley suggests a viable alternative to his own era's predilection for violence.

Thus, Longley's translation of Tibullus is simultaneously a translation into English *and* into the Northern Ireland of the 1970s. In his autobiographical "Tuppenny Stung," Longley writes that "in Ulster culture apartheid is sustained to the mutual impoverishment of both communities."[40] As Longley recalls Tibullus's Rome, where simple, rural occupations and simple material culture—cups made of beechwood—are offered in lieu of military conflict and its weaponry, he likewise offers a commentary on his own violence-ridden Northern Ireland:

> Blame the affluent society: no killings when
> The cup on the dinner table was made of beechwood,
> And no barricades or ghettoes when the shepherd
> Snoozed among sheep that weren't even thoroughbreds.

The pastoral vision is disrupted by modern diction that highlights ongoing cultural disruptions: barricades, used by authorities to separate fighting Catholics and Protestants, and ghettoes, which represent both the historic segregation of Catholics from Protestants and Europe's earlier segregation of Jews, the deadly consequences of which cannot escape the reader. His meshing of ancient and modern idioms and imagery invites the reader to consider the parallels between Tibullus's Rome and Longley's Northern Ireland, in which the poet's own impulses are thwarted by all-consuming violence:

> I would like to have been alive in the good old days
> Before the horrors of modern warfare and warcries
> Stepping up my pulse rate. Alas, as things turn out
> I've been press-ganged into service, and for all I know
> Someone's polishing a spear with my number on it.
> God of my Fathers, look after me like a child!
> And don't be embarrassed by this handmade statue
> Carved out of bog oak by my great-great-grandfather
> Before the mass-production of religious art
> When the wooden god stood simply in a narrow shrine.

Longley, while rendering Tibullus's first-century religious sensibility that embodies the transition from paganism to Christianity, offers a commentary on the state of religion in his own twentieth-century Northern Ireland: the transition from indigenous Celtic religion to Roman Christianity, in which one might imagine an Irish grandfather having carved a statue out of bog oak as opposed to purchasing the mass-produced statues available at any novena. In both cases, the transition provoked violent reprisals, compounded in

Northern Ireland by yet another transition—from Catholicism to Protestant-ism, producing a seemingly irreconcilable conflict between Christianity's two main forms.

Like Tibullus, Longley envisions "Peace personified: oxen under the curved yoke; / Compost for the vines, grape-juice turning into wine" where, "if there are skirmishes, guerilla tactics, / It's only lovers quarrelling." He concludes, "As for me, I want a woman / To come and fondle my ears of wheat and let apples / Overflow between her breasts. I shall call her Peace." In this series of miraculous transformations, peace is personified, grape juice turned to wine (a natural process that recalls Christ's miracle at Cana as well as communion), the scythe triumphs over the spear, the distinction between human and nonhuman nature is erased, and "war as a love-metaphor shades into love as a war-cure."[41] For Longley, the imagined pastoral retreat is a well-balanced ecosystem.

"On Mweelrea" sets war aside entirely to focus instead on lovers who find themselves absorbed in the landscape, ultimately becoming indistinguishable from it. Peter McDonald observes that "going underground, entering the landscape at a more intimate level than the visitor, takes the lover literally into the world of nature poetry."[42] In order to achieve this sense of oneness with nature, Longley depicts for the reader the lovers' gradual relinquishment of their ties to culture—leaving all of their "jugs and cups behind." The water's pulse becomes indistinguishable from the speaker's pulse; the lover's "maid-enhair" indistinguishable from that of the landscape; the "wash of blood and light and water" from her body indistinguishable from the uncut poppies in stubbly fields. This blurring of the distinction between subject and setting is one of the hallmarks of environmental writing, which continually challenges the privileged position that human beings have assumed in the universe—at the expense of the environment that they thereby feel entitled to degrade. Neil Everndon, who cites ecology's denial of "the subject-object relationship upon which science rests" as the source of its subversiveness, advocates in *The Social Creation of Nature* an intersubjective consciousness in which the con-cept of "self" is diffused and identified with the environment.[43]

"The Linen Industry" may be read as an elegy for an entire industry that flourished in Northern Ireland until cotton displaced linen, ending the live-lihoods of thousands of linen workers and threatening whole communities sustained by the linen industry. Although the elegy relies on the classical mo-tif of transformation, it is not the dead person who is transformed but the linen fields themselves—into the cloth that then allows the lovers to recreate the linen field, whether in the form of sheets, clothing, or ultimately burial shrouds. Neil Corcoran, punning on Herrick's "Upon Julia's Clothes," ob-serves that the poem "takes the clothes back to their original liquefaction, when they were flax in peaty water."[44] The symbol of transformation, the butterfly, appears as a bow on the woman's bodice, "a butterfly attending the embroidered flowers," conflating nature and culture in the manner character-istic of post-pastoral.

Longley's poem "Metamorphoses" directly treats this central trope of pastoral elegy, drawing on Ovid's tales of metamorphosis to render death for the subject as "rain . . . hollow[ing] out a font / And fill[ing] her eye in," "fell[ing] her like timber," transforming her to water in which she sleeps and sinks, "snuggling in its own embrace." Whereas Sarah Broom contends that Longley's poetry sees "Ovidian and other forms of metamorphosis and mu-tability . . . as troubling and disturbing,"[45] Longley's increasing use of the imagery of metamorphosis is correlated to his increasing reliance on the ele-giac mode; his growing preoccupation with death and the transformations it leads to is not necessarily disturbing but merely a product of his growing tendency to view the self as part of nature and death as an integral part of the natural process.

Broom finds in Longley's approach to Irish and British cultural pasts a reluc-tance "to establish any vision of a lost unity or paradisal state" but instead to address traumatic episodes such as World War I or the Holocaust. Broom con-siders Longley's translations from the *Odyssey* and the *Iliad* in *Gorse Fires* and *The Ghost Orchid* to be a departure from this approach, because these original texts are grounded in a conception of a Golden Age corresponding to Mircea Eliade's "nostalgia for origins":

> The Greeks of that era looked back on the Mycenaean culture as representing a time when things were fundamentally different: heroes were semi-divine; the gods were close to humanity; the division between mortality and immor-tality was indefinite and permeable; and there was a sense of unity, order, and energy in the world. The public retellings of these myths may have functioned to allow "a periodic return to the mythical time at the beginning of things, to the 'Great Time.'"[46]

Yet *Gorse Fires* (1991), which features seven Homeric poems that focus on Odysseus' return to home, family, love, nurture, represents not so much a departure from Longley's earlier approach as an additional means by which to elaborate on his earlier themes, as he merges Homeric landscapes "with those of the idyllic west of Ireland."[47]

"Between Hovers" features the traditional characters and setting of classi-cal pastoral. Elmer Kennedy-Andrews observes that like the shepherds of clas-sical pastoral, the speaker and his friend Joe O'Toole are spirits of the rural place. Joe's death is viewed from within the context of nature, linked first to a dead badger they ran over in their car, then to a dying otter the speaker sees some time after his friend's funeral. Despite the pastoral setting, the poem is "haunted by awareness of threat"—the cancer that takes Joe's life and the car, symbol of a destructive technological modernity that has invaded the pastoral simplicities of "an ancient, vestigially pagan, folkloric, vulnerable landscape." Longley finds a parallel "between the beauty of nature's innocent creatures and the human worth and goodness of the individual who has died."[48] Rather than attend the conventional funeral ceremony for his friend, Longley opts to return alone to the site later, to watch "a dying otter gaze right through me / At the islands in Clew Bay, as though it were only / Between hovers and not too far from the holt." The image of the otter is consolatory: Joe's death, like that of the otter, is reconceived as "between hovers"—a transitional rather than a final state. Longley's depiction of death as a transitional state is characteristic of post-pastoral, which entails an acceptance of the cyclical nature of the universe as well as the trajectory that humans share with all creatures.[49]

Longley has acknowledged the tremendous influence that his time spent in Carrigskeewaun, County Mayo, has had on his development as a poet. Notably, he does so in terms that are simultaneously personal and environmental: "The human habitat in that part of Mayo is precarious, isolated and vulnerable, its history complex. The landscape is haunted by . . . the ghosts of lazy-beds abandoned during the Famine. The bones of the landscape make me feel in my own bones how provisional dwelling and home are."[50] In "Remembering Carrigskeewaun," Longley conjures the classical pastoral world but this time by means of the traditional Irish cottage, thereby taking himself back to childhood, to a time prior to the Irish troubles and also, presumably, to a time less troubled by the impact of environmental loss. Nature and culture merge: the chimney becomes a voice box recalling animals and home, "a hollow between the waves." Longley justifies his environmental approach to landscape as an oblique means of placing the Troubles in perspective: "In my Mayo poems I am not trying to escape from political violence. I want the light from Carrigskeewaun to irradiate the northern darkness. Describing the world in a meticulous way is a consecration and a stay against damaging dogmatism."[51]

In "Laertes," a translation from *The Odyssey*, nostalgia for a lost landscape is again merged with nostalgia for childhood, as Longley is "faced with the dilemma of how to deal with the fact that, in Homer, Odysseus tests his father at length before revealing who he is, a process which seems cruel as well as awkward and unrealistic to the modern reader."[52] Longley suggests that Odysseus waits because his explanation would be too tedious, his father too comfortable as he is, and he prefers for his father to recognize him in that garden setting and remember him as he was. In order for them to truly know each other and resume their former relationship, they have to imaginatively return to that simple world—which might well be Longley's way of justifying his choice of the pastoral mode for addressing the Troubles.

> But the whole story is one catalogue after another,
> So he waited for images from that formal garden,
> Evidence of a childhood spent traipsing after his father
> And asking for everything he saw, the thirteen pear-trees,
> Ten apple-trees, forty fig-trees, the fifty rows of vines
> Ripening at different times for a continuous supply.

Sarah Broom writes that "the list of trees and plants from Laertes' garden represents the familiarity and certainty of childhood," although "the poignancy is gained through the recognition that such certainty and simplicity have been lost."[53] Longley's lists also reflect his debt to the tradition of pastoral elegy—which, as early as the idylls of Theocritus, featured catalogues of flowers, culminating in the flowers with which the Miltonic Lycidas's laureate hearse is strewn. Yet Longley's elegiac lists, "at once more artful and more tentative and indirect," significantly name not the dead but natural phenomena—flowers, plants, animals, or birds—"which are juxtaposed obliquely with the fact of human death,"[54] thereby forcing a reconsideration of anthropocentric assessments of the human place in the universe. Again, the mere act of reminding the reader of the human relationship to nature in the midst of despair over human loss is presented as a consolation.

Just as in "Greengrocer," where the list of commonplace gifts is a kind of cornucopia, "Ghetto" elegizes the nameless, otherwise forgotten victims of war, providing consolation by means not of rhetoric or argument but of a list of the names of varieties of potatoes:[55]

> My delivery of Irish Peace, Beauty of Hebron, Home
> Guard, Arran Banners, Kerr's Pinks, resistant to eelworm,
> Resignation, common scab, terror, frost, potato-blight.

Lyon notes that the meticulousness of the list "appears crazed," but the names themselves are significant: "Irish peace," suggesting a panacea in the midst of Troubles; "Beauty of Hebron," with its promise of a homeland, anticipates a peaceful resolution to the Jewish plight. Finally, the qualities of the potatoes such as "Kerr's Pinks," resistant to "Resignation, common scab, terror, frost" recall simultaneously the plight of soldiers who fought in World War I, Holocaust victims, and Irish famine victims. It is important to remember that the famine, too, has been widely regarded as a kind of genocide—a preventable catastrophe that wiped out half the Irish population, that some refer to as "the great hunger" because the English continued to import grain from Ireland even while the Irish were starving. Longley significantly offers his gift of potatoes, Ireland's primary source of sustenance for centuries, as a protection against suffering, an antidote to the plight they faced.

"The Ice-Cream Man" commemorates the murder of the Longleys' ice-cream man on Belfast's Lisburn Road. Significantly, the act of violence itself is referred to in only one line, underscoring the poem's central purpose as elegiac and consolatory. The poem, as Longley himself has indicated, is addressed to his daughter, whose commemorative gesture of laying carnations outside the ice-cream man's shop prompts him to provide an extended list of burren flowers—a figurative "wreath" for the dead that corresponds not only to the elaborate list of flowers brought to deck the hearse in "Lycidas" but also to those catalogued by Perdita in *The Winter's Tale*, act 4, in which Perdita and Polixenes argue over her banning of cultivated flowers—"our carnations and streak'd gillyvors"—from the flowers she distributes at the sheep-shearing feast. Longley proffers an abundant tribute of wildflowers of "great, creating nature" in lieu of the hackneyed gift of carnations.56 Although Broom claims that the litany of flowers is not imbued with any explanatory or redemptive significance, but is rather to calm and console the child (at the very least it provides a substitute to the litany of flavors offered by the ice-cream man),57 the list compels us to consider the symbolic significance of the flowers. In contrast to the cultivated, relatively scentless, merely decorative carnations, Longley's flowers have curative powers; the listing of them itself performs a healing function, affirming nature's beauty and continuance in the face of death and loss. Flowers are symbols of hope, of transformation, and they are especially significant in the setting of the burren, where seemingly dry, desolate sheets of limestone conceal water in underground streams or turlocks.

The burren has also recently been the focus of environmental campaigns, whether to halt the removal of the limestone plates taken by tourists as souvenirs, or the disturbance and destruction of rare and endangered plant and animal species which inhabit the region. Longley's allusion to the complex and fragile ecosystem of the burren serves both to emblematize the fragility of the human lives lost to violence in the North and place those losses within the larger context of environmental loss.58

Although Peter McDonald suggests that Longley's style adopts "a delicacy which seems to resist the formulas of explanation and consolation,"59 Longley's list of flowers is five times as long as his daughter's—as though to respond to her grief with a cornucopia of consolation. Furthermore, the long, pulsing, heavily accented sentence containing the list of flowers serves as a persistent affirmation of the life force, of an innocence that exists despite and beyond the deadly circumstances. Thus Elmer Kennedy-Andrews concludes that "although no explicit connection is made between the death of the ice-cream man and the incantatory recital of wild flowers, the kind of consolation the poem offers lies at a deeper level than of logical statement."60

Another poem informed by classical poetry, "The Campfires" is based on a scene from *The Iliad,* book 8, in which the Trojan army waits at dawn around campfires for the battle to begin. By interspersing the diction of World War I ("no man's land") and the Vietnam War ("killing fields") with the place-names of the west of Ireland, the poem links past and present, classical Greece and contemporary Ireland. Brian John writes that "the stars illuminating the Co. Mayo landscape resemble the camp-fires of the Trojan army before Ilium, and the soldiers relaxing prior to the battle are juxtaposed with the shepherd smiling 'on his luminous townland' on a similarly balmy night."[61] Longley's use of place-names recalls the traditional Irish poetry *dinnseanchas,* which imbues place-names with spiritual significance that resonates beyond the temporal. His idealized evocation of the west of Ireland places it in the realm of imagination and defines it as pastoral paradise: with balmy nights, resplendent constellations, dazzling moon, smiling shepherd, bountiful salmon, men relaxing in the fields, and horses munching on oats and barley. The deliberately pastoral and idyllic imagery, enhanced by relatively regular hexameters that create a sense of balance, creates a more striking contrast with "the armies preparing for battle."[62] Peacock recognizes the poem's environmental thrust: "no constituent of the natural cycle is privileged, and the human recognition of this shared existence is strangely consoling."[63] Again, Longley's reconsideration of the human place in the natural world is a source of consolation that likewise is its own implicit commentary on war.

"Baucis and Philemon" is based on the Greek tale of an elderly couple who unwittingly host the gods Jupiter and Mercury, disguised as humans. Longley describes the pair living next to a bog, in a cottage "thatched with straw / And reeds from the bog." Longley implies that their simple dwelling, the homely meal they serve, rural background, proximity to and harmony with nature (the setting is a sanctuary for birds) make them open to accommodate the gods who, in human form, had been previously rejected at a thousand houses. When they notice that the wine in the jug renews itself as fast as it is poured, they recognize the divine nature of their guests and apologize for the humble fare. The gods offer them immunity from the destruction that awaits their neighbors, their house is transformed into a temple over which they are appointed guardians, and they are granted their wish to die together. Upon their deaths, they are transformed into trees—an oak and a linden tree—which are gradually grafted together. Death's transformation again highlights the attainment of oneness with nature. The poem concludes with an elegiac blessing of flowers as Longley adds his bouquet to the others in the trees. As in earlier poems, Longley localizes the setting, situating it near a bog, and ending with advice that brings to mind Northern Ireland rather than Greece:

Treat those whom God loves as your local gods—a
Blackthorn
Or a standing stone.

The Northern Irish equivalent of the grafting together of Baucis and Philemon is represented in the combination of blackthorn—the most popular source of wood for walking sticks since the depletion of Ireland's oak supply, as well as the official symbol of the authority of the RUC—and standing stone, found throughout the Celtic world and associated with the religious rites of the indigenous people of Ireland.[64] Notably, the poet's parting advice is consistent with that of ecology: to treat inanimate nature with the same reverence once accorded nature deities.

The title poem of *The Ghost Orchid* (1994)[65] celebrates a wild orchid that is extremely rare in Britain and nonexistent in Ireland, and that Longley seeks to keep alive, at least figuratively, by adding "to its few remaining sites"[66] in a stanza dedicated to it. By giving the orchid human qualities—leaves "like flakes of skin," flesh-colored petals that bruise easily—Longley simultaneously celebrates a nearly extinct flower and reminds us of the fragility of human existence.

The Weather in Japan (2000) reflects Longley's increasing preoccupation with poems that are "ways of learning about dying"—whether about the death of human intimacy or death in the natural world.[67] The poems in *The Weather in Japan* ask "what type of art might best heal yet best stay true to the pain . . . Each frequently pastoral act of consolation is accompanied, then, by an acknowledgment of the extreme difficulty art has in delivering that consolation."[68] The book also reflects Longley's growing preoccupation with collapsing the distinction between art and nature, and with deanthropocentrizing nature, which ultimately troubles his relationship to classical pastoral elegy.

The Weather in Japan begins with an epigraph from James Wright's "A Sprig of Bay," and is dedicated to the memory of Sean Dunne (1956–95). Longley begins by walking through a rundown orchard, glimpsing its "original plan." His setting, dominated by a lofty bay tree, recalls the original, prelapsarian garden, with its central tree, through which God's "original plan" for the garden to serve as an idyllic home for humankind was thwarted. He drinks spring water in his friend's memory and picks a sprig of the bay his friend had once used for seasoning beans. The sprig of bay acquires new significance: in classical poetry bay constituted the laurel wreaths that crowned victorious athletes and was a reward for poetic achievement. Bay is thus a fitting tribute for his dead friend, whose personal significance to the poet is presumably as deserving of laurels as the considerably more public achievements of classical laureates.

Longley notes that the last turf was stacked—both a poignant reminder of the loss of his friend, who can no longer stack the turf—but also the loss of a way of life. The turf was used for "Old Head and the hookers," "hookers" referring to old-fashioned fishing boats no longer used for commercial fishing and elegized in Irish poems such as Richard Murphy's "The Last Galway Hooker." Transformed through the poet's imagination into a boy, Dunne as well as his way of life are figuratively reborn, and the primary intention of pastoral elegy is thereby fulfilled.

"The War Graves" provides a grim parody of pastoral: instead of drills for wheat, the Germans drilled holes for dynamite, and now the task of sowing seeds is left to field mice because the men are dead. Here, the world of war and death has supplanted the life-sustaining world of rural work, just as in Virgil's *Georgics* the farmer's way of life has been temporarily supplanted by that of the soldier's. The only hope left is that some day the farmer's hoe will overturn weapons; that is, the farmer's life-affirming work will prevail. The graves are decorated with flowers—"brookweed and fairy flax"—recalling a time when woods and fields were thought to be peopled with fairies, when people believed that consultation with the dead could really take place. By reviving these past practices and describing violets that thrive in the mine craters, the poem suggests the possibility for renewal, rejuvenation for nature and the war dead alike. Yet Longley reminds the reader that this pastoral paradise surrounded by birds, lambs, and flowers is "only an imaginary harvest home."

The comet at Edward Thomas's grave evokes the pathetic fallacy, an elegiac convention that creates the impression that nature itself responds to the loss. For example, a comet that appeared shortly after Julius Caesar's death was taken as a sign that nature had acknowledged his loss. Sacks writes that in ancient elegy the figure of the vegetation god

> appears to reverse man's submission to nature or to its changing seasons. Instead of grieving over the inhuman operation of nature or time, a setting and process on which he is unavoidably dependent, man creates a fiction whereby nature and its changes, the occasions of his grief, appear to depend on him. The withering vegetation is now no more the *cause* of human grief but rather the mourner or even the effect of a human-divine loss—the death of such figures as Adonis, Thammuz, Persephone, or Dionysus. Thus the so-called pathetic fallacy of nature's lament, one of the prominent elegiac conventions so frequently criticized for artifice and contrivance, actually has a naturalistic basis in the notation of seasonal change.[69]

As discussed in chapter 2, the pathetic fallacy's recognition of the relationship between nature and human nature renders it an essential trope of environmental writing. From the nettle bed at Wilfred Owen's grave, the narrator and his companion pick a celandine, "the flower that outwits winter." Their gesture to outwit winter, or death, for Edward Thomas also suggests that Thomas himself has become "the flower that outwits winter" through his poetic legacy.

In "The Evening Star," an elegy in memory of Catherine Mercer, who died at only two years and two months, nature seems to respond with a consolatory gesture: on the day they buried her, "so many crocuses and snowdrops came out for you / I tried to isolate from those galaxies one flower." Longley invokes the pathetic fallacy first by observing that the earliest flowers of spring actually appear for her sake to pay tribute to her, and appropriately too, because spring has a short life as had the girl. Longley writes that in his attempt to isolate from those galaxies one flower, a snowdrop—an evening star—appears in the sky at dayligone. The transformation from lowly snowdrop to lofty star suggests hope for an analogous transformation of the little girl. Further, it is "the star in Sappho's epigram" that "brings back everything that shiny daybreak / Scatters, which brings the sheep and brings the goat / And brings the wean back home to her mammy." Longley here offers the traditional consolation of pastoral, that through the evening star, all that has been scattered, lost, will be brought home—and the girl, herself a "wean," will likewise be brought back to her mother, back to life. Longley's poem, addressed to the girl, has the quality of a nursery rhyme, with its simple, repetitive catalogue of animals relished by small children, and the pastoral setting common to such rhymes.

"The Altar Cloth," dedicated to Marie Ewart, again associates death with a falling meteor, this time one that for a split second seemed headed for her house in the Piazza Vechia:

> Wherever you are I would have in your vicinity
> Wild figs ripening along the bumpiest side-road
> And, even if an adder dozes near that carpet,
> Masses of cyclamens on the path to the waterfall.

Longley's gift of flowers appears this time in a pastoral landscape where, despite the evil that lurks in the vicinity, prolific nature, with its life-sustaining waterfall, ultimately prevails.

"An Elegy" is in memory of George MacKay Brown, a poet known as the "Bard of Orkney":

> After thirty years I remember the rusty scythe
> That summarised in the thatch the deserted village,
>
> And the anchor painted silver so that between showers
> Between Hoy and Stromness it reflected the sunshine.
>
> Now that the anchor catches the light on the ocean floor.
> The scythe too is gleaming in some underwater room.

Ling comments that the poem imagines the "deserted village" death leaves behind,[70] one of Longley's many allusions to Goldsmith's "The Deserted Village." In more comprehensive terms, the poem elegizes not only the poet who died, but the community and way of life that the poet had himself elegized. Brown is notable for his epic poem cycle *Fishermen with Ploughs*, which elegizes the people of the Orkney of his childhood as well as their way of life, which entailed a close relationship with the land and sea. Brown describes an idyllic childhood in Orkney, where he worked as a milk delivery boy with the local milkman, delivering by horse and cart until his world was dramatically transformed by World War II. When he left school in 1940, there were German air raids. Brown's pastoral elegiac evocation of a landscape and people transformed by industrialization and war would have special appeal for Longley.

Asked in an interview if the home he's talking about, this natural world, is an innocent world, Longley replies,

> I wish it was an innocent world. It's increasingly menaced as well. I don't quite understand why it's the west of Ireland that I use to embody my themes. I really just have not written about the city in which I live. Perhaps it's just because I find birds more inspiring than aeroplanes, and trees and shrubs more inspiring than lamp-posts and telegraph poles. . . . I hate the term but I suppose in some ways I'm a nature poet . . . deep down I suspect that cities will disappear. I love looking at holes in the roads when the workmen are digging up gas-pipes or whatever and you realise that cities are evanescent as anything else.[71]

Longley's wishful thinking echoes Virgil's *Georgics*, which conveys his longing for an end to warfare in the idealizing terms of pastoral, anticipating a time when the farmer will prevail over the soldier and the landscape will flourish once again.

Yet Longley's most recent collection, *Snow Water* (2004), dispenses as well with the traditional pastoral subject, moving even further away from anthropocentric elegy to a more comprehensive effort to figuratively restore lost life. Where traditional pastoral would reflect the same sorts of anthropocentric assumptions that an ecocritical viewpoint would presumably reject, its emphasis on the harmony between nature and human nature to some degree anticipates ecology, to the extent that Glen Love argues that "a redefined pastoral might emerge," one that insists on our "implacable connection to a nature finally resistant to our controlling and ideologizing tendencies."[72] Love concludes that "a viable pastoral for the future might well find its healing vision not in the simplicity of the garden but in the complexity of the old-growth forest or of the microwilderness in the ground beneath our feet."[73]

Thus, rather than making his primary goal the celebration and elegizing of human beings, Longley celebrates nature, and the consolation he offers is the hope for its renewal. Longley celebrates the metamorphosis of its flora—"as beautiful as bog asphodel in flower / is bog asphodel in seed"—as well as its fauna, from pheasant to skunk to the nearly extinct Irish hare. In recent interviews, he has spoken of human beings *as* animals, whose primary concern should be "how we get on with the other animals."[74] When he elegizes human beings, their transformations merge them with the animal world: one is transformed into a snipe, and another, Kenneth Koch, is promised a heron to watch over him. Longley's concise description of Edward Thomas's career trajectory invites comparison with Longley's own: "The nature poet turned into war poet as if / He could cure death with the rub of a dock leaf." The ease with which Thomas accomplished this transformation is the quality sought after by Longley throughout this collection, as he reckons with the reality of human death within the broad context of nature. Unlike Montague, Longley never states a course of action; rather, he strives to depict the natural world in all of its complexity in order to bring the reader to a more sophisticated understanding and appreciation of the ecosystem.

Longley's concluding poem, "Feathers on water / a snow fall of swans / snow water," with its minimalist style reminiscent of Japanese haiku, could not be more unlike the most celebrated Irish poem about swans, Yeats's "The Wild Swans at Coole," in which the swans' loss is registered solely in terms of its effect on the speaker. Dispensing with the lyric "I," and thus with the self-referentiality and rigid subject/object dichotomy that it inevitably promotes, Longley's poem merges swans with water, feathers with snow, snow with water, and implicitly, the speaker with nature. The poem's refusal to distinguish between human and animal, nor even between animate and inanimate, provides its own oblique answer to one of ecology's fundamental questions, as expressed by Neal Everndon: "Where do you draw the line between one creature and another? Where does one organism stop and another begin? Is there even a boundary between you and the non-living world. . . . how, in short, can you make sense out of the concept of man as a discrete entity?"[75]

CHAPTER 4

Learning the Lingua Franca of a Lost Land

Eavan Boland's Suburban Pastoral

In her 1988 homage to Elizabeth Bishop, "An Un-Romantic American," Eavan Boland describes her first encounter with Bishop's work, a poem titled "The Moose" in an anthology of American poetry she had been sent for review:

> As I read Elizabeth Bishop's poem, this night I knew began to give way to the quicker, more magical dark of hers. As I followed the rhythmic slides of the short stanzas, with their skids and recoveries, my sense of place yielded to hers. The turning of mortice locks and the breathing of children became a terrain of "neat, clapboard churches" and the poplars stirring became the "hairy, scratchy, splintery" dark of the New Brunswick woods. The Gulf-stream Irish night turned to the "shifting, salty, thin" fog near Bass River. And I was lost in and to the poem.[1]

After reading "The Moose," Boland bought Bishop's books, studied her poems, and "tried to unravel the secrets of her prose."[2] "The Moose" appeared in Bishop's 1976 collection *Geography III*, and while Boland does not specify the date she first encountered Bishop, by 1980, when *Night Feed*, her collection of poetry, was published, Bishop's influence on Boland seems evident. Boland's essay on Bishop emphasized Bishop's "sense of place" and its role in transforming her own sense of place. Her subsequent poetry likewise attests to the transformative power of Bishop's distinctive version of pastoral.

Both Mark Seidl and Robert Don Adams have examined Bishop's poetry as pastoral: Seidl contends that Bishop "experienced her world and, accordingly, shaped her work in terms of a complex version of the old pastoral opposition between country and city."[3] Bishop reinvents the traditional genre as a vital, modern mode of self-definition—one that would be particularly appealing to a postcolonial Irish woman poet like Boland: Bishop's pastoral provides the means for critiquing the exploitation of nature for the sake of modernity, the oppression of a colonized people, and the postcolonial social hierarchy it perpetuated, in which women, by virtue of their gender as well as their colonial status, have been doubly colonized.

Appropriately then, Boland includes in *Night Feed* a poem entitled "The New Pastoral," which presents suburban Dublin as a potential site for pastoral, thereby anticipating a new direction in Boland's poetry that closely follows Bishop's own employment of pastoral. Boland, like Bishop, reacts against the Romantic tendency to represent nature as contingent on one's own consciousness, favoring instead a more closely observed nature to which respect and awe are due. In Darwin's wake, it is all the more difficult to maintain either the Romantic conception of nature or the Christian belief from which it arose: that nature's primary purpose is to respond to the needs and wants of humankind. For women in particular, this conception of nature has always been problematic: the patriarchal delineation of woman *as* nature effectively prevented her from imposing her will on it.

Prior to *Night Feed*, Boland occasionally employs pastoral imagery, finding intersections between ancient Irish nature poetry and classical poetry. Her first collection, *New Territory*, includes a triptych based on the Irish legend of Lir, "Elegy for a Youth Changed into a Swan," the characteristically Celtic celebration and worship of trees. "O sap of the green forest like a sea / Rise in the sycamore and roan, / Rise in the wild plum and chestnut tree" is followed by her translation of the Horatian ode, "O Fons Bandusiae," which is equally celebratory of its woodland setting. In Boland's translation, gifts in honor of the titular Bandusian spring are carried to a woodland shrine, where a green oak is celebrated. The site of celebration, the oak tree, and the spring that is apostrophized all have parallels in Celtic tradition, in which sacred groves were sites for worship, oak trees were venerated above all others, and bodies of water were considered divine emanations, associated particularly with goddesses. Despite her early identification of a connection between classical pastoral and her own national identity, as well as her two poems set in the suburbs that would later inspire her "suburban pastoral" ("Suburban

Woman," and "Ode to Suburbia"), Boland does not yet make full use of the pastoral tradition to integrate her main thematic concerns.

Her tendency to use apostrophe, however, anticipates the general direction of her later poetry. Helena Feder observes that the poetic technique of apostrophe, maligned by critics who were embarrassed by poets' use of the vocative to address inanimate objects, is ultimately a discourse that "recognizes alienation from nature and formalizes the attempt to restore our connectedness with it."[4] As Boland's poetry becomes increasingly sensitive to the separateness of humans and nature, it becomes commensurately aware of the need to restore a sense of interconnectedness.

Boland's admiration for Bishop had been initially focused on her exemplary role for women writers who are outside the predominantly male national literary tradition. The difficulties Boland faced, as an Irish woman poet, of finding a place in an Irish literary tradition that had been "for more than a hundred years almost exclusively male," are addressed in *In Her Own Image* (1980), published immediately prior to *Night Feed*. *In Her Own Image*, its title obviously a challenge to the conventional patriarchal notion that "man" was created in a male God's image, seeks to restore women's voices, challenging traditional representations of them as muses for male poets and objects of male desire lacking any subjectivity of their own. Boland views Bishop as a writer who, in spite of her marginalization both as a woman and as a Canadian, managed to find a place for herself in the American literary tradition. Boland praises Bishop for remaining "wryly outside" of that group of male poets who represent the national experience in terms of their own private and public identities. Bishop's work, according to Boland, is thereby infused with the same sense of exile that characterizes Irish writing—allowing her to depict experiences "with the precision and surprise of the traveler, the inner emigré who sees them for the first time and may not see them again."[5]

Boland's essay begins by contrasting Bishop's approach to the subject/object relationship with that of the Romantic poet. Boland makes the critical distinction—"Before Wordsworth poetry had a subject. After Wordsworth, its prevalent subject was the poet's own subjectivity"—which means that the Romantic poet "is never likely to lose track of the boundaries and divisions of his own world, and for the best of all possible reasons: because, in most instances, he has invented it."[6] As though to emphasize the way this practice transcends national boundaries, Boland cites as examples the Irish poet Yeats, associated with "the mossy stone of Thoor Ballylee"; the English Wordsworth, whose "outlines of Tintern Abbey" are likewise the contours of his own soul; and the American Whitman and "the graphite shine of Brooklyn Bridge." She concludes, "These are not, as we read of them, volatile or shifting jetsam of an outside world. They are fragments of an inner universe, securely anchored in an inner vision."[7]

Distinguishing more precisely between these male Romantic poets and Bishop, Boland writes,

> It is more difficult to point out the absence of the Romantic emphasis than its presence. Yet I see such absences in Elizabeth Bishop's work. One of the compelling evidences of it is her refusal to exercise the privileges and powers of the Romantic mechanism. She never suggests that her fishhouses and hymn-loving seals, her Nova Scotia kitchens and Tantramar marshes depend on her. She never intimates to us, as Yeats might in "The Wild Swans at Coole" or Byron in "Childe Harold," that these objects will vanish without her intervention. Her earth is not represented as a dramatized fragment of her consciousness. Instead, she celebrates the separateness, the awesome detachment of the exterior universe.[8]

Undoubtedly alluding to the familiar description of Irish literature as "a broken tradition," Boland remarks that Bishop's images, "if they exist alone . . . remain part of a fractured world."[9] Boland, like Bishop, may be drawn to the genre of pastoral because of its traditional capacity to convey a "fractured world"—to accommodate and express historic tensions between city and country—that in turn may be used to address tensions created by class conflict, gender oppression, political struggle, warfare, and colonization. "Suburban Woman" describes "town and country at each other's throat" prior to the emergence of suburbia, and in "Ode to Suburbia," the suburbs encroach upon the "shy countryside." Irish writers from Goldsmith to Heaney have relied on the traditional association of Ireland with the countryside and England with the city to offer a critique of the impact of British colonization on the land. As Sidney Burris observes of Seamus Heaney's Irish pastoral in *The Poetry of Resistance: Seamus Heaney and the Pastoral Tradition*, pastoral poetry since Virgil has sought to counterpoint "the joys of the landowner with the miseries of the dispossessed."[10] Yet Boland's sense of dispossession arises not merely from her status as an Irish writer but also from her status as a woman, dispossessed by patriarchal structures. Whereas Longley occasionally enjoys disrupting the gender binary, as in "Mr. 10½," Boland as a woman poet searching for her own voice in a predominantly masculine tradition feels a greater need to challenge it systematically than the male poets in this study.

Boland's description of the magical transformation that occurred while she was reading Bishop's poem suggests yet another reason for her employment of pastoral. The motif of transformation is a hallmark of the pastoral tradition. Pastoral depicts not only the transformational forces of nature commonly manifested in weather and seasonal changes,[11] but suggests a more comprehensive view of human nature, breaking down the distinction between nature and human nature by depicting the continual transformation of one into the other. In *Virgil's Pastoral Art*, Michael Putnam maintains, "Virgil remains guiltless of the modern misconception that nature and human nature are somehow different and separable."[12] Ecology, incidentally, rests on the same premise: that western philosophy's dualistic separation of human from nature is the root of environmental crisis.[13]

Whereas the first three books of Virgil's *Georgics* concern the seasonal and climatic transformations more commonly associated with the pastoral tradition, book 4 reminds the reader of the potential for human transformation:

> As Aristaeus visits Cyrene's underwater dwelling, captures multiform Proteus and listens to the tale of Orpheus, the reader watches his initiation—and is himself initiated—into the components of nature hidden from ordinary sight and into the artist's deepest self. Cyrene's realm explains nature's essence as well as her essential divinity. The capture of Proteus tests the georgic artist's courage physically to tame, which means to gain full knowledge of, a metamorphic nature capable of assuming infinite shapes. But to hear of Orpheus is to have elucidated the terrifying dilemma of the artist forever torn between his mortal and his divine side.[14]

Water, the universal source of being, is the essence from whence Aristaeus, Proteus, and indeed all nature spring. Proteus incorporates the infinite substances that derive from this essence (the prophet himself, a priest of Neptune, descends finally into Ocean). Proteus represents "the infinite particularity into which such a mass can turn itself," personifying nature's capacity for metamorphosis and embodying the innumerable objects of the external world.[15] The metaphor of shape-shifting, common in Irish myth, conveys the harmony in nature as well as the unity of all things–providing particularly apt metaphors to express the identity of colonized people, the woman poet, and women in general for whom centuries of dichotomization had favored their oppressors and relegated them to separate and unequal status.

Andrew Auge examines the way in which Boland renders the transformative power of nature in her brilliant recasting of the *dinnseanchas*, especially in the long poem "Anna Liffey." In their traditional form, such poems involve "a celebration of rootedness," an umbilical binding of mother tongue to motherland. Boland instead conceives of Irish national identity as having "an origin like water," a concept that inspired the title for her 1987 collection of poems. Boland's metaphor of water represents the fluidity of identity, both to challenge static definitions of nationhood and to reassert the role of women, traditionally regarded as outside the process of national definition. Water has long been a symbol of women, presumably because their identities have been considered fluid and malleable—awaiting definition by men—and also because of humanity's ultimate origin in the water of amniotic fluid.

Auge attributes "Anna Liffey" with engaging in the same kind of etymo-
logical speculation that characterized the *dinnseanchas*. Tracing the linguistic
origin of the river back to the mythic *Life*, a territorial goddess figure, the
speaker describes how "the river took its name from the land, / The land took
its name from a woman," suggesting a "primordial unity [that] eventually
gives way to the speaker's realization of her own ultimate groundlessness."[16]

As early as *New Territory*, Boland relies on the motif of transformation:
the "Children of Lir" triptych discussed earlier is based on a tale of transformation in which the children's jealous stepmother Aiofe transforms them
into swans and curses them to remain so for 900 years.[17] This tale of transformation became popular in nineteenth-century Ireland, perhaps because it
seems to anticipate and emblematize England's long colonial domination of
Ireland. From *Night Feed* on, however, Boland's poems of transformation
increasingly focus on the changes the women undergo, observing that the
women in Greek myth "who fled the hot breath of a god pursuing" were
usually forced to undergo changes to escape one or another male deity who
sought to capture, subdue, and impregnate—hence necessitating "the hour
of change, of metamorphosis, / of shape-shifting instabilities." Her myths
of transformation include that of Demeter, the Greek earth mother from
whom all growing plants emanate; Daphne, the Greek goddess transformed
into a laurel in order to escape Apollo; Etain, the Celtic goddess imbued with
the druidic power to transform herself in to a fly to escape Aengus; and the
mermaids in Irish mythology, who could be deprived of their shape-shifting
freedom when a human male managed to take an article of their clothing.

Throughout *Night Feed*, Boland continues to rely on metaphors of transformation to characterize female identity. In "The Woman Changes Her Skin,"
the traditional feminine domain of the bath provides a space in which transformation is possible. "The Woman Turns Herself into a Fish" intimates the
basis for mermaid myths common to island nations like Ireland. The process
of transformation serves to "unpod" the seed, "flatten the paps," "eclipse
in these hips" the menstrual flow—allowing her to rid herself of all vestiges
of the feminine that have traditionally been used to justify her oppression.
"The Woman in the Furshop," who is gradually transformed into the wild
animal she wears as a coat, reverses the process by which patriarchal culture
has tamed the wildness out of women in order to render them more suitable
for a life of domesticity and submission to male authority.

Boland concludes that a radical source of Bishop's vision is "the feeling
she expresses, of perceiving a world she cannot control,"[18] observing that at
times she seems "uncertain, and unwilling to be certain, of where her own
consciousness ends and the observed world begins."[19] For Boland as well as
for Bishop, nature is not simply the product of human consciousness; rather,
humans *are* nature and their consciousness is a product of it. Thus, poetry

has the power to reveal but not to control the natural world, and although human beings can hope to respond to and form connections with the natural world, they cannot hope for their response to be returned, or to impose their views on it. Mark Seidl observes that "recognition of the alienness of nature is the principal link between Bishop's pastoral and the very tradition it works to revise."[20] Compared to the natural world of Romantic poetry, Bishop's world is unresponsive in human terms. In her poem, "The Fish," for example, the fish shifts its eyes "a little, but not, / to return [her] stare."[21]

Boland, like Bishop, suggests that her own heightened sense of the unresponsiveness of nature has also been conditioned by the historic status of women. Boland's poem "It's a Woman's World" distinguishes between the world of men, whose contributions are acknowledged in history, and that of women, "defined / by what we forget, / by what we will never be." Women, therefore, rather than romanticizing their role in the universe by positing oneness with nature, see the world perhaps more truly:

> By night our windows moth our children to the flame
> of hearth not history. . . . that woman there,
> craned to the starry mystery
> is merely getting a breath of evening air, while this one here—
> her mouth
> a burning plume—
> she's no fire-eater,
> just my frosty neighbour, coming home.

In Bishop's reading, "the tendency of modern pastoral since Wordsworth had been . . . to inflate the individual ego at the expense of nature."[22] Bishop searched instead for a version of pastoral that would enable self-definition while respecting nature's otherness.

Boland likewise seeks a role for herself that does not impose her own consciousness on the natural world but rather gleans knowledge from it. In order to accomplish this goal, the poet must rely on what Boland describes as "the volatile or shifting jetsam of an outside world." Guy Rotella writes that Bishop's poems have the "lowest density of generalization that it is possible for poems to contain," and describes how she once wrote to Lowell to correct an error he had made about raccoons: "My passion for accuracy may strike you as old-maidish—but since we do float on an unknown sea I think we should examine the other floating things that come our way very carefully; who knows what might depend on it?" He further observes, "For Bishop, the effort to know and render the literal with precision is a way to steady the self, to stay afloat. This does not mean that she trusts to observation, art, or knowledge as vessels of salvation; they are leaky boats. But she does believe they can help us survive."[23] Committing herself to the most accurate observation she can sustain, Bishop nonetheless insists that no knowledge or form is objective or authorized. Rotella concludes that Bishop "makes meaningful works of art that threaten whatever meanings they imply."[24] Like Bishop, Boland gradually found that she could make her poetry only from the "chance sights," the ordinary objects and experiences of her day-to-day life there. Rather than mirroring the Irish male mythic tradition, Boland strove for a "revised way of seeing, rather than the thing that's seen,"[25] and has emphasized that the best nature poets have preferred the lexicon of the "overlooked and disregarded," the "devalued."[26] Peter Kupillas suggests, "These modifiers acquire new meaning when we consider that the experiences from which she writes and the objects about which she writes have been, in a traditionally patriarchal society, part of the domain of women and therefore regarded as 'trivial,' 'private,' lacking in universality and not the proper subjects of Irish poetry."[27]

Because women undergo childbirth and hence are relegated primary responsibility for child rearing, they have long been confined to lives of domesticity, considered less inherently interesting, valuable, or "universal" in appeal than those of their male counterparts. But Boland reminds the reader of the universality of women's ordinary experiences of childbirth and child rearing. In "Before Spring," seedlings planted in pots are moved to sunny beds after the frost is past and "the pride . . . in giving life" is transferred from seedling to newborn child, "little seed-head." In "Envoi," Boland invokes a muse in classical poetic fashion, but this time the muse is asked to bless the ordinary and sanctify the common, in an ostensibly ordinary setting that nonetheless has great potential for the extraordinary. Suburban Dublin at Easter time, redolent with clematis and winter-flowering jasmine, is about to awaken into spring, a process of revivification that, not coincidentally, marks the celebration of the resurrection of Christ. The poet anticipates finally putting her hand in the muse's side, finally having faith that her seemingly ordinary experiences are worthy of immortalizing. Similarly, in "The Garden," the Edenic setting of the garden with its central apple tree features not Adam and Eve but mother and daughter, for whom Boland avers, "It's our turn in this garden." Although Marvell and his successors allude in their garden poems to the Garden of Eden, their pastoral excludes women and sexuality. Marvell's garden and meadow instead evoke a prelapsarian paradise before the "luckless Apple," and indeed Eve, were introduced.[28] Poggioli observes that Marvell's "Garden" pushes even further the opposition between the pastoral of love and the pastoral of self, depriving the latter "of melancholy's bittersweet taste" but seasoning it "with a mirthful and witty misogyny":

Such was that happy Garden-state,
While man there walk'd without a mate . . .
Two paradises 'twere in one
To live in Paradise alone.

Marvell "proved that the pastoral remains a masculine dreamworld even when it abandons the realm of sex."[29] Not coincidentally, his male-dominated pastoral emphasizes the primacy of individual perception. By reincorporating the feminine into the pastoral landscape, Boland thereby reincorporates sexuality and a collective vision.

Much of the conflict in Bishop's poetry is grounded in the old pastoral opposition between country and city, an opposition that, in an industrialized society, inevitably entails a response to technology; Boland's increasing reliance on this opposition in her suburban pastoral suggests Bishop's influence. Whereas Bishop's earlier poetry reveals a deep suspicion of modernity, later in her career, she came to believe that nature and human progress could be reconciled. Mark Seidl considers her poem "The Moose" pivotal in its effort to subsume the seemingly opposing values of country and city within a broad vision of community:

> Not until she completed that long-gestating poem, "The Moose" . . . did she finally make her peace with modernity. In this poem, the egoism implicit in modernity as she conceives of it disappears as human needs and values blend with and complement those of nature, yielding communal relations in which the poet can fully participate.[30]

Opening with a series of impressions of the Nova Scotian landscape, the poem then shifts to a focus on passengers on a bus. Whereas moving machines in Bishop's poetry "typically betoken psychic distress or impending destruction," the bus in "The Moose" instead "fosters the speaker's growing awareness of human community,"[31] reflecting Bishop's gradual acceptance of technology as a fact of life. Seidl observes,

> Just as modernity enhances, rather than fragments, human community, so too does nature, as Bishop injects into the community a strong dose of pastoral harmony. Before the bus helps the speaker into the realm of communal experience, it rolls into a fog "shifting, salty, thin," a fog that recalls the mist in "Cape Breton" in that it draws all things into a larger order. But rather than containing a technological threat as in the earlier poem, the fog here reinforces a set of already established interconnections . . . Natural processes and creatures intertwine with each other and, in turn, with harmless human cultivations.[32]

In "The Moose," human technology and cultivation merge with nature, eventually forming a whole that is embodied in the bus passengers' experience of community.

Likewise, Boland's suburban pastoral melds the labor-saving technology of the contemporary household with images of traditional pastoral: classical pastoral's herds of sheep have been replaced by the "switch and tick" of "new herds"—modern appliances such as dishwashers, washing machines, toasters, dryers, and irons. Whereas both Montague and Heaney are nostalgic for the more primitive implements of the rural world, these labor-saving devices, in freeing women from many domestic responsibilities, have enabled women to approach the condition of pastoral harmony that was previously the provenance of men. In the sequence poem "Domestic Interior," section 2 ("Monotony"), the persona's arms sheaf nappies rather than grain, and her altars, her "warm shrines," unlike the oracle at Delphi who received gifts of grain, are washing machines and dryers. In section 6, "The Muse Mother," Boland's modern-day sibyl, "lymning hymns sung / to belly wheat or a woman," is glimpsed through a window, holding a nappy liner.

The pastoral harmony in "The Moose" seems to be a product of the moose's gender. Bishop insists on this through a passenger's exclamation—"Look! It's a she!'"—as well as through the speaker's more subtle associations of the female moose with domesticity: she is "safe as houses," as home, the hearth, structures traditionally associated with the female and maternal.[33] "That a female creature," writes Joanne Feit Diehl, is the occasion for this unprecedented experience "is itself not unexpected: such a gesture participates in the reaffirmation of maternal power," a power embodying "a female strangeness that constitutes an inherently subversive notion of the Sublime."[34]

Similarly, Boland's poem "The New Pastoral" depicts the suburbs as a woman's domain, by day abandoned by its upper-middle-class male inhabitants in favor of the urban work world, thus leaving it dominated by a female presence and perspective. Jody Allen-Randolph observes that "the suburb, where identity and creativity are often 'assaulted' and even lost" is for Boland "also a place where identity might be retrieved."[35] "The New Pastoral" opens with the lines, "The first man had flint to spark. He had a wheel to read his world. / I'm in the dark." Boland suggests that while males have received the credit for the discoveries that produced technology, women have figuratively been left "in the dark" because their contributions have been overlooked, their work attributed to "anonymous." Males have also traditionally been the pastoral poets as well as the subjects of the pastoral landscape (grounded as the pastoral tradition is in homosexuality, many pastoral poems entirely omit women from consideration, focusing instead on a male love object).[36] Boland's "new pastoral" breaks from these traditions by acknowledging Boland as author of her poem, and thus creator of her own world, and by explicitly contrasting her vision with that of men's. She writes that she is "a lost, last inhabitant— / displaced person / in a pastoral chaos."

Boland's pastoral is "chaos" not only because of the traditional dichotomy between male and female, civilization and nature, order and chaos, but also because of a consciousness of the pervasiveness of decay—a rarity in male pastoral poetry. The male persona in the famous "Passionate Shepherd to His Love," for example, fails to register that the beauty of the natural world and the nymph will inevitably fade; hence, the female response in "The Nymph's Reply":

> Thy gowns, thy shoes, thy beds of roses,
> Thy cap, thy kirtle, and thy posies
> Soon break, soon wither, soon forgotten—
> In folly ripe, in reason rotten.[37]

Boland's narrator reveals a similar awareness of human mortality as well as nature's inevitable process of decay: "Can I unbruise these sprouts or cleanse this mud flesh / till it roots again? / Can I make whole / this lamb's knuckle, butchered from its last crooked suckling?" Unlike the shepherd poet, who vicariously tends the lambs without any thought to their eventual fate at the hands of butchers, Boland's housewife narrator encounters the lamb only after it has been butchered and thus has no other choice but to be conscious of death, of deterioration, of loss, of chaos. Boland's "new pastoral" is thus also post-pastoral in its attentiveness to nature's cycles of birth and decay, life and death.

Furthermore, Boland emphasizes that women's roles in her pastoral involve real work as opposed to "otium"—the pleasurable, artificial work presumably engaged in by poet shepherds. Otium, the Latin word for leisure, peace, freedom from business, ease, is the subject of a Horatian ode that contrasts the endless pursuit of wealth and glory with a simple, pastoral existence—implying that the latter lifestyle involves no real work at all:

> Around your great farm house you can hear the lowing
> Of your many herds of fine Sicilian cattle;
> Your fine race-mare is whinnying in your stable;
> You wear the finest garments
>
> Double-dyed with African purple dye.
> To me the Fates have given a little house,
> And a certain talent for rendering Grecian verses,
> And scorn for the envious.[38]

Boland's last line, "I danced once on a frieze," is an allusion to Keats's "Ode on a Grecian Urn" (inspired by his visit to an exhibition of the Elgin Marbles and its Parthenon frieze), whose depiction of a pastoral scene of unchanging natural beauty and eternal love contrasts sharply with the narrator's own world, with its deep sensitivity to the passing of time: "Ah, happy, happy boughs! That cannot shed / Your leaves, nor ever bid the Spring adieu."[39] Yet her allusion also underscores her awareness that she, as a woman, has traditionally been only the object of pastoral longing, never the subject. Her reference to dancing "once on a frieze" recalls the age-old artistic practice of idealizing the female as independent of time, unchangeable, while all else around her is subject to change. Yet this representation also leaves her frozen in time, unable to act in reality, unable to change or influence anything, while men are granted agency. The world's greatest discoveries and innovations— fire and the wheel—are attributed to male ingenuity, implying that they have the power to shape the world to suit them. But Boland puts this representation in the past tense, implying that she has rewritten her own role and, by extension, that of women's, in pastoral as well as in reality. Although women were long at the mercy of males who depicted them in terms of timeless beauty, Boland instead attempts to capture the real woman—subject to all the forces of time and capable of acting within them. Thus her remonstrance, "I want a poem I can grow old in."

Boland's sequence poem "Domestic Interior" is replete with pastoral conventions—but rather than focussing, as classical pastoral had, on the male shepherd's love for a nymph or another male shepherd, it concerns the relationship between a mother and a daughter. The poem begins with a section titled "Night Feed," which describes the narrator's getting up at dawn for the "night feed" of her infant daughter. Associating the daughter's infancy with that of earth, the poem intersperses images of beginning (birth, dawn, infancy, opening daisies, the early bird) with images that anticipate change and growth ("mercurial rainwater," "worms turning"). Peter Kupillas observes that the mother, the "finder [who] is keeper" at this dawn meeting, recognizes that the first half of the old singsong adage presages later loss.[40] Losers will ultimately be weepers, as

> Worms turn.
> Stars go in.
> Even the moon is losing face.
> Poplars stilt for dawn
> And we begin
> The long fall from grace.

Thus the poem that opens with images of purity and innocence—daisies, rainwater, and sleeping infants—closes with images of death—their own, and that of nature. As Boland relocates the pastoral realm in the suburbs in section 2, "Monotony," she writes,

> I grow in and down
> to an old spiral,
> a well of questions,
> an oracle: will it tell me—am I
> at these altars,
> warm shrines,
> washing machines, dryers
> with their incense
> of men and infants
> priestess
> or sacrifice?

"An oracle" is appositive to the narrative "I"; the narrator presents herself as an oracle, or the one who communicates the message of the oracle.

The oracle to whom she refers was associated in Greek legend with pungent fumes, clouded memories, riddles, and profound wisdom. Centuries before the birth of Christ, devout pilgrims journeyed to Delphi to ask her advice on sites to build cities, laws to enact, and prayers to say. According to legend, a shepherd named Kouretas noticed his goats behaving strangely near a certain opening in the earth. When he told others about it, some investigated the fumes, went into trances, and began mumbling prophecies. A woman was appointed to serve as the official oracle, but because her prophecies were often equivocally phrased, many supplicants misinterpreted her advice.[41] Thus, on the traditional site of pastoral, a woman's vision was acknowledged as essential, and its legendary potential for ambiguity provides an apt metaphor for poetry. Boland thereby implies that the female poetic vision is just as essential to the contemporary world as the oracle's had been to the ancient world.

In the third section, "Hymn," Boland opens by stating, "a lamb would perish out there,"[42] yet another reminder that hers is indeed a new pastoral in a new setting—not the classical pastoral of male shepherds and lambs in a timeless world. In "Hymn," Boland imbues the connection between mother and child with sacramental value: the lullaby that the mother sings to the infant at bedtime becomes a hymn.[43] Given her fascination with the myth of Demeter and Persephone, Boland undoubtedly alludes here to the Homeric hymns, the second of which is dedicated to Demeter and concerns her relationship with and long search for her daughter Persephone following her abduction to the underworld by Pluto. Upon Persephone's return, Demeter promptly restores the land to a rich pastoral paradise: "And rich-crowned Demeter did not refuse but straightway made fruit to spring up from the rich lands, so that the whole wide earth was laden with leaves and flowers. Then she went, and . . . showed the conduct of her rites and taught them all her mysteries . . . awful mysteries which no one may in any way transgress or pry into or utter, for deep awe of the gods checks the voice."[44] Thus the seemingly mundane nurturing acts of the mother are imbued with all of the transformative power and mystery of earth itself.

Sidney Burris regards the myth of Persephone, who is doomed to spend winters in the underworld as punishment for having eaten a few pomegranate seeds, as emblematic of the Greek seasonal cycle, out of which emerged the entire pastoral tradition:

> The etymological history of the word "pomegranate" claims an essentially pastoral lineage . . . its Latin root "granatus" means, simply "having many seeds," . . . the Babylonians had thrown [pomegranates] on the floor of the bridal chamber—the fat, ripe, pomegranates would burst open, scattering their seeds and, it was hoped, their fertility, on the newly married couple.[45]

The irony that the male-centered pastoral tradition evolved from a story of women, fertility, and birth is not lost on Boland, and the Demeter/Persephone myth remains integral to her oeuvre.

The myth's centrality for Boland undoubtedly stems from its capacity to counter the myth that has been integral to Irish national identity: while Ireland has been depicted for centuries as a woman victimized, and in need of rescue, by men, the myth of Demeter and Persephone features a dramatic rescue undertaken by a woman. Clair Wills writes that "the representation of the Irish land as a woman stolen, raped, possessed by the alien invader is not merely one mythic narrative among many, but, in a literary context, it is *the* myth, its permutations so various and ubiquitous it can be hard to recognize them for what they are."[46] Whereas Wills contends that "the trope functions not only as the means by which the poet can lament the loss of the land, but also, through his linguistic embodiment of it, the means by which he may repossess it," Boland as a female poet, whose story is conveyed by a female narrator, crucially alters the myth and reappropriates the lost woman as well as the lost land. Heaney and Montague uncritically rely on the sovereignty myth in which woman is embodied in the land; Boland, as well as McGuckian and Ní Dhomhnaill, restores female agency in a variety of ways.

In "Endings," Boland returns to the myth, describing a mother who reflects on her own mortality and the eventual loss of her infant daughter, drawing a parallel between her and the apple trees outside her window:

If I lean
I can see
what it is the branches end in: The leaf.
The reach.
The blossom
The abandon.

The connection between nature and human nature, integral to the pastoral tradition, is evident here and indeed throughout "Domestic Interior." In particular, Boland's references to flowers and trees—daisies, poplars, apple trees, rowan trees, jasmine—recall the floral and arboreal catalogues of pastoral poetry, yet they also enable Boland to create a uniquely feminine pastoral. Patricia Haberstroh observes that "as she has done in many of her poems, Boland often turns to images of flowers and woods to embody feelings; the life cycle in the natural world reminds her speakers of the limitations of maternal joy."[47] Peter Kupillas observes that flowers, blossoms, or fruit are often metaphors for Boland's children, indeed, for all children.[48]

Yet Boland also relies on these natural elements to transform traditional representations of the female. Alicia Ostriker explores the ways in which contemporary women poets employ traditional images for the female body—flower, water, earth—retaining the gender identification of these images but transforming their attributes so that flower means force instead of frailty, water means safety instead of death, and earth means creative imagination instead of passive generativeness.[49] Both Bishop and Boland are drawn to descriptions of nature that have similar transformative power. In "At the Fishhouses," Bishop describes water that burns as if it were "a transmutation of fire"; in "The Harbour," Boland emphasizes that water prevails against presumably more durable materials such as granite and iron: "An ocean forgot an empire and the armed ships under it changed: to slime weed and cold salt and rust."

The Journey (1987) includes some of Boland's most heartfelt meditations on national identity. In "Mise Eire," "my Ireland," Ireland is "land of the Gulf Stream, the small farm, the scalded memory" to which she vows she will not return, although its influence on her poetry remains pervasive. Previously, in *Night Feed*, her childhood spent away from Ireland was described as a loss not of land but of "the habit of land." Even after leaving Ireland as an adult, she continues to regard the land as a means of self-definition. She creates a miniature pastoral retreat in a bottle garden—revisioning it as a "globe" that contains the sun itself. In "Listen. This is the Noise of Myth," she explores the human impulse to seek pastoral retreats and, by association, to create pastoral poems that serve as figurative retreats. Although her poem seems to be based on the legend of Diarmuid and Grainne (who fled from Grainne's husband Finn McCool after Grainne placed a *geasa* on Diarmuid) the spare details of her opening stanza, repeated in various ways throughout the poem, could just as easily allude to Adam and Eve or any mythical account of humanity's fall from grace:

> This is the story of a man and woman
> under a willow and beside a weir
> near a river in a wooded clearing.
> They are fugitives. Intimates of myth.

Boland underscores the archetypal elements of this story of lovers who flee as a result of "self-deception, sin," and are forced to encounter a "sequence of evicted possibilities." Their story, Boland suggests, arises from the human need to explain the cyclical nature of the seasons and indeed all of life. During their flight, each time the lovers find a temporary retreat, they are confronted anew with cold and death, "the fields still gardened by their ice, / the trees stitched with snow overnight," which forces them to flee again until

> the woods flooded and buds
> blunted from the chestnut and the foxglove
> put its big leaves out and chaffinches
> chinked and flirted in the branches of the ash.

The myth of Demeter and Persephone, likewise an attempt to explain the cyclical nature of life, is given contemporary resonance in Boland's "Suburban Woman: A Detail":

> This is not the season
> when the goddess rose
> out of seed, out of wheat,
> out of thawed water
> and went, distracted and astray,
> to find her daughter.

Outside History (1990)[50] includes the poem "Object Lessons," in which a cup depicting the traditional pastoral scene is eventually shattered, emblematic of the eventual destruction of all the pastoral retreats that human beings create to shelter themselves from the inevitability of their own deaths: "a hunting scene . . . Linen spread out in a meadow. / Pitchers of wine clouding in the shadow . . . A lady smiling as the huntsman kissed her: / the way the land looks before disaster." Boland writes of the time before

> we knew the details of
> this pastoral scene were merely
> veiled warnings
> of the shiver
> of presentiment

She recognizes the necessity of attributing human agency to the inevitable disaster—in this case, represented by her and her husband's oversight in neglecting to sand and seal the floorboards on which the cup fell.

Despite the impermanence and deceptive safety of pastoral retreats, poems throughout *Outside History* continue to describe them as places where nature's transformative power is made manifest. The sequence poem "Outside History" is replete with garden imagery that emphasizes nature's transformations. Section 3, "The Making of an Irish Goddess" features the seasonal transformations of the Persephone story as Ceres, the Roman version of Demeter, descends into the underworld to reclaim her daughter. The scars of the earth where presumably her daughter made her entry and exit are analogous to the furrows made for the seeds that lie dormant through winter as well as the scars of childbirth, suggesting that the birth process itself, which results in the first in a series of separations between mother and daughter, is as much an inspiration for the myth as is the seasonal cycle. Section 4, "White Hawthorne" concerns a plant that, in Irish folklore, is sometimes referred to as the fairy bush and is considered bad luck to cut. Thus, despite its allure, the poet is reluctant to touch it or bring it indoors for fear that "a child might die." Like water, hawthorn has transformative power that allows it to "re-define the land." Section 5, "Daphne Heard with Horror the Address of the God," describes a garden with a laurel hedge, alluding to the laurel into which Daphne was transformed in order to escape Apollo's sexual advances. In "Midnight Flowers," the mere flip of a light switch makes a garden appear. "Distances" includes a reference to the town of Carrickfergus, which has been immortalized in song as a pastoral retreat: "Inside the perfect / music that basalt and sandstone coastal town" is captured "in the scentless afternoon of a ballad measure."

In a Time of Violence (1994)[51] includes poems in which awareness of famine in nineteenth-century Ireland and civil strife that has characterized twentieth-century Ireland undermines the pastoral vision. "That the Science of Cartography Is Limited" describes the narrator and her husband's trip to the border of Connacht, where they enter a wood fragrant with balsam, sweet pine, and cypress. The idyllic setting conceals a famine road that the Irish were required to build in exchange for food. The third poem in the sequence, also set in famine Ireland, "March 1 1847. By the first post," takes the form of a letter composed by an Anglo-Irish girl to her friend in London. Amid the pastoral backdrop of a springtime redolent with daffodils and harebells is the unwelcome evidence of disease and death caused by famine. The narrator endures the stench of death by pressing a cloth "sprinkled with bay rum & rose attar" against her mouth and sees a dead woman lying "across the Kells Road with her baby—in full view." One recalls that for critics like Barrell and Bull, pastoral tradition after the eighteenth century was critiqued for being especially escapist. In Ireland in particular, the Anglo-Irish response to the famine would certainly have exacerbated the charge of escapism, yet Boland's attempt to restore these scenes to history results in a complex pastoral indeed.

"The Pomegranate" returns to the Persephone story, which Boland confesses is "the only story I have ever loved," primarily because she can "enter it anywhere." Searching for her own daughter at bedtime, the poet enters the tale as Ceres, resolving to being "ready to make any bargain to keep her," and carrying her back "past whitebeams / and wasps and honey-scented buddleias." Even when surrounded by summer's bounty and beauty, she is aware that "winter was in store for every leaf," and that her daughter, too, must one day enter the story as Ceres.

The Lost Land (1998)[52] continues to explore the Persephone story, but this time it is employed to examine Ireland's colonial legacy. Whereas the title poem begins by portraying Boland's personal relation to the legend—as a woman faced with her daughters' leaving—its final line, "*Ireland. Absence. Daughter.*" provides a transition to the next poem, "Mother Ireland," which imbues the traditional representation of Ireland as mother with all of the implications of the Persephone myth.

The Lost Land also uses the traditional pastoral motif of the transformative power of nature as a means of addressing Ireland's colonial legacy. Poets since Virgil relied on a similar technique to suggest that the rhythms of nature have the power to overcome the relatively transitory upheavals of civilization. In the *Georgics* passage quoted in the introduction, the farmer's plough uncovers rusted weapons of war as the forces of nature gradually subsume evidence of human strife.

Boland associates the colonizer with presumably durable substances— granite and steel—whereas the Irish, dispossessed of their land, are associated with water in various forms—rain, ocean, and rivers. In "The Harbour," she writes,

> City of shadows and of the gradual
> capitulations to the last invader
> this is the final one: signed in water
> and witnessed in granite and ugly bronze and gun-metal.

In "The Scar," she describes the River Liffey, which

> hides
> the long ships, the muskets and the burning domes. . . .
> And those versions of the Irish rain
> which change the features
> of a granite face.

"The Colonists" succinctly portrays the triumph of nature over civilization, of the land over its colonizers: "The river is still there. But not their town."

Boland's essay on Bishop acknowledges the way in which Bishop, torn between continents (North America and South America) and between countries (Canada and the United States) "frequently uses place as an index of loss and almost never as a measure of identity."[53] Boland, whose childhood was divided between Ireland, England, and the United States, and whose country of origin was deeply divided through the process of colonization, feels similar diffidence about the issue of national identity. In *The Lost Land*, Boland's suburban Dublin setting incorporates the pastoral tension between urban and rural worlds as a means of resurrecting Ireland's colonial past: "the old pale ditch can be seen / less than half a mile from my house." The suburbs represent not only the boundary between rural and urban but also the traditional boundary between Norman conquerors and the indigenous Irish population, between England and Ireland, between the Pale and that which lies "beyond the pale." The pale ditch's "ancient barrier of mud and brambles," once the symbol of conquest, is now described in terms of pastoral that celebrates the landscape. It is now "a mere rise of coarse grass, / a rowan tree and some thinned-out spruce, / where a child plays at twilight." Boland writes, "I was born on this side of the Pale. I speak with the forked tongue of colony," yet she suggests that language may ultimately be a way of restoring harmony, healing the divisions. As she speculates about the identity of the colonizers who once settled on the land, she alludes to the abyss that opened up when Persephone was abducted by Pluto:

> Who came here under the cover of darkness
> from Glenmalure and the Wicklow hills
> to the limits of this boundary? Who whispered
> the old names for love to this earth
> and anger and ownership as it opened
> the abyss of their future at their feet?

Even the title of her collection, *The Lost Land*, expresses the fundamental condition of loss and dispossession that is the inheritance of the pastoral poet. In the first section of the book, "Colony," Boland's opening poem, "My Country in Darkness," expresses the loss of the *filii*, the Irish poets who, upon the Flight of the Earls in the eighteenth century, lost their patrons, their livelihood, and ultimately their art: they are doomed to practice "a dead art in a dying land." Because their poetry was a repository of Irish art and culture, their loss is emblematic of that of the entire Gaelic world: "The Gaelic world stretches out under a hawthorn tree / and burns in the rain." Hawthorne trees were used to form the hedgerows in Ireland that were essential to conducting "hedge schools" hidden from view of the English, where the Irish could continue to promulgate the language and culture that had been outlawed. Boland sets her poem "after the wolves and before the elms"; the last wolf in Ireland was killed in 1786, a time when large settlements of Scots and English increased the population to the extent that it encroached on the wolves' habitats. The English elm, native to England, was planted by colonists in Ireland and Wales. In the eighteenth century, landowners planted them at intervals along the hedges that enclosed farmland.[54] Elms appear in "A Dream of Colony" in front of a colonist's house, where "gradually the elms beside us / shook themselves into leaves. / And laid out under us their undiseased shadows." The diseases that will one day overtake the elms are symbolic of the blight brought by the colonial enterprise that will one day tear the nation asunder.

In the poem "A Habitable Grief," Boland describes being an Irish child in England:

> I learned
> a second language there
> which has stood me in good stead:
> the lingua franca of a lost land.

She refers, of course, to the Irish language, which England, as part of its colonial enterprise, outlawed for centuries, contributing to its near extinction. Throughout *The Lost Land*, however, Boland insinuates that just as Demeter managed to reclaim the land as well as her daughter Persephone, Ireland can be reclaimed from the devastation of colonization and women from the legacy of patriarchal oppression. Both may be reclaimed through the power of language; thus, the poet's own words may be regarded as steps toward reclamation.

CHAPTER 5

"In My Handkerchief of a Garden"

Medbh McGuckian's Miniature Pastoral Retreats

Medbh McGuckian's book *The Flower Master,* more than any of her subsequent collections of poetry, relies on the conventions of pastoral poetry.
Replete with natural imagery, mentioning flowers, plants, fruits, and seeds in
every poem but one ("The 'Singer'"), it establishes contrasts between nature
and civilization, city and country, ultimately privileging the values associated
with the countryside—simplicity, innocence, honesty, and harmony with nature. The poems' persona, as well as the reader, is afforded the traditional
solace of pastoral: withdrawal into the pastoral world is undertaken in order
to gain new strength and knowledge with which to confront the problems of
the external world.[1] Just as pastoral retreat in Virgil's *Eclogues* is the means
of confronting the evil of political expropriation, McGuckian's pastoral resonates with and responds to the conflicts in her world—both the political and
social conflicts of Northern Ireland and the conflicts that characterize gender
relations in patriarchal society. More recently, she has returned to the pastoral
mode (these later poems will be discussed at the end of the chapter), though
without the sustained pastoral imagery and conventions that characterize *The
Flower Master.*

In *The Flower Master,* gardens refer to the primal garden in western tradition, the Garden of Eden. Christian pastoral builds on Arcadian imagery not
only dialectically, as a means of conceiving of paradise, but also substantially,

as the body of paradise itself.[2] Friedman observes that in the effort to reconcile the literary myth of a primitive golden age with the Christian vision of prelapsarian Eden, the garden was the most important element, "the setting that lies at the heart of the myth, the scene in which takes place the drama of the birth of the mind." Like the pastures of Virgil and Theocritus, the garden became the emblem for a legendary time when humanity and the created world existed in unexamined harmony. Each real and imaginary garden was ultimately "to be seen as a version, however inadequate, of the protected and ultimately beautiful *locus amenus* in which Christ woos the beloved Spirit."[3]

Women's experience of nature has traditionally been restricted to the domestic sphere and has long been more likely to occur in the garden than in the more spacious pastures of classical poetry. McGuckian's pastoral retreats are thus found in gardens, flower arrangements, sun-traps, greenhouses, trees and flowers themselves, the female body that serves as a haven for the developing embryo, and ultimately the child born of that body. McGuckian explains that *The Flower Master* was written during her first pregnancy, its poems inspired by her own gestation, labor, and delivery; thus, the restricted space of the womb serves as the ultimate emblem for McGuckian's minimalist pastoral retreat.[4]

Terry Gifford observes that "for many post-pastoral ecofeminist writers, Arcadia might be located within the body," and Clair Wills suggests that for McGuckian, her own body becomes the means for reading public and political events, thereby challenging church and state control of female bodies, sexuality, and reproduction.[5] Because women's traditional association with nature is compounded in Ireland both by "Catholic representations of the female as virgin handmaiden or equally desexualized mother, and with the nationalist trope of Ireland as the motherland," McGuckian's exploration of her own maternal sexuality allows her to "author" her own interior, "in defiance of the elision of the woman's body in traditional representations of femininity."[6]

Although McGuckian's rendering of nature relies on garden imagery reminiscent of the Christian pastoral tradition of Marvell and his poetic successors, her pastoral retreats in *The Flower Master* virtually always incorporate aspects of eastern traditions, evoking in particular the small-scale, minimalist style of the Japanese tradition of gardening. Her choice of a minimalist pastoral setting—a "handkerchief of a garden"—partially reflects her urban context: born and raised in Belfast, where she grew up without a garden,[7] and now the director of the graduate program in creative writing at Queen's University Belfast, McGuckian writes of a very different world than that of rural poets like Heaney or Montague or, for that matter, the naturalist poet Longley, who owes his considerably more expansive vistas of burrens and meadows to his County Mayo sojourns.

McGuckian's incorporation of eastern influences into her version of pastoral may also be viewed as the result of a long tradition for Irish as well as for modern writers. In his study of Oriental influences on Irish literature, *Irish Orientalism,* Joeseph Lennon explains that the Orient, especially Japan, "came to stand for an unadulterated traditional culture from which modern Ireland could learn,"[8] and provided a vision of a premodern, pre-Christian, precolonial culture[9] associated with spiritual health, antimaterialism, and antirationalism.[10] Celtic revivalists who wanted to develop the representations of the Celtic otherworld ("fairyland") in literature turned to the Orient for models. Yeats found in Asian literature remedies for modern ills as well as "parallels to what he saw as a vanishing Celtic Ireland."[11] In an 1886 letter to Katharine Tynan, Yeats likens the Orient with fairyland: "it is almost all a flight into fairy land from the real world, and a summons to that flight."[12] Wilde had equated Orientalism with lushness and unbridled sensuality,[13] and while his assumptions might simply be dismissed as another case of the eroticization of the "other," the image of the Orient offered a welcome respite from the strictures of Irish Catholicism that dominated Ireland as well as the homophobic British legal system with which he was soon to have a personal confrontation.

Modernists found in the eastern tradition possibilities for resisting modern culture. Asian minimalism seemed to offer an essential antidote for consumerism and conspicuous consumption. One school of ikebana (Japanese flower arranging), sogetsu, founded in the 1920s, gained popularity in the west because it was the easiest to translate into the languages of other cultures through its more democratic approach (flower arranging had traditionally been restricted to the upper class—performed by priests, noblemen, and warriors) and its emphasis on individuality and originality in creating arrangements; its founder, Sofu Teshigahara, has been called "the Picasso of ikebana."[14] Sogetsu coincides roughly with the modernist movement and with imagism in particular. Wheeler observes that McGuckian's allusions to ikebana in "The Flower Master" intersect with literary modernism's preoccupations with eastern tradition.[15]

The Flower Master alludes in its title, as well as in many of its poems, to Japanese flower arranging, experts of which are typically referred to as flower masters.[16] Introduced in the seventh century by the Japanese ambassador to China, who founded the first school of floral art, the Ikenobo, flower arranging in the east has evolved quite differently from the purely decorative art often trivialized and feminized in western culture (anecdotal evidence may be found in one American man's reaction to the St. Louis Botanical Gardens: "eh, you've seen one flower, you've seen 'em all," met with a sigh of dismay from his wife). Rather, its conventions and symbolism are as highly developed and complex as those of the western literary tradition of pastoral. The practice of flower arranging emphasizes the bond between humanity and nature, enabling the artist to represent nature on a small scale, thereby recreating a pastoral retreat within domestic and urban spaces. Likewise, the Japanese garden, often miniature due to lack of space, seeks to recreate the natural landscape—usually in the form of a mountainscape with waterfalls and tumbling streams—each element in harmony with its surroundings down to the smallest detail. Wheeler observes that although McGuckian superficially seems to echo Baudelaire and his *Fleurs du Mal,* in fact, the immediate "master of the poem seems to be not Baudelaire . . . but a teacher of ikebana, instilling the principles of Japanese flower arrangement."[17] McGuckian's references to the Japanese festival of moon viewing and to the tea ceremony, as well as her own statements in an interview with the author, confirm that Japanese culture figures centrally in her collection.[18]

The title poem is written in first-person plural, presumably from the perspective of women, their "scissors in brocade." "Like foxgloves," plants that prefer full sun but can adjust to partial shade, they have "come to terms with shade," or have become comfortable in their garden and, perhaps more broadly, comfortable with the ambiguity that "shade" connotes. They know the names and needs of all the plants—foxgloves, daffodils, violets, feverfew, bluebells, and so forth. In the biblical account of creation, the task of naming fell to the man and occurred prior to the creation of the woman. While the act of naming was, and is, regarded as a male prerogative that grants the right of possession to the namer, in McGuckian's poem, the female, not the male, is "flower master"; moreover, she views the world in collective terms rather than through the individual perception privileged in western culture and associated with men. The women have also mastered all of the garden tasks, knowing not only how to straighten and prune flowers but how to get them to respond: how to "stroke gently the necks of daffodils / and make them throw their heads back to the sun." Their power to make nature respond to them introduces a central motif of pastoral poetry, the "pathetic fallacy," which, as Peter Sacks observes, "appears to reverse man's submission to nature,"[19] granting humans at least imaginative power over forces to which they are subjected. While the pathetic fallacy is often the province of pastoral elegy, in which nature itself is depicted as mourning the death of the subject, McGuckian presents a life-affirming image, in which the women's power over nature is all-encompassing—physical, erotic, and emotional.

The gardening tasks are carried out for a "special guest" soon to arrive, presumably male, who, upon entering the garden "must stoop to our low doorway," or must adjust his standards to theirs, yielding to the power of the flower master—and thereby in this case to women's traditional sphere. In its embrace of a sheltered, more domestic space, the whole poem maintains a different attitude toward poetry and womanhood. The first-person plural speakers compliantly engage in the lessons: "we come to terms with shade, with the principle / of enfolding space," a process of accepting the environment rather than imposing human principles on it. The flower master's students learn to bend and arrange seasonally appropriate plants into works of art with symbolic correspondences, emblematic of the poet's own art of shaping and arranging words. This "strategy of bending rather than cutting"[20] again indicates a preference for shaping the environment to suit its human inhabitants rather than aggressively altering it, even destroying it, to conform to their wishes.

Wheeler contends that "the meditative function of ikebana . . . illuminates the entire collection," noting that McGuckian avoids symmetry, instead creating a tripartite arrangement in loyalty to ikebana's aesthetics, in which arrangements consist of three main lines.[21] Just as ikebana requires strict attention to personal insight and a "direct, non-analytic expression of the theme in the simplest terms possible,"[22] McGuckian's poetry demands departure from western style analysis and its characteristic privileging of objectivity in thought and symmetry in aesthetics. Its worldview, at least in western culture, is regarded as traditionally feminine: more reliant on insight than on reason, more fraught with ambiguity and "shade" than men's, thereby more reflective of women's experience of the body.

McGuckian's speaker studies under "the school of the grass moon," a translation of the school founded by the previously mentioned Sofu Teshigahara in 1927. Although ikebana originated as a masculine discipline and remained male-dominated until the twentieth century, schools like Sogetsuryu encouraged the participation of women as well.[23] Coupled with McGuckian's references to the Japanese festival Tsukimi, literally "moon viewing," the motif of the moon is associated with the female reproductive cycle and with female sexuality in general. In a conversation with Nuala Ní Dhomhnaill, McGuckian explains that *The Flower Master* is about "flowers . . . sex and flowers." Patricia Haberstroh writes that "one of the most startling aspects of . . . *The Flower Master,* is its focus on sexuality and the way in which gender lines are sometimes blurred . . . she constantly stresses the sexual nature of the subjects and speakers of these poems, and her flower images suggest both sex and gender roles."[24]

The pastoral retreats in *The Flower Master* thus differ in another important respect from much of the garden poetry in the western pastoral tradition since Christianity: they are eroticized. Although the Garden of Eden—the inspiration for garden poetry—is associated with the human awakening into the awareness of sexuality, the pastoral tradition evolved in such a way as to exclude sexuality from the garden. As discussed in the previous chapter, the pastoral of Marvell and his successors excludes women and sexuality, evoking instead a prelapsarian paradise before Eve made an appearance.[25] By reincorporating the feminine into the pastoral landscape, McGuckian, like Boland, thereby reincorporates sexuality and a collective vision.

Incidentally, although sexuality had been a key component of Theocritus's pastoral, his idylls were more often homoerotic, his love objects more likely to be young boys than women. Rictor Norton, in *The Homosexual Pastoral Tradition* claims,

> If any particular genre can be called a homosexual genre, the evidence would point most convincingly to the pastoral tradition—from Theocritus' *Idylls* to the chapter entitled "Bee and Orchid" in Marcel Proust's *Cities of the Plain*, from Walt Whitman's *Calamus Leaves* to A. E. Housman's *Shropshire Lad*, from Mark Twain's *Huckleberry Finn* to Richard Amory's underground pulp novel *Song of the Loon*, from Gerard Manley Hopkins's ballads on boys bathing to Sanford Friedman's *Totempole*, from all the Greek poets' praise of boys in the gymnasia to all the flashbacks to adolescent experience in Boy Scout camps in American gay fiction in the 1960s. In its origins, homosexual love was an integral part of the pastoral tradition.[26]

The Flower Master's focus on specifically female erotic experience has invited comparison with another collection of garden poetry—H.D.'s *Sea Garden*— that also eroticizes its gardens, relying on flower imagery to describe female sexuality. McGuckian's "sea-fans with sea-lavender" invoke H.D.'s many sea flowers.[27] More substantially, however, McGuckian's "Flower Master" echoes H.D.'s "Sheltered Garden"—from the catalogues of flowers and the sheltered garden setting, to its desire to seek freedom from confining gender restrictions, albeit H.D. expresses her desire in more radical terms:

> O to blot out this garden
> to forget, to find a new beauty
> in some terrible
> wind-tortured place.

Rather than seeking figurative exile from paradise, McGuckian is instead content to remain in the garden, renegotiating the conditions by which women have inhabited the garden in the first place.

Because the anatomical structure of the flower is associated with female sexuality (McGuckian cites Georgia O'Keefe as an obvious example), McGuckian's flower garden setting in her first book is the place in which female power may be appropriated. Pastoral poetry, in its fusion of agricultural and sexual imagery originally "suggested conscious intercourse with earth, though its imagery was traditionally male, to the female earth."[28] McGuckian contends that women writers may simultaneously identify with "both flower and flower-gardener,"[29] figuratively describing their experience of the body in terms of developing blossoms and their literary labor as cultivation or flower arrangement. Because the flower serves as both the plant's reproductive structure and a traditional emblem of feminine and poetic beauty, it has proven an effective trope for female poets negotiating a double role as creators of beauty and aesthetic objects. It also provides figurative language for discussing a range of issues relevant to women writers, including sexuality, reproduction, and the relations between the natural and the artificial, wilderness and domestication,[30] thereby incorporating the central tension of pastoral.

McGuckian's 1993 revision of *The Flower Master* highlights seasonal and floral motifs, accentuating the amalgamation of violence and sexuality that pervades the volume,[31] relying on flowers and their traditional associations with feminine beauty to establish aesthetic values and explore the status of the female poet. Her reordering of the poems also enhances her structural focus on marriage, pregnancy, and childbirth. Yet in an interview, McGuckian emphasizes that her references to mastery refer not only to patriarchy but to the legacy of colonialism in Northern Ireland.[32] Thus, her decision to open her revised *Flower Master* with the poem "Smoke," set in Belfast on Orange Day, is a reminder that her references to violence also address the tensions inherent in the divided culture of Northern Ireland.

Thomas Docherty observes that many of *The Flower Master*'s poems "are concerned with different kinds of initiation rites and with the transgressions of borders or boundaries." Though the borders are sometimes geographical, they are more often symbolic: the border between infancy and adulthood, between an Edenic garden and a secular world, and between male and female.[33] In "Smoke," the border is between the urban houses and the country hills, reflecting the traditional division in pastoral poetry. Yet it also alerts the reader to the division between Protestant and Catholic. Sarah Fulford observes that McGuckian's reference to Orange Day—"that snake of orange motion"—would be lost on a reader without knowledge of Ireland.[34] On Orange Day, July 12, Northern Irish Protestants hold parades and build bonfires to commemorate the 1690 victory of William of Orange over the Catholic population.

Yet McGuckian invites the reader to see the poem on multiple levels: although it suggests the encroachment of Protestants on the Catholic community, her reference to the burning of whins more generally alludes to the seasonal bonfires common in Celtic tradition, still a familiar Irish Halloween custom originating with the Celtic season of Samhain. Perhaps because whins are highly invasive as well as highly flammable and the spines of the mature plants can damage the livestock that eat them, they were traditionally thrown into bonfires and are to this day controlled by burning.[35] Controlled burning, while a common practice to make wildfires more manageable, has been criticized by environmentalists, most recently following the 2009 Australian wildfires, when controlled burning was considered by some to be a culprit in the fires. Arguing that controlled fires harm fauna and their habitats as well as emit carbon dioxide, many environmentalists maintain that the landscape should simply be left alone.[36] The seemingly uncontainable whins, as well as the smoke that threatens the urban world of houses—the civilized world represented by the anonymous "they" who "set the whins on fire along the road," "so sure what they can do"—are simultaneously metaphors for the power of nature, human attempts to control nature, colonial appropriation of land, and the uncontainability of human nature: "I am unable even / To contain myself."

Having thus invited her reader to see the correspondences between nature and human nature, McGuckian explores other borders. "Faith" beautifully examines the border between childhood and old age, life and death, beginning, "My grandmother led us to believe in snow / as an old man in the sky shaking / feathers down from his mattress over the world." Her grandmother, despite her old age, had created a childhood world for her of benevolent intentionality, of faith and wonder, evocative of the pastoral realm, and it is to this world she strives to return. She weaves through the poem a series of falling images that bring together the grandmother's fate, the girl's awareness of her own eventual fate, and the many spiritual blessings that fall from their mortal states, including the promise of reincarnation or transformation: snow, her grandmother's sloughed off skin, coins, a shower of roses, Virgil's souls, autumn leaves. St. Therese, who described her life as "a little way of spiritual childhood," promised upon her death "a shower of roses";[37] Virgil's souls were permitted life after death in the Elysian fields; Zeus poured his divine form down to earth in a shower of gold coins; and finally, falling autumn leaves are emblems of human mortality, as in the "Golden Grove unleaving" in Gerard Manley Hopkins' "Spring and Fall."

"Spring" likewise features a childhood world of "street lamps swollen as crocuses," introducing another motif that runs throughout the book: depicting the phenomena of the civilized world as natural elements, thereby conjuring a version of pastoral out of the cityscape. Recognizing the value of urban landscapes as well as wilderness, thereby collapsing the traditional dichotomy between nature and culture, is cited in Lawrence Buell's *Writing for an Endangered World* as central to current ecocritical practice. The narrator arises from bed with her sister to "stare at the February moon," introducing imagery of the moon that will appear throughout the collection, concerned as it is with women's reproductive cycles but also with Japanese moon viewing.

"The 'Singer'" describes her childhood, when she sat studying at her mother's old sewing machine. The mounting pressure of annual exams is contrasted with the carefree world of shouting children outside her window, and she imagines the phenomena of the civilized world as natural elements: "A car was thunder, / The ticking of a clock was heavy rain." As she sits, she presses on the sewing machine's treadle: "There were nights / I sent the disconnected wheels / Spinning madly round and round / 'Til the empty bobbin rattled in its case." Relying on ancient associations of the spinning wheel with fate, Mc-Guckian depicts the increasingly complicated world of adulthood as disconnected, mad, empty of significant causal relations. Yet the "singer" of the title is a double entendre, also referring to the poet's role as "singer," attempting to impose design on what would appear to be a chaotic world.

The next poem, "Eavesdropper," had originally been the first poem of the collection, and had been titled "That Year." "Eavesdropper," set in puberty, might well have been placed later in the collection in order to portray the natural progression from childhood through adolescence. McGuckian's revision of the poem's last line is significant: "I wanted curtainings and cushionings, / The grass is no bed after dark" becomes "the grass is an eavesdropper's bed." Whereas the first version suggests that the grass provides no retreat, no protection at all for the tormented adolescent, the second portrays it as the means for satisfying her curiosity (she is the titular eavesdropper): with her head pressed against it, she can learn something of the world that has thus far evaded her. Attaining knowledge of the world through which one simultaneously gains self-knowledge is the traditional consolation of pastoral.

In "Mr. McGregor's Garden," McGuckian's setting is of course the one place forbidden to Peter Rabbit, who risks being shot by Mr. McGregor and ending up in rabbit stew. The garden, conceived as both the most tempting, delicious place and the most forbidden and perilous alludes, as do many poems in the collection, to the Garden of Eden, once lost and always remembered with nostalgia, fraught with temptations and potential for loss. McGuckian's opening lines—"Some women save their sanity with needles, / I complicate my life with studies / of my favourite rabbit's head"—contrast her choices in life to those of women who have chosen the domestic path, represented by [knitting] needles, or those who have found drug use to be the only means of coping with the dual pressures of being women in a male-dominated, violence-ridden Northern Ireland. Given the poem's title and setting, McGuckian views the traditional pastoral retreat of the garden as a viable alternative.

The poem's allusions to Peter Rabbit also serve to highlight the way in which the poet/persona's life choices invite comparison with Beatrix Potter, a Victorian woman for whom life's choices were even narrower, and who chose the life of the mind, the life of art, over domestic life. Potter, denied formal education because she was a girl, found a career in writing and illustrating children's books that represent the Lake District as a pastoral paradise, became a farmer who sought to preserve traditional farming methods, and left her land to the National Trust after fighting for years to protect it from tourism and industry. Potter's "favourite rabbit's head" was of course Peter, a character based on her pet rabbit Peter Piper.[38]

McGuckian's rabbit's head might also refer to the rabbit's head used to demonstrate theories of visual perception, in which the head is also a drawing of a duck, depending on how one chooses to view it. Docherty describes how the head "demonstrate[s] a particular boundary in the way we see. It is impossible to see both at once, yet it is also impossible to see the volatility, the shift as the rabbit crosses the threshold of perception to become a duck."[39] The possibility of two entirely different interpretations of the drawing, which cannot be maintained simultaneously, is a challenge to the value that the post-Enlightenment world has placed on the objectively verifiable—those things that we can see with our own eyes. Even those things are subject to interpretation, and the value of subjectivity is restored. The subjective/objective, body/mind dualism is often extended to animal/human and female/male in order to posit the inherent inferiority of animals and females. Greg Garrard suggests that only by avoiding the "neurotic obsessiveness" of the dichotomizing western philosophical tradition can the anthropo- and androcentric dualism be undermined.[40]

From childhood, Potter kept her pets, including rabbits, toads, and hedgehogs, in boxes—hence, "my resident toad in his flannel box," followed by the description of the hedgehog, which appears in Beatrix Potter's world as Mrs. Tiggy-winkle, the harried washerwoman who does laundry for Potter's entire animal world. In McGuckian's poem, the hedgehog becomes a male version of the harried housewife.[41] This transformation is consistent with gender role reversal throughout the collection, where the "master" as well as the traditionally male roles of writer and flower arranger are female. Having grown up with rigidly prescribed gender roles and viewing her decision to be a poet as a challenge to these prescribed roles, McGuckian takes delight in challenging them in her poetry by deconstructing hierarchical language.[42] Gifford reminds us that "Arcadia is a borderland in which not only shape-changing is possible, but also status, role and . . . gender changing too."[43]

McGuckian's speaker is one of the many artists and poets in *The Flower Master* for whom art is both an escape from their more mundane lives and a form of self-expression. In this setting, as in other garden settings, the forces of nature yield to its inhabitants, and thus her hedgehog's sleep is "under his control / And not the weather's."

Naming in Edenic fashion the creatures in her garden, McGuckian also describes the "fungi," the "dry-rot," the "slimy veil" under some flowers. Just as the rabbit's head exhibits "vulgar volatility," nature alternates between life and death, warmth and frost: beautiful purple flowers belie a slimy veil. During the 1890s, Potter devoted her attention to natural history, particularly fungi, painting her earliest studies of fungi in the Lake District while on holiday. She devoted much of the next ten years to the subject, painting hundreds of watercolors of all varieties of fungi and presenting a paper on spore germination to the Linnean Society in 1897. Although the scientific community rejected her findings at the time, experts now consider them correct.[44] That McGuckian's "ladylike sketching" reveals the "slimy veil" on the spiky flower heads reminds the reader that her explorations of the natural world are likewise explorations of sexuality and gender relations.

"The Long Engagement" describes sitting "In a quiet, eastward-facing room, / And [making] a thread from the fibres of the five signs / Leading to the eight valleys, my lush palace gate." McGuckian presumably alludes to Buddhism, for which the end of the life of heavenly beings is foreshadowed by five signs of decay: their clothes gather dust, their floral garlands wilt, they begin to sweat; their bodies begin to stink, and they become restless.[45] The "eight valleys" refer to Buddha's eightfold path to end suffering and attain Nirvana—the eradication of all desires. In one Buddhist tale that survives as a Noh play, a fisherman finds a feather robe that belongs to a heavenly being who is bathing, and he refuses to return it unless she performs the celebrated dance of heaven—a dance that she used to perform at the palace of the moon. Without the robe, she cannot return to heaven.[46] The story parallels the mermaid tales found in Ireland, in which a man succeeds in abducting a mermaid by taking an article of her clothing—her cloak or her cap—and hiding it so she is compelled to live the life of a mortal woman. The heavenly feathers are reminiscent of McGuckian's early description of snow as feathers from heaven. Both tales of females coerced by males allude to gender relations, particularly the condition of women under patriarchy.

McGuckian then contrasts the safe, predictable relationship of her great-grandparents with the relationship she has chosen:

> A dead loss, my mother counts you,
> Setting my teeth on edge at all hours,
> Getting me to break the lychee's skin.
> She underestimates the taste of sacrifice,
> The irrelevance of distances,
> Cat's eyes, the cleanness of hands.

The lychee, a rare fruit originating in south China, is red and heart-shaped, thus a symbol of romance and love. Lady Yang Kuei Fei, the imperial concubine of Hsuan Tsung (AD 712–756) had a passion for fresh lychee fruit. To woo her, the emperor had them brought from southern China to his palace 600 miles north, dispatching guards mounted on fast horses to deliver them while they were still fresh.[47] McGuckian plays on the lychee's associations with love and passion, portraying the act of breaking its skin as a sexual initiation, the loss of virginity. The act of eating the lychee parallels that of Eve and the fruit of Eden, likewise regarded as a sexual initiation, and an awakening into the awareness of humanity's mortal ("fallen") condition. McGuckian's poem "Problem Girl" had featured an Eve-like girl eating her apple, or "lychees," delineating a degeneracy from religious life into secularity.[48]

"Slips" recreates a pastoral realm of simple rural pursuits and pleasures, a world in which nature supplies one's every need:

> The studied poverty of a moon roof,
> The earthenware of dairies cooled by apple trees,
> The apple tree that makes the whitest wash. . . .
> My childhood is preserved as a nation's history,
> My favourite fairytales the shells
> Leased by the hermit crab.

With the sky as one's roof, there is no need for traditional housing, electric lighting, or refrigeration—all the trappings of modernity. Her favorite fairytales, "shells leased by the hermit crab," refer to the sound one hears when holding a shell up to one's ear (actually the sound is an echo of the workings of one's ear), but more broadly suggest that in this setting she enjoys a kind of self-sufficiency, with nature rather than books supplying her stories (Dickinson's "the simple truth that Nature told in tender majesty"). This setting, devoid of urban incursions, restores youth and innocence—"my mother's slimness restored to her"—preserving her childhood. McGuckian's reference to the apple tree that "makes the whitest wash" alludes to red gum or Angophora, which early European settlers found in abundance around the colony of Port Jackson, and which became known as the apple tree. When burned, its high potash content improved the quality of whitewash and clay mortar.[49] As usual, however, the apple tree reference is likewise to the Garden of Eden, whose central tree has long been depicted as an apple tree: indulgence in its fruit required figurative "whitewashing"—covering up the truth, as well as a more fundamental cleansing, which restores the sinner to a state of grace.

In "The Sofa," McGuckian presumably addresses a former lover who has attempted to reenter her life:

> Since I was child enough to forget
> That you loathe poetry, you ask for some—
> About nature, greenery, insects, and, of course,
>
> The sun—surely that would be to open
> An already open window? To celebrate
> The impudence of flowers?

Although her "impudence of flowers" might refer to a common type of fuchsia,[50] it also echoes a Gwendolyn Brooks poem, "A Catch of Shy Fish," in which an "impudence of . . . flowers" becomes a "ripe rebuke" for an old, sick man. Throughout the collection, McGuckian clearly recognizes the transformative power of nature as well as the power of poetry to convey it: hence, her question here is a rebuke to one unable to recognize either. The poem continues by explaining her preference for another, who does indeed recognize the power of nature and of poetry, and, by association, her, demonstrated through the simple gesture of buying her flowers for her name day.

In "To My Grandmother," McGuckian celebrates the life of the woman whom she had chosen to feature on the cover of her revised *Flower Master,* which, coupled with her decision to dedicate the revised collection to "my mother, without my father," prepares the reader for a collection that devotes more attention to the women in her life. Her elegy begins with an expression of remorse for a life beyond hope of recovery: "I would revive you with a swallow's nest," alluding to the Chinese belief that eating swallow's nests increases longevity;[51] "sedate your eyes with rippleseed," alluding to the traditional Chinese medicine used to heal eyes.[52] McGuckian wishes to push a chrysanthemum stone into her grandmother's sleeve, "without [her] noticing its reaching far, its going, its returning," a gesture that expresses her desire to bring her grandmother back to life. The chrysanthemum stone, which occurs naturally in the Hunan region of China, contains mineral deposits that resemble chrysanthemums, and like chrysanthemums, the stone symbolizes happiness and a life of ease.[53] In the poem's closing line, the rice and mussels with which she would like to fill her grandmother's mouth, as though the grandmother were herself a sparrow, are also symbols for longevity. McGuckian's vision of an ideal world in which "the heart should rule the summer, ringing like a sickle over / the need to make life hard" is expressed in this poem which restores her grandmother's life and depicts an eternal summer and a harmonious nature.

"The Seed-Picture" refers to seed pictures traditionally made at Halloween and its reference to "the clairvoyance of seed work" to the use of seeds for auguries, common around the Celtic festival of Samhain, whose modern incarnation is Halloween. The persona refers to the children who come to her "since the split." Her efforts to bond all the seeds "in one continuous skin," though literally describing the act of unifying all the seeds into one picture, refer as well to the attempt to provide a sense of continuity to these children, as well as to the composition of the poem itself. The act of capturing and containing these seeds "since the split" expresses the natural process of seeds being planted, split open, and growing into new plants, producing more seeds. Samhain, associated with the harvest and the gathering of seeds, was likewise the season of death, and McGuckian's seed-picture is the means for conveying the interrelationship between life and death as well as the harmony between nature and human nature. To see the interconnection between seeds and humans requires an ecological perspective that sees "how all things are interdependent, even those apparently most separate."[54]

"The Sun-Trap" refers to the greenhouse that enables its owners to extract as much warmth as possible from "the sickly Irish weather." She writes that "the hygroscope says orchid, though in winter it stays blue." A hygroscope indicates the degree of humidity of the air, relying on a vegetable or animal fiber, which, as it contracts with moisture, moves an index around a graduated scale. In one type of hygroscope, the moisture makes a small male or female figure emerge from a toy house.[55] The hygroscope thus becomes, in several ways, a metaphor for the couple's relationship: the orchid, the flower associated with sexuality, warmth, and the exotic, contrasts with blue, a cool color associated with depression. Three boundaries are transgressed: First, by trapping the sun within the space of the house, a transgressed boundary produces warmth inside, contrasting with the sickly rain and threatening weather of the outside. Second, the "sun-trap" is metaphoric for the search for human warmth of some kind, which involves transgressing boundaries of self in order to recognize a "kindred spirit." Finally, Thomas Docherty cites "near-explicit references to incest," a transgression of familial boundaries involving the speaker and a cousin once-removed.[56]

"Gladiolus," new to the 1993 edition of McGuckian's volume, is among McGuckian's many flower poems (for example, "Tulips") that find in flowers models for human behavior: "Its only aim the art / Of making oneself loved" as "it grows in transit with the satiny moons / Of honesty." McGuckian describes her gladiolus as if she had found it in a gardener's manual, meticulously remarking its "stately flowers," the shade and structure of the foliage, and its method of reproduction. Thrifty and eager to please, McGuckian's gladiolus "will not exhaust the ground." While the flower steps "free of its own / Foliage," exercising a limited freedom, the words "border plant" and "collared" suggest containment. The gladiolus that exists as a poetic object also generates art—if one interprets "making oneself loved" as a creative endeavor. Her flower's method of survival involves not endurance of a hostile world but manipulation of its own appeal and a susceptibility to the "roguish draught" that lays the ovules open for pollination: passivity is a stereotypically feminine characteristic.[57]

"The Orchid House" refers, of course, to the greenhouse that has been used in the west for orchid cultivation since the nineteenth century, when orchids were in such demand that English gardeners devised a means for replicating the conditions under which orchids grew in the tropics. Throughout the four poems in the sequence, McGuckian describes flowers—orchids, gentians, and begonias—that thrive in the perfect, pest-free, sunny, climate-controlled miniature pastoral retreats of glasshouses. With their fragrance, their "pleats and tucks," their swellings, and their propensity to "yield themselves," they are metaphoric for women, and in particular the pregnant persona, who "sprout[s] willowy as any sweet begonia."

Orchids, which originated in China or Japan three to four thousand years ago, are noteworthy for diversity as well as their beauty. Jakob Breyne, a seventeenth century German botanist, wrote, "If nature ever showed her playfulness in the formation of plants, this is visible in the most striking way among the orchids. They take on the form of little birds, of lizards, of insects . . . a man, a woman . . . sometimes like a clown who excites our laughter."[58] McGuckian likewise praises their multiplicity of form: "moths, the gloss of mirrors, Christmas / stars." Like all flowers, orchids are associated with sexuality. According to legend, Theophrastus, a student of Plato, noted the round paired bulbs of one common European orchid and gave it the name *orchis* from the Greek word for testicle. Because the bulbs of common European orchids resembled testicles, medieval botanists considered them aphrodisiacs, using dried and pulverized tubers in love potions.[59] McGuckian, too, sees them as emblems for human sexuality, though, in keeping with her gender role reversal, not specifically male. She plays on their resemblance to either sex: "So I tell them underground in pairs . . . their helmets blushing / Red-brown when they marry."

"Gateposts" depicts an Irish version of a pastoral retreat, an idealized rural world of thatched cottages, hearth fires, and pastoral labor:

> He says it's unlucky to widen the house
> And leaves the gateposts holding up the fairies.
> He lays his lazy-beds and burns the river,
> He builds turf-castles,
> And sprigs the corn with apple-mint.
>
> She spreads heather on the floor
> And sifts the oatmeal ark for thin-bread farls:
> All through the blue month, July,
> She tosses stones in basins to the sun,
> And watches for the trout in the holy well.

Iron gates with stone pillar gateposts are common in Northern Ireland and may have originated in prehistoric times because of their resemblance to standing stones or to the portal stones that guarded the entrance to megalithic graves. In his book *Irish Folk Ways* (1957), Estyn Evans explains that pillars at farmyard entrances were often described "as the man and wife of the house, and one of the pair may have a flat top whereon, it is said, the fairies like to dance."[60] The apparent preparation for the birth of a child (for whom he contemplates widening the house) involves invocations to nature to ensure success.

"Lazy Beds" refers to the labor-saving method of breaking in new ground, which involves not removing the sod·but simply turning it over onto the tubers themselves, most commonly potatoes.[61] Apple mint, also known as corn mint, produces scents that seem to repel pests or mask the scents that attract them. Heather, considered a "feminine herb," was traditionally used for protection against violence and rape, and supposedly opens the portals between the mortal world and fairy world. Making an offering of heather on Beltane Eve was thought to attract good fae to one's garden. In Irish myth, wells and springs are closely identified with goddesses, and depicted as originating in the Otherworld—that parallel dimension whose inhabitants have the power to control the natural forces of this world. It was believed that drinking from these holy waters or bathing in them would bestow the power of the Otherworld in the form of poetic inspiration, wisdom, or healing. Supernatural fish, especially salmon or trout, are still said to appear in a well's depths to those seeking omens for the future. The fish motif may derive from a belief that well goddesses could take the form of a fish, which would in turn have originated from the life-giving power of water.[62]

"The Sunbench" describes a miniature pastoral retreat, and seems to refer to a turf bench with a wooden or stone frame that was common in medieval gardens. The poem also refers to "petals lolling in a knot garden," an allusion to the intricate patterns of lawn hedges, usually of box, that originated with the Tudors.[63] As in many of the poems in the collection, McGuckian's retreat is likewise the fetus-sheltering body "voluptuous with rapid growth," which has summered "seed leaves," the developing embryo, and now prepares for delivery.

"The Dowry Murder" alludes to the Indian practice of *sati*—the ritual burning of wives performed by their husbands and in-laws, usually mothers-in-law:[64]

> the part
> Of my body that deals with it needs churching,
> Where I keep a secret house, a room within
> A room, or an organic, touch-dry garden
> Where I sit upon my hair.

The narrator who sits on her hair, helpless, delicate, awaiting some fate, recalls Rapunzel, shut away by an enchantress in a tower in the woods. In some versions of the tale, she is made pregnant by a prince who has used her long hair as a rope with which to climb up the tower and gain access to her room. The orangery outside the tower was a common feature of royal and aristocratic residences from the seventeenth to the nineteenth centuries, originating in Italy's Renaissance gardens.[65] The exotic pastoral retreat, the "secret house," and the "room within a room" refer not only to the setting of the Rapunzel story but to the narrator's own body as she awaits the birth of a child. Though the pregnant persona is the one reading the railway novel "that ends / With the bride's sari catching fire," her own poem ends with the man's head falling off in a drawer, suggesting that he, not she, is the murder victim this time—a John the Baptist whose head on a platter was requested by Salome.

The title of the sequence poem "Lucina" alludes to the Roman goddess of childbirth, who eased the pain and ensured safe delivery. Lucina later became an epithet of Juno,[66] as "she who brings children into the light" (Latin: *lux*). Again, the body itself serves as a pastoral retreat for the growing embryo:

> That's how my body fools itself on the calendar,
> Its once-white bean fields monitor
> A lip-soft ferning, little shell-pink gardens,
> Their wedding-day petals ending in a point.

In addition to flowers and an abundance of trees—lacewood, willow, ash, tulip, hawthorne—McGuckian's garden imagery includes herbal lore associated with pregnancy and childbirth: southernwood tied in a muslin bag and placed between the breasts, which reputedly alleviates morning sickness and stimulates labor; dill, used in traditional children's medicines primarily to cure indigestion.[67] The scientific name for southernwood is *Artemisia abrotanum*, one of a class of medicinal herbs named for the Greek goddess Artemis, also associated with childbirth and the moon.[68] The moon, associated with the menstrual cycle and with fertility in general, is the basis for much of the poem's imagery: "the fattening moon," "the moon pond." Imagery of lactation occurs in nearly every section: full breasts, ponds "creamy" with fish, "milkless bluish breasts, "milky blue," "silvery breasts," "a measure of milk," and a "milk-fevered lady." Other fertility imagery includes eggs, May Day, "a loaf broken open," and impregnation by an otter—an allusion to the story of the Irish king Lugaid mac Con, whose mother was impregnated by an otter while bathing. Later, when Lugaid suffered from insomnia, his otter-father cured him by taking him beneath the waves, the mythical site of the Irish otherworld.[69] Irish mythology's placement of the otherworld's actual entry point in the natural world, and its frequent depiction of humans and animals capable of shape-shifting into one another, anticipates principles of environmentalism such as the immanence of nature and the interdependence between humans and nature.

In "The Aphrodisiac," a woman retreats from "the menacings of love" into "a garden you could visit blindfold / For its Scent alone," and in "The

Flitting," the woman herself is a "garden escape"—a pastoral retreat:

> She seems a garden escape in her unconscious
> Solidarity with darkness, clove-scented
> As an orchid taking fifteen years to bloom,
> And turning clockwise as the honeysuckle.

The children sheltered in the womb ultimately become pastoral retreats themselves, but not without compromises. "Flitting," an Irish expression for moving from one house to another, refers to the poet's attempts to maintain the dual identity of artist and mother, inhabiting both the poem and the house. "Stanzas" are literally rooms or dwelling places; the poet's growing family necessitates moving house as well as temporarily giving up writing; and children might be said to have inhabited the "house" of their mother (the pregnant Sylvia Plath described herself as a "ponderous house"); thus, "flitting" might also refer to their movements within the womb, through which the mother gradually faces the reality of her pregnancy.

The poet covers the "cuts" with reproductions of Dutch realist art and, while describing a female figure in one of the paintings (a Vermeer), declares, "Her narrative secretes its own values, as mine might / If I paint the half of me that welcomes death." "Flitting" means not only to move quickly and lightly or to move from one abode to another, but also, in Scots dialect, to die. The house as body costs the speaker so much that "now my own life hits me in the throat." The house that permits the children's life to flourish ultimately threatens the poet's desire for immortality, which has heretofore been her primary reason for being. Finally, pregnancy forces a woman to confront her own mortality, as her life is rendered expendable compared to the developing fetus and her quest for immortality through art must be postponed:

> I postpone my immortality for my children,
> Little rock-roses, cushioned
> In long-flowering sea-thrift and metrics,
> Lacking elemental memories.

Ultimately, then, her children become beautiful pastoral retreats that serve as inspirations for her poetry and sustain her art.

"The Truth Room" opens with the lines,

> If I were to plant a tree in my handkerchief
> Of a garden, it would be a tree of heaven
> Which will grow in ash or gravel—like the jewelweed,
> Its roots will travel stone, its seeds
> Fall fast in a still room.

Anabel Patterson has discussed the significance of trees in the pastoral tradition, noting that Petrarch's reading of Virgil created its own mini-tradition within the larger trajectory of pastoral.[70] Whereas the classical tradition had equated the beechen shade under which Tityrus reposes with imperial protection, Sir Philip Sidney and his predecessors used an orange tree to represent the protective role of the Dutch house of Orange in northern Europe. By the middle of the seventeenth century, the metaphor of the protective oak was preferred, used first to describe Charles I and later, by Marvell, to describe Cromwell, the "sacred oak" of the Puritan revolution.[71] McGuckian's tree, not merely a symbol of earthly power, is an *axis mundi* that serves to unite earth and heaven, real and ideal, and is thus emblematic of the role that nature has in her poetry. Later, in "The Mast Year," with its detailed, versified instructions to gardeners, its descriptions of the habits of trees—oak, pine, beech, birch, alder, and sycamore, and its reference to beekeepers who "love the windbreak sycamore"—is reminiscent of Virgil's *Georgics*.

"The Heiress" alludes to women's dispossession from the land in Irish legal history, as the woman in this poem must depend on inheriting through her son. Clair Wills contends that McGuckian allies the position of women to that of Gaelic Ulster—defeated and dispossessed and resigned to retreating to more barren ground—citing McGuckian's own statement that the poem is based on the story of Mary, Queen of Scots, who was denied inheritance in favor of her son, who became King James of England, and during whose reign the major plantation of Ulster was carried out.[72] Sarah Fulford observes, "Like Cathleen Ni Houlihan, McGuckian's female figure is the dispossessed woman who is homeless and wandering along the shore; she is exiled from History or time, as we know it."[73]

Whereas the Irish nation is routinely feminized, the women themselves, like the character in McGuckian's poem, have been disconnected from the farmland, not permitted to engage in "delicate Adam work" or "man's work" of tilling the soil. Yet the man's work is "delicate," a word that is more evocative of women's work or a lady's embroidery, suggesting that skilled labor need not necessarily be viewed within traditional conceptions of masculinity. Even so, the female figure in the poem remains uninvolved with the man's work, and essentially out of sight, since she is told to "'stay out of the low / Fields' and out of the sun."[74] Fulford observes that the poem makes a connection between agricultural work on the land and the temporal: "Where the furrow is this year the ridge / Will be next," suggests the interdependence of time and space, reflecting seasonal change and crop rotation.[75] Fulford contends, "Although she is part of 'pure' nature, 'a place for fawns,' she is uninvolved in his manipulation of nature except to the extent that she is connected with the natural and is also manipulated or told what to do by him.

By implication, both woman and nature are colonized or taken over by the male who penetrate their dark places or 'low fields.'"[76] Richard Kerridge addresses the way in which the traditional association between woman and land leads to ecofeminism's argument "that the beliefs and institutions which oppress women are largely those who cause environmental damage."[77] Here, McGuckian challenges the traditional association of women with the natural, the material, the emotional, and the particular, whereas men presumably occupy the realm of culture, the nonmaterial, the rational, and the abstract.[78]

After the publication of *The Flower Master*, McGuckian's poetry departs from the pastoral tradition, dispensing with its imagery and conventions as well as the tensions on which pastoral traditionally depends. Of these poems, McGuckian has explained that "the environment is an inner one, the sea and sky are mental attributes . . . I suppose it is the old microcosm thing. I do tend to explore the delicate balance of the human or female organism."[79]

Her next collection, *Venus and the Rain,* is more concerned with imagery of sea and sky (Venus as both the goddess of love who rose from the sea, and the second planet from the sun). *On Ballycastle Beach* also focuses on sea imagery, highlighted by her cover illustration by Jack B. Yeats showing a person dwarfed by a merging sea and sky. McGuckian refers to many of the poems as "seascapes." In the title poem, the snow obliterates the landscape's distinctive features so that the boundaries separating the natural elements from one another, and the human figure from nature, eventually disappear.[80] These are the boundaries on which pastoral depends, and though those boundaries are permeable, they create the generative tensions integral to pastoral. In *Marconi's Cottage,* seasons are emblematic of contrasting and conflicting states of mind (every season, in fact, is represented at some point in the poem), but nature is so contingent on mind that it disappears as a separate entity.

With the publication of *Drawing Ballerinas* (2001), however, McGuckian seems to have returned to the themes of her earlier work, marking a concomitant return to motifs associated with pastoral. The note to her title poem explains that it was written to commemorate Ann Frances Owens, who died in the Abercorn café explosion. The juxtaposition, in the same note, of a victim of the Troubles with Matisse's response to violence in wartime France—drawing ballerinas—suggests that McGuckian has rediscovered an artistic response to violence. The imagery in her poetry is once again that of the pastoral retreat that shelters its subjects from violence: "a machine-gun / in its nest, a crease in the middle of a flower," "moonflowers at the edge of war." Many of the poems obliquely parallel Northern Irish violence with that the Holocaust. In "A Perfume Called 'My Youth,'" the line "by a hedged path, / where to walk in a wood was to be fired at," recalls the Nazis' deceptive practice of executing Jews in wooded areas of the concentration camp.

At Dachau, for example, where Jews entered beneath a sign that read "Arbeit macht frei," suggesting that if they only worked hard enough they could regain freedom, many were led down a woodland path whose pristine beauty proved equally deceptive, because it led to an execution site near which they were buried in mass graves.

The poems are replete with the pastoral imagery that characterized her earlier poems—from green glens to the "blue bloom" of gardens to the body that serves as a pastoral retreat. In "The Colony Room," a lover's body is "all woods, roots and flowers," and "durable as paradise." "The Frost Fair" refers to "the brightening, endangered earth . . . the year's first angel," suggesting that McGuckian, like the other contemporary poets in this study, has incorporated an awareness of environmental threat, as well as of nature as an entity in its own right, that is characteristic of post-pastoral. Glen Love's plea, that "we need to redefine pastoral in terms of a new and more complex understanding of nature,"[81] is answered in the poetry of Medbh McGuckian.

CHAPTER 6

"When Ireland Was Still under a Spell"

Miraculous Transformations in the Poetry of Nuala Ní Dhomhnaill

In *Southern Review*'s 1995 special issue on contemporary Irish poetry and criticism, a recurring theme is the woman poet's continued efforts to focus attention on the place of women in Irish culture—an effort that has often entailed rejecting the traditional iconography employed by male poets in favor of incorporating women as symbol—Mother Ireland, Queen Medbh, Grainne O'Malley, the hag of Beare—and imaginatively restoring their presence to the Irish landscape. *Southern Review* includes a *comhrá* featuring McGuckian and Ní Dhomhnaill, in which both discuss their relation to landscape, to language, and to the worldview of Irish mythology. McGuckian characterizes the human relationship to the natural world in the poetry of Nuala Ní Dhomhnaill:

> What I find most valuable and authentic is Nuala's relationship to nature. Nature is part of this Platonic ideal for Heaney and others, but Nuala is the only poet in the world, except for Tsvetaeva . . . who has the same dynamism and the same feeling of being at one with the world. Not an observer of it but having it . . . being a microcosm, so that when you talk about the sky or the sea or a tree or vegetation, you've been inside it or it's been inside you. The

whole reciprocity there is very, very different from Yeats's "When my arms wrap you round I press / My heart upon the loveliness" of the world . . . We are the world that the poem is celebrating, but we are also the poem and we are also the celebration.[1]

Declan Kiberd's *Inventing Ireland* discusses the way in which postcolonial writers have rejected classic realism in order to distance themselves from the standards by which their countries' colonizers had designated them as "other." Citing Salman Rushdie's search for a form that would "allow the miraculous and the mundane to coexist at the same level,"[2] Kiberd examines how writers of the Irish literary revival sought to find this form by drawing on Irish folklore and religious beliefs; writers like Joyce gradually shifted from classic realism to portrayals of a more subjective reality. Stephen Slemon argues that the formal technique of magical realism, which mixes the fantastic and the realistic, allows for the creation of works that encode within themselves "a residuum of resistance toward the imperial center and its totalizing systems of generic classification."[3]

Ní Dhomhnaill's rendering of nature, with its emphasis on the reciprocity of landscape and self, human and animal, sacred and mundane, fantastic and realistic, may be viewed as an attempt to revive the Celtic worldview as reflected in Irish poetry that predates English colonization. By privileging the traditional Irish worldview, Ní Dhomhnaill's poetry is an implicit challenge to the colonizer's worldview. The tacit assumption in her poetry, like that of the other poets in this study, is not only that Ireland is far more than the sum of the natural resources extracted for centuries by its colonizers, but it is also more than the western worldview, with its emphasis on the rational and its rigid distinction between objective and subjective, can comprehend.

Oona Frawley's *Irish Pastoral* observes that early Celtic poetry was influenced by the pastoral tradition. Whereas Yeats and other revivalists preferred to believe that this pastoral was a sentimental pastoral, reflecting lived pastoral existence rather than literary tradition, Frawley points out that it is just as much a literary tradition as classical poetry had been. Terry Gifford's *Pastoral* cites the tendency of critics to entirely overlook Gaelic language pastoral traditions even as recent poetry has been increasingly likely to rely on pastoral to engage with urgent contemporary issues.[4]

By returning to ancient Celtic traditions—which portray a close relation between woman and land, embodied in the figure of the all-powerful earth mother—Ní Dhomhnaill simultaneously reclaims power for women; just as postcolonial writers invite their readers to look beneath the surface of the power structure, Ní Dhomhnaill continually reminds us that there is more to the feminine than meets the eye. Gillian Rose, in *Feminism and Geography*, articulates her concept of "paradoxical space": although in popular and academic discourses, landscape—as the passive, objectified Other that awaits the gaze for signification—plays the feminine role, alternative readings of a space "beyond patriarchy" must be attempted.[5] Paradoxically, the reclaimed metaphor of land-as-woman, so often used to control and dominate women and the natural environment, offers a space where an alternative feminine identity can be attempted.[6] Thus Ní Dhomhnaill's gender as well as her nationality figure into her claim that the subjective reality of her poetry is as valid as the ostensibly "objective" reality of classic realism.

Her challenge to the binaries of body/mind, subjective/objective, nature/ human, woman/man ultimately transcends both national and gender concerns, however, to defy a western tradition grounded in Enlightenment thought that reduced nature to quantifiable aspects, removed the immanence from nature, and located supernatural qualities and properties "only in the mind, not in the objects themselves."[7]

Ní Dhomhnaill's decision to write and publish in Irish, which distinguishes her from the other poets in this study, is integral to her effort to convey the simultaneous existence of the otherworldly and the worldly: an awareness of the differences between the Irish language and the English language enhances an understanding of the disparity between precolonial Irish and postcolonial British worldviews. Her allusions to shape-shifting or transformation in Irish folklore and mythology (shape-shifting is also an essential characteristic of classical pastoral) expresses the harmony between nature and human nature depicted in pastoral poetry. But these allusions are also the means by which she taps the transformative power of the Irish oral tradition in order to convey the need for more fundamental transformations in the western worldview.

John Wilson Foster observes in *Nature in Ireland* that the metamorphosis of human beings into animals (often maidens into swans) is a motif in saga literature and later folktales: "The recurrence of metamorphosis amounts to a Celtic view of the natural world as deceptive, fluid, essentially formal rather than substantial, without fixity in the identity of species (but not, of course, evolutionary)." Foster emphasizes that nature is not merely whimsical: the formulas of shape-changing convey the values of Celtic society. While he suggests that the capriciousness of Irish weather might account for the prevalence of metamorphosis, factors such as the succession of cultures on the island, the dictates of narrative interest in an oral culture, and the advisability of concealment and disguise in a circumscribed and dangerous society also led to the prevalence of transformations in Celtic folklore.[8] The transformation process testifies less to organic notions of similarity than to the presence of an unseen dimension of life, because animals, birds and trees were links for the Celts to the Otherworld.[9] Yet metamorphosis also occurs frequently in the western pastoral tradition, most notably in Virgil's *Georgics,* in which

Proteus's many transformations emblematize nature's transformative power and attest to divine immanence.

Although Ní Dhomhnaill's poems of transformation feature metaphors from Celtic rather than classical mythology, several pastoral conventions are pervasive, such as the reciprocal relation between nature and human nature, the motif of transformation, a worldview that allows for the presence of the natural and supernatural, and the concept of a pastoral retreat that manifests the growing tension between nature and civilization.

Seamus Heaney has characterized pre-Christian Ireland as a time when "the landscape was sacramental, instinct with signs, implying a system of reality beyond the visible realties."[10] Even early Irish Christianity maintained the belief in "the seamlessness of sacred and secular spheres"[11] to a greater extent than other branches of the church, incorporating Ireland's holy wells, springs, sacred mounds, and hills into its ecclesiastical rituals. The Irish nature writing genre called *dinnseanchas,* defined by Seamus Heaney as "poems and tales which relate the original meanings of place names and constitute a form of mythological etymology,"[12] embodies such a worldview.

In Ní Dhomhnaill's article, "Dinnseanchas: The Naming of High or Holy Places," she contends that "a renewed interest in *dinnseanchas* may enable us to share our love and admiration and wonder of the land of Ireland and can cater in an imaginative way for the need of many for a place to belong to so that we may love and cherish it rather than merely killing each other over it."[13] She thus slightly redefines *dinnseanchas* for a contemporary audience increasingly attuned to valuing the land for its own sake rather than for its role in a nationalist agenda. In her poems about nature, Ní Dhomhnaill not only draws on rich layers of associations in the *dinnseanchas* to explain the origins of the places she encounters, she also applies the worldview reflected in them to figuratively transform her contemporary landscape: its seemingly objective features—standing stones, burial mounds, hills, springs, and bogs— thereby acquire spiritual resonance.

Kenneth Jackson's observation, in *Studies in Early Celtic Nature Poetry,* about the connection between nature and human nature in early Celtic nature poetry, could also describe Ní Dhomhnaill's approach:

> Hermit poems and the elegies and early Fenian poems, the best in early Celtic nature poetry, are concerned most vitally with the singer's own reactions to his surroundings; not with making a descriptive catalogue about the various things he sees, but with telling us how he feels about them and how they harmonise or clash with his own particular mood . . . in the best of Irish and Welsh nature poetry, it is the emotion, not the sun, that matters.[14]

Ní Dhomhnaill's effort to portray a world in which the subjective and the objective are equally essential recalls the worldview of ancient Irish poetry, and is likewise a characteristic of post-pastoral. It is also a reminder that, contrary to the modus operandi of Ireland's colonizers and the Ireland of the "Celtic Tiger," the Irish landscape is not merely a repository of resources to be exploited; rather, it has intrinsic value and is rich with the potential for insights into self and culture.

Ní Dhomhnaill's use of Irish folklore to reestablish Irish identity and thereby counter the ravages of Anglicization is a well-established practice. In the nineteenth century, Lady Wilde, in a long essay on "The American Irish," links Irish folklore with Irish nationalism, chronicling the wrongs wreaked on Ireland by Elizabeth, Cromwell, and William III that culminated in the bitter uprising of 1798 and condemning English education policy, which left Irish people ignorant of their own history and traditions.[15] Sean O'Sullivan writes that the movement for a national literature "uncorked the native folklore bottled in the Irish tongue. . . . Who would know the national culture of modern Ireland must be aware of her folklore and folklorists."[16]

In "Driving West," Ní Dhomhnaill describes a drive across the Dingle Peninsula, a region resonant with folkloric salience:

> I've crossed the Conor Pass a thousand times
> if I've gone once, yet each time it unveils
> new stories, revelations clear to me
> as rocks along the road, as actual
> as words articulated.

As Ní Dhomhnaill recollects the folklore associated with the Dingle Peninsula, she draws on the collective subjectivity from which the folklore emerged—a world that cannot be substantiated but that nonetheless provides a kind of truth that is just as indispensable as the truth of the "real"— objectively verifiable—world. The "rocks along the road" might allude to ogham stones, boundary markers that are more prevalent on the Dingle Peninsula than elsewhere, and often bear the name of Duibhne (Dingle is known as "Corca Duibhne" in Irish), a local Celtic goddess and ancestress of the people of this region.[17] Like many Celtic goddesses, Duibhne was closely associated with the land and thought to bring it protection and fertility. Thus, the physical features of the landscape are imbued with spiritual and imaginative significance.

"Driving West" mentions place-names—Loch Geal, Cnocán Éagóir, and Dún an Óir—all of which use Irish words for features of the landscape (lake, hill or mountain, and fort, respectively) and allude to Irish folklore associated with the places. Although the place-names she mentions receive scant attention in history texts, they have undeniable cultural significance. Loch Geal, in Ní Dhomhnaill's County Kerry, was reputedly the home of a monster known as "An Carabuncail" (carbuncle) because her outer skin was covered with jewels and shells that shined and glistened, lighting up the night sky as far as the eye could see. She showed herself every seventh year, appearing at night and almost invariably on Christmas night, lighting the countryside so brightly that people could see well enough to count all the sheep and goats.[18] Dun an Óir was originally an Iron Age promontory fort, within which an invasion force of about 600 Spaniards and Italians built another fort in 1580. They came to support the Catholic Irish against the Protestant English, who successfully bombarded the fort from land and sea and then slaughtered all survivors, including many innocent local inhabitants. Folk memory of the massacre is so strong that a memorial was erected on the site in 1980.[19] Dun an Óir means "fort of gold" in Irish—a reference to the legend of buried treasure by a member of a family of chieftains once prominent in Wexford in the thirteenth century. The legendary gold turned out to be nothing more than igneous rocks that contained a variety of minerals, but no trace of gold or silver, left by an Elizabethan explorer, after which they were incorporated into the fort.[20] By blending the historical and folkloric significance of these places, Ní Dhomhnaill's naming of them enables her to reclaim them imaginatively.

"Gaineamh Shuraic" ("Quicksand") similarly incorporates relics of folklore with those of reality, as when Ní Dhomhnaill describes the narrator's psyche as a dark cave replete with bog holes and hollows:

> Down there there's ancient wood and bogdeal:
> the Fianna's bones are there at rest
> with rustless swords—and a drowned girl,
> a noose around her neck.[21]

According to Irish legend, the Fianna were a third-century band of warriors charged with defending Ireland from foreign invasion. The drowned girl, on the other hand, was a real person whose corpse was recovered from a bog, and whose history may be found in P. V. Glob's *Bog People,* a book that chronicles the recovery of hundreds of Iron Age people from bogs throughout Europe, and is the inspiration for Seamus Heaney's *North.* Glob describes a young girl with a band over her eyes and a noose around her neck, who had apparently been drowned by the weight of a big stone and birch branches placed upon her body.[22] Especially during the Celtic Iron Age (the four centuries before Christ), the goddess Nerthus to whom these victims were sacrificed is associated with matriarchal Celtic religion.[23] Ní Dhomhnaill has acknowledged her reading of Heaney, and her poem may allude to his well-known poem "Punishment," which describes a girl who was recovered from a bog with a noose around her neck, perhaps as punishment for adultery, and is widely considered Heaney's commentary on the abuse of Catholic girls who dated British soldiers. By melding two seemingly disparate visions of reality —the world of ancient religion, relegated today to the seemingly innocuous categories of myth, folklore, and legend, and the objectively verifiable world of anthropology—Ní Dhomhnaill suggests that these realms deserve equal status. The former is the product of a pre-scientific worldview espoused by the Gaelic-speaking Irish, while the latter relic, the object of archaeological study, may be seen as the product of the scientific revolution and of the conquerors, the English. One of the unforeseen consequences of the scientific revolution was the tendency to regard earth as *not* living, merely a passive entity that exists solely for scientific inquiry and human exploitation; Carolyn Merchant describes the way in which

> the removal of animistic, organic assumptions about the cosmos constituted the death of nature—the most far-reaching effect of the Scientific Revolution. Because nature was now viewed as a system of dead, inert particulars moved by external, rather than inherent forces, the mechanical framework itself could legitimate the manipulation of nature.[24]

Ní Dhomhnaill's act of resistance to imperialism thus extends to the entire western tradition, which she argues has evolved in such a way as to be inadequate—a "total sham"—because it has emphasized rational discourse to the exclusion of myth. Ní Dhomhnaill regards myth as "a basic, fundamental structuring of our reality, a narrative that we place on the chaos of sensation to make sense of our lives. The myth of the end of myth-making is the worst myth of all; it means that the unconscious has been finally cut off and is irretrievable."[25]

Ní Dhomhnaill thus concentrates her literary efforts on rendering the images and beliefs associated with the Irish otherworld. Of her poetry, she states, "I don't want to be limited by a restriction against mixing of realms. I mean Shakespeare did the same thing. But after Bacon it was very hard."[26] In other words, whereas Shakespeare would freely incorporate otherworldly beings into his plays, after the scientific revolution writers became increasingly reluctant to include in "serious" work these beings that had no basis in reality (the form known as the short story makes a decisive break with the folktale in the nineteenth century). In Ní Dhomhnaill's writings, the otherworldly realm is accessed by way of the *sidh*, the fairies, for it was at the fairy mound—the intersection of the "real" world and the otherworld, the temporal realm and the imaginative realm—that the potential for self-recovery is made possible through the powers of otherworldly beings. Her poetry evokes images of "an immortal dwelling place wherein the most expressive urgings and forms of individual selfhood may reside without political restriction or fear of cultural displacement."[27]

In "The Lay of Loughadoon," Ní Dhomhnaill's children ask her to tell them folktales while out on a walk, and when she does, she transforms their sense of reality until they begin to feel they can actually see "the giants, monks, and the Knights of the Red Branch [jostling] each other on one bench." She accomplishes this transformation of the landscape by recalling the folk significance of its components. The Loughadoon Valley features many ancient archaeological monuments and cooking sites dating from the Bronze Age and figuring in early Irish literature.[28] Ní Dhomhnaill accomplishes her transformation by recalling the time

> When Ireland was still under a spell
> and every sheep had two heads forsooth
> and before the Inexhaustible Cow had been milked into the sieve
> and oak-trees grew in the Big Bog
> where the Fianna went in chase of deer.

This world of myth and folklore is characterized by abundance and inexhaustibility, much as the Irish otherworld was traditionally described.[29] The "inexhaustible cow" to which she refers, Glas Ghailbhlann, was reputed in Irish folklore to have an inexhaustible supply of milk that signified prosperity.[30] Oak trees, sacred to the Celts, once flourished in Ireland but were cut down by the English particularly during the Elizabethan era. She then refers to a megalithic tomb or burial mound next to an ancient cooking pit, ostensibly where Finn and the Fianna bathed and cooked their meals. Her allusions to Celtic religion and folklore return the reader imaginatively to an era prior to English colonization and also prior to the scientific revolution, a time when magical transformation would still have been deemed possible.

Her obvious mixing of real and mythical animals—the hornless deer, the stag of many tines, the red-eared hound, the wild ox, the boar, the wolf in its den, the griffin, and an array of birds—alerts the reader to the pervasiveness and value of myth in her zoological catalogue: all of the animals she mentions have strong associations with the otherworld. Otherworldly deer and stags with extra antlers occur frequently in Irish mythology. The stag's role in the vernacular tradition is largely that of an otherworld animal, "luring the living into the realms of the gods, or facilitating the fulfilment of some prophecy by allowing itself to be hunted and eaten, no doubt, like the otherworld pigs, to rise up alive and whole afterwards."[31] In Irish folk and myth traditions, animals with red ears like Ní Dhomhnaill's hound were associated with the Irish otherworld because their color was red. The boar figures in Irish mythology as a prognostic animal, and the literatures are full of references to beings metamorphosed in pig form, to pigs' otherworld origins, and "to great supernatural otherworld pigs which bring a trail of death and disaster behind them."[32] Celtic tribal gods were sometimes conceived of as manifesting themselves as wolves, and one tribe in Ireland even claimed descent from wolves.[33] In Celtic culture (as well as many others), birds were invariably associated with the otherworld.

By the time the narrator's tale is told, the children have so fully come to identify with the characters of folklore and myth that they understand their language: "But we saw ahead of us the red-legged chough / and the stone-chat / and we'd listened to them loud and long enough / to understand what the ravens said." In Irish folklore, ravens invariably appear in prophetic roles, whether their appearance is natural or otherwise. Future events were frequently divined from the flight and cries of ravens, and certain people were believed to have the "language of the birds," to understand the speech of ravens and carry on conversations with them.[34] Because ravens were associated with the otherworldly, the children's newly discovered ability to understand them is by association an ability to perceive nature as a unity of seen and unseen forces as well as to become active participants in the world of mythology. Furthermore, the apparently inexhaustible variety of this world attests to the inexhaustibility of the imagination in its effort to re-vision a world prior to English conquest. MacKillop notes that "evidence from all areas of Celtic culture, from the ancient to all the vernaculars, demonstrates a belief in life materially surviving the expiration of the body."[35] By inviting readers to envision an otherworld that is parallel to their "real" world, Ní Dhomhnaill likewise beckons them to expand their concept of postcolonial Ireland.

In poems such as "At Raven's Rock," Ní Dhomhnaill again relies on the alleged prophetic power of ravens to imbue an ostensibly ordinary place with magical significance. All of the components of the landscape, from "the magic ring of the rapids" to "a sprig of St. John's Wort in a cleft" to "the graceful birch that gleams and the ever-verdant holly," are infused with the magical properties traditionally assigned in Irish folklore to certain bodies of water, herbs, plants, and trees. Ní Dhomhnaill continues, "I shake a hawthorn and it teems / haws, a couple of which I eat in lieu / of the filbert / eaten by the Salmon of Knowledge." *Eó fis,* the "salmon of wisdom," is believed to be one of the forms adopted by the otherworld god, and many legends refer to the sacred salmon. Finn McCool traditionally obtained his supernatural wisdom by sucking the thumb he burned when cooking the salmon of Linn Feic. The salmon is also frequently featured in tales of transformation. Anne Ross cites two Irish tales in which cooking salmon and dividing it among those present prompts a severed head to speak.[36] Both the salmon and the trout are associated with wells and springs, and a traditional belief in the otherworldly knowledge and wisdom of the salmon and trout is stressed throughout early Irish literatures.

Ní Dhomhnaill's conclusion suggests that her recollection of this story of transformation has effected her own imaginative transformation:

> I press my cheek
> to the rock. I compose myself. All at once I'm delivered
> from danger, earth-bound, able to hold in check
> the monsters of the imagination, the demons of the air.

Ní Dhomhnaill's presence at Raven's Rock, her figurative act of eating the salmon, and finally, her identification with the subjective aspects of the landscape, are the means by which she wards off the destructive forces around her. By drawing on the collective imagination, she succeeds in dispelling private delusions. That a simple encounter with nature becomes the means by which Ní Dhomhnaill "compose[s]" herself (finds inner peace *and* creates herself) and wards off "monsters of the imagination" appears ironic to a modern sensibility inclined to view such "earth-bound" beliefs as mere superstitions—"monsters of imagination." It suggests that one's identity is formed, nurtured, and secured by just such subjective aspects of the landscape.

In "The Race," Ní Dhomhnaill's road trip through the small towns of western Ireland provides an occasion to explore Irish landmarks of folkloric import:

> Like a mad lion, like a wild bull, like one
> of the crazy pigs in the Fenian cycle
> or the hero leaping upon the giant with his fringe of swinging silk,
> I drive at high speed through
> the small midland towns of Ireland,
> catching up with the wind ahead
> while the wind behind me whirls and dies.

The "crazy pigs in the Fenian cycle" are treacherous, transformed otherworld animals, whose purpose is to lead the Fenian warriors to some otherworld abode. The favorite food of the pigs, the acorn, is the fruit of the most venerated of Celtic trees, the oak, which must have increased pigs' otherworld associations.[37] In her rearview mirror, Ní Dhomhnaill's narrator sees "sun glowing red behind [her] on the horizon, a vast blazing crimson sphere like the heart of the Great Cow of the Smith-God when she was milked through a sieve, the blood dripping as in a holy picture." Her experience leads her to wonder, "when Deirdre saw the calf's blood on the snow did it ever dawn on her what the raven was?" According to legend, the raven foretells Deirdre's fate: the king of Scotland, Conor Mac Nessa, ordered Deirdre's lover Naoise killed, captured Deirdre, and forced her to submit to him, which led her to commit suicide by dashing her head on a rock. Animal blood was used for purposes of divination and ravens were regarded as birds of ill omen—so the calf's blood and the raven are a particularly ominous combination. The Mórrígan, the great goddess who reputedly possessed the power of transformation, often appears as a raven throughout the Ulster and mythological cycles, hovering over the battle field, foretelling slaughter, and later feeding on the slain.[38]

A reference to the Irish Great Mother, Ollmháthair Mhór, concludes the poem: "and thou, dark mother, cave of wonders, / since it's to you that we spin on our violent course, / is it true what they say that your kiss is sweeter than Spanish wine, Greek honey, or the golden mead / of the Norse?" The ancient Irish believed that over and above the local mother goddesses, there were even more powerful mothers—the nurturers of the gods themselves. The great mother was invariably associated with the earth, and in another poem, simply entitled "Ollmháthair Mhór," Ní Dhomhnaill reminds the reader of the environmental and personal consequences of failing to revere the Great Mother:

> The fringe of your cloak is on the horizon:
> you will wrap us in *your* great-coat of clay,
> we'll be extinguished with kisses, drenched with bitter tears
> of acid rain—our own home-brewed rain.

While still an undergraduate, Ní Dhomhnaill wrote a series of poems based on Mor, and she has continued to allude to Mor and other Celtic goddesses in order to address contemporary Irish gender relations and, in particular, Irish women's virtual exclusion from the process of nation building. Joe Cleary traces the theory of "The Great Mother" to Bachofen's book *Das Mutterrecht,* which maintained that matriarchy, not patriarchy, was the original social form. Bachofen constructed the matriarchal stage of human history "as a condition of harmony with nature and a lost epoch of human happiness" prior to the arrival of the much more conflict-ridden patriarchal stage. Despite twentieth-century Euro-American anthropology's eventual rejection of the theory, Cleary maintains that the pervasiveness of the "Great Mother" in popular culture indicates a dissatisfaction "with some or other element in the project of modernity."[39]

Ní Dhomhnaill's reliance on the theory of the Great Mother reflects her dissatisfaction with a modern sensibility that continues to equate masculinity with strength and femininity with weakness and passivity. She invites her readers to return to a much older way of conceiving of the female: "The strength derived from bonding to the 'earth energies' is a woman's natural inheritance, although social and religious authorities have conspired to discourage women from such earthly affinities."[40] Ecofeminist critical discourse, incidentally, has likewise challenged the closely related dichotomy that equates woman with nature and man with culture, privileging man and thereby justifying male exploitation of both women and nature. Ecofeminism contends that such an ideology, which provided the justification for colonization, continues to underpin a blatantly exploitative relationship with the natural world. Thus landscape that is gendered feminine but is constructed as active rather than passive, as dialogical rather than monological, as subversive rather than hegemonic, and as the site of feminine rather than masculine fantasies, "might disrupt gender codings for women and environmentalists alike."[41]

The hag of Beara is associated with a whole group of goddesses in Celtic religion whose attributes may be found in Sheila ni Gig, Roisin Dubh, Cathleen ni Houlihan, and others—who were feared and deified because they held the power of life and death. "Hag Energy" is Ní Dhomhnaill's term for what writing in Irish provides: "Irish in the Irish context is the language of the Mothers, because everything that has been done to women had been done to Irish. It has been marginalised, its status has been taken from it, it has been reduced to the language of small farmers and fishermen, yet it has survived."[42] The Irish language, pushed into remote pockets of western Ireland, escaped the influence of the politics of nation building and was presumably neither industrialized nor patriarchalized: as such, it is suited for re-creating a landscape that accommodates feminist and postcolonial ways of seeing.

Ní Dhomhnaill's decision to write and publish in Irish, which grows out of the need to acknowledge the simultaneous existence of the otherworldly and the worldly, likewise permits her to convey a worldview that implicitly challenges the English worldview. Ní Dhomhnaill contends that the difference between the Irish language and the English language underscores this distinction between pre-scientific and post-scientific cultures. She writes,

> Irish deals with the world in a narrative, non-conceptual way, which is not the same at all as a non-intellectual way, it just means that whereas conceptual thought exercised only the intelligence, narrative forms of thought exercise the heart and the imagination, and other parts of the human organism beside the purely intellectual. For instance, Irish has a whole attitude to "an saol eile," the preternatural or "the Other World" which is totally impossible to translate into English, where the post-Enlightenment language has a built-in prejudice against it.[43]

Deborah McWilliams writes that Ní Dhomhnaill "is ardent in her conviction that 'one of the few, genuinely alternative cultural strands now [is] the Irish language tradition," because, as she observes, "the Irish language didn't go through the Renaissance . . . [or] the Reformation . . . [or] the Enlightenment . . . [or] the Victorian era. [Rather] it fell out of history."[44] At least officially it fell out of history during the period in which it was outlawed in Ireland; it continues to be spoken in the isolated regions, but these regions, she would argue, remained relatively untouched by the intellectual movements of mainstream culture.

Thus, the Irish language itself embodies a culture, an alternative way of seeing the world and of representing reality. In the poem titled "The Language Issue," from which the title of her third collection of poetry, *Pharaoh's Daughter*,[45] is taken, Ní Dhomhnaill finds an analogy for her effort to save the Irish language in the biblical story of Moses and the bulrushes:

> I place my hope on the water
> in this little boat
> of the language, the way a body might put an infant . . .
> Not knowing where it might end up;
> in the lap, perhaps,
> of some Pharaoh's daughter.

When the story of Moses and the bulrushes takes place, the Israelites were in bondage to the Egyptians. The effort of Moses's sister to protect her brother ultimately preserved not only her brother but an entire people. Beyond that, it preserved an entire culture, a way of life, a tradition whose influence was ultimately felt around the world. Similarly, Ní Dhomhnaill's purpose is to preserve Irish culture by preserving its folklore and language—and in turn, she hopes that this culture will have an influence on a worldview. She relies on Irish language and Irish folklore in an effort to retrieve something essential to both: a vision of reality that has been lost. Stephen Slemon, discussing the double vision or "metaphysical clash" produced when colonization imposes a foreign language on an indigenous population, writes that the postcolonial text "recapitulates a dialectical struggle within language, a dialectic between 'codes of recognition' inherent within the inherited language and those imagined, utopian, and future-oriented codes that aspire toward a language of expressive, local realism, and a set of 'original relations' with the world."[46]

Ní Dhomhnaill's poem "Aubade" expresses this dialectical struggle, both through her tactic of placing the poem in its original Irish opposite the English translation of it and through her reliance on a type of poem, the aubade, or dawn song, imported from England but carefully reshaped to reflect a decidedly different setting and worldview. Opening the poem with the contention that "it's all the same to morning what it dawns on," she proceeds to challenge the arrogant assumptions of the conventional aubade. In John Donne's "The Sun Rising," probably the best-known aubade in the English language, the lover's world is depicted as a universe so complete in itself that the natural elements outside his window seem irrelevant and annoying (he insults the sun and orders it away as one would, at one time, have ordered a servant). Ní Dhomhnaill's poem is much more circumspect and serious: rather than depicting the lovers as the center of the universe, Ní Dhomhnaill depicts them as part of the natural setting, amid jackdaws, mallards, moorhens, and oystercatchers. As in the traditional aubade, the sun is coming up and the lovers are in bed together, "yawning in unison before they do it again"—but there is an underlying tension in this poem that isn't usually found in an aubade—the bickering and the blitz—and finally, the responsibility we have for our children, which John Donne would no doubt consider out of place in a love poem. In Ní Dhomhnaill's version of the aubade, lilies and roses are not merely the components in an idealized description of a woman's beauty but are worthy of observation in their own right.

In the final stanza, the parents' only legacy for their children is broken bowls—alluding to the brokenness of Irish tradition in terms of language, culture, and religion. Yet, she concludes, it is preferable to give them broken bowls than no bowls at all—better to give them a broken tradition that is an amalgamation of Irish English and Irish Gaelic, Catholic and Protestant, Celt and Saxon than to leave them utterly at the mercy of their own resources.

Thus, Ní Dhomhnaill "aspires not only to call attention to the language issue in contemporary Ireland, but also to revive, within the Irish philosophic tradition, the pre-modern belief in the simultaneous existence of at least two realms of being: the worldly or natural, and the otherworldly, or preternatural."[47] Ní Dhomhnaill contends, "The Gaeltacht language I grew up with fell out of history before the Enlightenment, and before many other things, including Victorian prudishness . . . Nor has Irish a prejudice against the otherworld. You talk about the otherworld in Irish and it's an intellectually credible attitude."[48]

Ní Dhomhnaill's frequent use of folktales involving transformation, or shape-shifting, from human to animal form, serve to remind the reader of the inseparable relation between the human and the animal world, and of the value of integrating precolonial folk vision with a contemporary worldview. James MacKillop observes that "transmigration of souls gives way to the widespread motif of shape-shifting, and the happy afterlife becomes concurrent with mortal life."[49] Anne Ross notes the way in which shape-shifting brings animals and humans "into a continual juxtaposition, their shapes and characteristics continuously merging and separating in the mythological legends."[50] Through the motif of transformation, Ní Dhomhnaill problematizes the western dichotomy of subject and object, nature and self, and instead asserts their interrelationship, even their inseparability. Ní Dhomhnaill's poetry relies on transformations to convey that "the whole of Western discourse is ripe for transformation and is transformable."

Shape-shifting legends, born out of dire need to cope with terrible situations, imply that the only hope for salvation is radical transformation. Bo Almqvist writes,

The once all but universal belief in transformation and enchantment forms the core of innumerable popular narratives. In a wide range of these we also meet with skins, hides, cloaks, feathercoats, etc., which are donned by magicians as they transform themselves into animals or cast over antagonists they want to turn into wild beasts or birds. Equally common is the motif that certain zoomorphic or semi-zoomorphic beings—whether expressly stated to be enchanted humans or not—are able to remove their animal coats and take on human shape.[51]

Shape-shifting, central to the classical pastoral tradition, is also common in Celtic mythology and often the source for Ní Dhomhnaill's many shape-shifters: ravens, hare, deer, water horses, hounds, hags, hawks, and mermaids. Her poems about mermaids—creatures caught between two realms, sea and land, and between two ways of being, natural and supernatural—are emblematic of the Irish modern condition. Mermaid folklore is of course most prevalent in fishing communities on islands—and in Ireland, it is also associated with the Gaeltacht, which, because of its remoteness, was less influenced by British culture and language and thus is widely regarded as more "Irish" than other regions. In folklore, mermaids were tricked by mortal men into leaving behind their sea lives; the men would hide some article of the mermaid's clothing—usually a cap or a cloak—in order to prevent their return to the sea. Jane Urquhart's novel *Away* uses the mermaid figure as a symbol for postcolonial Ireland; when the protagonist, allegedly a former mermaid, emigrates from her homeland to Canada during the famine, her desperate need to get back to the water ultimately results in her death. Ní Dhomhnaill's mermaids, because they come from a different realm than humans, operate under totally different sets of principles and have strikingly different concepts of reality that likewise represent challenges to patriarchal and imperialist hegemonies.

In her poem "The Mermaid in the Labour Ward," the human realm is equated with mortality and pain (the "curse of Eve" was to suffer labor pains), the mermaid's realm with prelapsarian tranquility. After the mermaid is forced to join the mortal realm, which represents the simultaneous entry into female domestic life, Ní Dhomhnaill writes,

> It's little wonder
> in the long months that followed,
> as her instep flattened
> and her arches dropped,
> if her mind went with them.[52]

In "The Mermaid," Ní Dhomhnaill writes from the mermaid's perspective, refreshingly distinct from that of the colorless lives of "landlocked" women bound by the social strictures imposed by patriarchy:

> Though I've got a fish's tale
> I'm not unbeautiful;
> my hair is long and yellow
> and there's a shine from my scales
> you won't see on landlocked women.
> Their eyes are like the stones
> but look into these eyes of mine
> and you will see the sturgeon
> and you will see fine seals
> gambolling in my pupils.
> Not without pain have I landed;
> I broke
> the natural law.[53]

Whereas the mermaid forgoes immortality by breaking the natural law—relinquishing her natural form for a mortal form—she maintains a viewpoint that mere mortals lack but that she is confident she can provide for them. Ní Dhomhnaill thereby expresses her intention to offer the same kind of vision to her readers.

Ní Dhomhnaill's poem "The Mermaid and Certain Words" relies on the image of the mermaid to depict an inversion of contemporary power relations in Ireland. The poem features a menacing Irish schoolmaster who makes the learning of Irish a punishment, but who is revealed to be "the fictitious creation of a deceptive mermaid, . . . used to camouflage a deeper knowledge of Irish folklore than any taught in schools." Although Ní Dhomhnaill's mermaid denies any knowledge of the sea, "life under the wave," or "those superstitions," her deceptions are ultimately exposed.[54]

> In the Department of Irish Folklore there is a full manuscript,
> from the Schools Compilation, written in her hand, written in water
> with a quill pen, on a tassel of seaweed as parchment.

Although mermaids have traditionally been portrayed as victims of mortal men and students as victims of bullying schoolmasters, this mermaid student ultimately prevails. Furthermore, she does so with lines "written in water," an allusion to young Lycidas, whose name was "writ in water" but also a particularly apt description of the oral tradition, which, though faced with extinction, is fluid enough to accommodate a variety of tellers and perspectives. Significantly, Ní Dhomhnaill suggests the oral tradition—and indeed the lore of women, whose work was too often attributed to "anonymous"—ultimately prevails against the seemingly stronger and more permanent written tradition. Yet the final irony is that the oral tradition may only be revived when a poet like Ní Dhomhnaill sets herself to the task of writing about it, of publishing poems based on documents transcribed by folklorists.

In "The Merfolk and the Written Word,"[55] Ní Dhomhnaill again associates mermaids with the oral tradition, describing the merfolk "literate in their own fish tongue," whose "Island School" is "closed down by the Department of Dried-Out Islands back in the '50s." Their plight is emblematic of that of Irish-speaking island dwellers (recalling, in particular, the 1950s evacuation of the Blaskets), and indeed of the plight of all Irish speakers after British colonization. She writes, "They never took to the pen / or cultivated the native prose text," suggesting that Ní Dhomhnaill's own use of the Irish oral tradition in her poetry is an act of defiance that enables her and her readers to imaginatively inhabit this folkloric realm.

In "Dora Dooley," Ní Dhomhnaill anticipates an encounter with the banshee Dora Dooley, "with her cloak of astrakhan / and a lap-dog under her oxtereen" triggered by her encounter with "a little, old, local lady" who is obviously a modern transformation of the legendary banshee. The *banshee,* from *bean,* a woman, and *sidhe,* a fairy, is an attendant fairy who follows families, prophesying the deaths of their members with her terrible wails.[56] The keen *(caoine),* the funeral cry of the peasantry, is said to be an imitation of her cry. When more than one banshee is present and they wail and sing in chorus, it is for the death of some holy or great one.[57] Ní Dhomhnaill's juxtaposition of the details of contemporary Irish life with those of Irish folklore suggests the presence of the extraordinary even in the seemingly ordinary details of Irish life, and it conjectures that folklore's origins lie in the embellishment on, extrapolation from, and enrichment of private, ordinary experience.

In "The Fairy Boat," Ní Dhomhnaill alludes to the legend that forms the basis for the 1994 film *The Secret of Roan Inish:* fairies who can transform themselves into seals. While picking dulse, three women see the fairies "go through a place so narrow only a seal might pass." The elders advise them to head home and say the rosary, "for this same vision had often come / to people out on the sea." Ní Dhomhnaill thus encapsulates Christianity's traditional response to Celtic religion—imposing its own rituals and myths in an effort to eradicate all traces of Celtic ones. Ní Dhomhnaill concludes the poem by noting that there were

> three who'd seen and three who hadn't
> the men rowing for dear life
> with their blue jerkins and red bonnets
> putting in at the Women's Cliff.

The implication is that the encounter with the fairies is just as likely to have really happened as not, and that the worldview reflected in the encounter is just as likely to be valid as that of the Christian worldview imposed on it. As in other poems, the red bonnets signify the men's association with the Celtic otherworld.

"The Lay of Loughadoon," discussed earlier, also alludes to a famous transformation—when their stepmother Aiofe transforms the children of Lir into swans, in effect exiling them to the water for nine hundred years:

> And I picked a tuft of wild thyme,
> "the herb of the son of the King of the Cloaks,"
> so the memory wouldn't dim
> of the spell cast by the lough.
>
> Because now, at evening, on a tributary
> of the Scoraid four swans move—
> Fionnuala and her brothers three—
> while below us, from the valley-mouth,
> come hound voices, and the view-halloo
> not of shepherds, no,
> but Fionn and the Fianna hunting high and low
> for that elusive, hornless doe.[58]

The legend has been used by Tynan, Yeats, and others as a covert commentary on Ireland under English domination. That Ní Dhomhnaill substitutes the characters of folklore and myth for the "real" inhabitants of the landscape—the children of Lir rather than real swans, Finn and the Fianna rather than shepherds—suggests how vital the folk vision remains for her. "The Lay of Loughadoon" suggests the power of orally transmitted folklore to transform one's perception of reality as well as the importance of the poet in channelling the folk vision, this time via the written word, to new generations of readers.

Ní Dhomhnaill's most recent collection of poetry, *The Water Horse* (2000), returns to the legend of the children of Lir in two poems, "The Tragic Legend of the Children of Lir" and "Fionnuala (after her change)." The latter poem makes an explicit connection between the swans' desire for transformation—a return to their "natural shape"—and the female persona's effort to break out of patriarchal and imperial strictures:

> Although our human voice remains
> To enchant the hearers,
> Our mind, our sense, our sweet music
> And even our Gaelic tongue remains,
> What would I not give
> To be free from the curse,
> The dread laws we obey,
> That took our natural shape away
> And gave us the blood and shape of birds.[59]

The 1995 *Southern Review* interview with Mebh McGuckian and Ní Dhomhnaill explores the common assumption that Ní Dhomhnaill is overly preoccupied with earth, sexuality, and the nonrational rather than the rational. Ní Dhomhnaill responds, "I am for a marrying of the logical with the non-rational, for combining 'male' energy with 'female' energy." Ní Dhomhnaill's many poems about transformation are the means by which she implores readers to consider the import of more comprehensive transformations in their views of themselves and the world.

In an essay in *Irish Writers and Religion*, Ní Dhomhnaill tells a tale from West Kerry that illustrates the value of transformation: "Mis and Dubh Ruis: A Parable of Psychic Transformation" concerns a girl, Mis, whose father the king dies, causing her to lose her sanity, thereafter restored by a harper, Dubh Ruis. Ní Dhomhnaill emphasizes the cultural significance of Mis's transformation: continuing to tell and heed tales in which transformation is deemed possible is the means by which we avoid capitulating to rationalist empiricism, circumvent the inbuilt biases of the England language and the worldview it embodies, and ultimately "break out of the dominant patriarchal ethos of the age."[60] Such a breakthrough requires an inner transformation analogous to the outer transformation that occurs in nature with the arrival of spring.

Ní Dhomhnaill's pastoral retreats likewise suggest that hers is a complex pastoral, designed not as an escape from the complexities of modernity but rather as the means by which to make sense of them. The Irish language poet Máire Mhac an tSaoi's introduction to Ní Dhomhnaill's *Selected Poems: Rogha Dánta* (1993) refers to the poet's "idyll of Irish rural life," which, although superficially simple-minded, constantly registers an awareness of the presence of death and has "an overt and articulated darker side."[61] Mhac an tSaoi locates certain characteristics in Ní Dhomhnaill's poetry that recall centuries of discourse on pastoral, contending that it allows readers to "put a name on the age-old nightmare that haunts the geometrically-defined gardens of our city housing estates, the nightmare that followed us in from the country." The tension between rural and urban, traditional and modern, is best highlighted from the vantage point of the pastoral retreat.

Pharaoh's Daughter (1990) features a series of pastoral retreats associated with precolonial, and thus, premodern Ireland. In "In Baile an tSléibhe" set in the Blasket Islands, which were evacuated in the 1950s, Ní Dhomhnaill attributes her gift of poetry to the poet Sean, her ancestor who lived there, and would of course have also written in Irish. In this setting, "a woman leading cows to drink saw a white trout leap from the stream to land alive inside her bucket," and "Cathair sheep wore silken spancels." This setting in which magic is possible and magical transformations commonplace is also idyllic—as fecund, lush, and beautiful as anything in the classical pastoral tradition:

> From April's end into
> the heart of June
> the wayside stream is veiled
> under conspiracies
> of yellow flag
> and fuschia;
> the yard is scented
> with mayweed
> or camomile.

The beautiful poem "Celebration," which apostrophizes a small bird, celebrates not only the bird but the landscape it inhabits:

> the cows low sweetly in river fields
> with grass and wild flag up to their ears
> chewing the cud with contented sighs,
> trust and patience in the solemn eyes
> though the butcher awaits them and liver-fluke
> hides in the cresses of every brook.

As in classical pastoral, the awareness of death permeates the idyllic scene, and the simple, rural activities in which the people participate, though characteristically Irish, provide the same kind of respite from despair: in place of the songs sung by Theocritus's shepherds, the rural Irish chant the decades of the rosary around a holy well "like corncrake-call or hum of bees / while fruitflies dust with eggs the blackberries." In both cases, human sounds are likened to those of nature, suggesting the natural harmony with nature that prevails among inhabitants of pastoral retreats.

As in classical pastoral, these pastoral retreats are also depicted as under siege from the outside world. In "As for the Quince," the woman who cuts down the quince tree in the yard does so with a Black and Decker saw; the original Irish version of the poem does not attempt to provide an Irish translation for the saw's brand nor for the English the young woman speaks, implying that there simply is no translation. These nontranslatable vestiges of colonization represent the incursion of English into the Irish language as a result of colonization, which led to the near extinction of Irish language and culture. Yet this poem is more broadly about the incursion of modernity, which brought with it environmental degradation such as deforestation, a process that began in Ireland in the sixteenth and seventeenth centuries but continued until the end of the 1990s.[62]

As in the poetry of Medbh McGuckian, lovers' bodies are often depicted as pastoral retreats. Ní Dhomhnaill's poems are often reminiscent of the biblical pastoral of the Song of Solomon: the lover is a cooling fountain, with temples like spring wells, eyes like mountain lakes. The pattern and type of imagery is Petrarchan, but this time, the poet is presumed to be female rather than male and the object of desire is female rather than male. With increasing mechanization, the notion of nature as a living organism was lost and with it, much of the source of power for women: "The passivity in the sphere of reproduction would be reasserted, sexual passion would eventually be repressed and the spirits would be removed from nature in coincidence with the waning of witch trials."63 The post-Enlightenment pastoral mode, although it viewed nature as benevolent, was a model created as an antidote to the pressures of urbanization and mechanization.64 Its typical rendering of both woman and nature as subordinate and passive is undermined, but Ní Dhomhnaill's depictions of them seek to restore agency as well as erotic power. In "Nude," the lover's skin smells of meadowsweet; in "The Unfaithful Wife," his body is as sweet as "a garden after a shower"; and in "Stronghold," there is a secret garden between his shoulder blades, with bees and olive trees, honey on the rushes, and trees in flower: "Winter never comes there / And the frosty breezes / Never blow there at all." In "Blodewedd," the poet herself is transformed through her lover's touch into pastoral retreat—"a grassy meadow fragrant in the sun." Ní Dhomhnaill's title refers to the Celtic goddess whose name means "face of flowers," conjured by magic to be the wife of Lleu, made from blossoms of oak, meadowsweet, and broom.

The Astrakhan Cloak (1992)65 continues to explore various versions of the pastoral retreat: "Deep-Freeze" presumably offers to its visitors a cornucopia, a land of plenty that gives forth "milk and honey, apples and peaches," but ultimately proves an inadequate substitute for Irish mythology's "cauldron of plenty" or Irish folklore's healing well, much less the concept of the Irish otherworld, with its promises of eternal youth and abundance. These relics of a past culture promised not merely material comforts but spiritual, and they were inevitably eclipsed by the process of modernization: "these are the strains of no Otherworldly musicians / but the hum of its alternating current." Muldoon's translation suggests a punning relation between the "alternating current" and "Otherworldly musicians," which reinforces the sense that modernity provides but a dim reflection of this pre-Enlightenment sensibility.

It is Ní Dhomhnaill's evocation of the precolonial Irish landscape—"when Ireland was still under a spell"—that allows for the simultaneous presence of the natural and supernatural, making magical transformation possible, from the little old local lady who appears as the banshee Dora Dooley to the poet's own transformation at Raven's Rock.

Finally, in "The Voyage" the poet's imagination takes her to the Isle of Enchantment, an earthly paradise believed to lie at the same latitude as Ireland but far out to sea, and sometimes associated with the Aran Islands. This island, which appears out of nowhere with "flowers and plants / and exotic nuts galore," bears traces of precolonial Ireland:

> As we studied the patchwork
> of farms and village streets
> the islanders came out in currachs
> with their arms full of treats.

This "non-existent island" with docks reminiscent of those in Galway, where people can pay to see exhibitions of "its mythology and natural resources, / its exports and fauna," could likewise describe contemporary Ireland as well, in which imaginative resources have been ignored or suppressed in favor of exploiting natural resources for export in the global economy. Ní Dhomhnaill implies that the Ireland that once existed will one day exist only in the imagination because the natural and imaginative resources that constituted it will be depleted.

The poem ends when the island, now free of sorcery, is once more submerged by a wave that breaks over the monastic settlement. The land now "under the wave" alludes to the Irish otherworld but is also reminiscent of Ireland following colonization, when both Catholicism and indigenous Celtic religion were suppressed by the British.

In *Rogha Dánta*, "We Are Damned, My Sisters" evokes precolonial Ireland, depicting it as a pastoral retreat:

> We spent nights in Eden's fields
> eating apples, gooseberries; roses
> behind our ears, singing songs
> around the gipsy bon-fires
> drinking and romping with sailors.

Irish "gypsies," also referred to as "tinkers" or "travellers," are considered indigenous rather than immigrant.

"Labysheedy" (The Silken Bed) is the anglicization of "Leaba Shioda," a reference to a small town (also sometimes spelled Labasheeda) in County Clare on the north bank of the River Shannon. The lover vows to make a silken bed for her beloved, described like a pastoral retreat for lovers, with "honeyed breezes / blowing over the Shannon," reminiscent of those described in the Song of Songs. The setting is replete with the simple pleasures of the pastoral retreat: milk poured from jugs at dinnertime, flowers picked to adorn the lover, and again, imagery reminiscent of the Song of Solomon:

your hair is a herd of goats
moving over rolling hills,
hills that have high cliffs
and two ravines.

In *The Water Horse* (2000), Ní Dhomhnaill relies on the classical myth considered by Burris and others to be integral to the pastoral tradition: the story of Demeter and Persephone. Though the poem marks a departure from her preference for Celtic myth, she adapts the story to a contemporary Irish setting, in which Persephone explains to her mother she couldn't resist the temptation of his BMW, his excellent credit rating, and his offer of velvet gowns, satin underthings, stately homes, and even a film career. His final offering, a crimson pomegranate dripping with blood-like seeds, seals Persephone's familiar fate: the pastoral retreat is abandoned at the expense of life itself, but in Ní Dhomhnaill's version, the trappings of modernity, western culture, and global capitalism are implicated in Persephone's fate. Once again, the incursion of modernity is made visible on the page: in the Irish version of the poem, "BMW" and "Hollywood" have no Irish equivalents and stand as permanent reminders of the pastoral retreat that has been sacrificed, never to be fully regained.

CONCLUSION

The Future of Pastoral

It seems evident by now that reports of pastoral's death, like that of Mark Twain over a hundred years ago, have been greatly exaggerated. Although Barrell and Bull traced its death to the ostensible erasure, in the nineteenth century, of the distinction between country and city; critics from Raymond Williams to Roger Sales charged it with a dangerous escapism that served to justify the exploitation of the lower class; and environmental critics have attacked its anthropocentric tendencies, recent ecocriticism has been equally quick to recognize its continued potential to address the human connection to the natural world in meaningful ways. Glen Love writes confidently about the future of pastoral, arguing for a redefinition that incorporates a "new and more complex understanding of nature": "A pastoral for the present and the future calls for a better science of nature, a greater understanding of its complexity, a more radical awareness of its primal energy and stability, and a more acute questioning of the values of the supposedly sophisticated society to which we are bound."[1]

Greg Garrard finds in the trope of the pastoral retreat a model for an ecological pastoral tradition:

> It ought not to be too pious, or too implausible, to associate the ecocriticism of the future with Eden's inflection of the Earth: attuned to environmental justice, but not dismissive of the claims of commerce and technology; shaped by knowledge of long-term environmental problems, but wary of apocalypticism; informed by artistic as well as scientific ecological insight;

and committed to the preservation of the biological diversity of the planet for all its inhabitants. It is a long way from the pastoral we started with, and it is a great-souled vision with its feet planted solidly on the ground.[2]

Terry Gifford argues in the last chapter of *Pastoral* for a continuation of the pastoral tradition that reflects a more complex understanding of the human relationship to nature, as well as an acknowledgment of specifically environmental threats to the pastoral retreat. He concedes that "of course, one of the extensions of the post-pastoral is specifically 'green' literature that engages directly with environmental issues."[3]

Certainly, contemporary Irish poets have written in direct response to various environmental threats that have simultaneously provided the impetus for popular protest. In Ireland, particularly since the 1970s, fears about the commodification of land and resources, the impact of globalization, and the loss of traditional ways of life have found outlets in various types of social protest involving roads, natural resources, waste management, globalization, and energy sources, which have often employed the rhetoric of cultural nationalism. Recently, plans to construct the M3 motorway on the landscape of Tara led to responses by a number of poets, including Seamus Heaney, Fred Johnston, and Paul Muldoon. Muldoon, who co-organized a gathering of poets and musicians to celebrate the place and protest the M3, includes on his website links to the "Save Tara" campaign, his *Times* editorial "Erin Go Faster" on behalf of Tara, and of course his 2006 poem "Tara of the Kings," which was set to music and played, for the first time, by Muldoon's band Rackett in August 2007. The Irish poet Eamonn Wall, also a scholar of Irish environmentalism and the author of *Writing the Irish West: Ecologies and Traditions* (2010), mourns the M3's incursion on Tara as emblematic of more widespread environmental degradation: "The great leaders will build a great road across Tara. The small men in the small towns will fell the last oak."[4]

Likewise, the "Shell to Sea" campaign, which arose when five men were jailed indefinitely for their refusal to permit Shell Oil to build on their land, led to a range of environmental protests involving similar collaborations between poets and musicians. Poet Louis De Paor, director of NUIG's Irish language program, collaborated with singer/songwriter John Spillane to write and record a song on behalf of the campaign. Citing the exploitation of natural resources as well as the environmental and health risks that the pipeline poses, protesters have drawn on traditional national discourses to make their case, taking out rosary beads at the site (County Mayo, site of the pipeline, has the highest percentage of Catholics in Ireland, and because of the history of English colonization, Catholicism has long been considered integral to Irish national identity) and putting up posters of Michael Davitt, Irish hero who founded the Land League.

While acknowledging the potential of more direct approaches to environmental issues, Gifford cautions against didacticism: "the danger that green literature becomes didactic in a simplistic way is really a danger that it loses its power as art and becomes reductive propaganda or vague 'right-on' rhetoric."[5] Gifford's fears that green literature might reach the point at which it is nothing more than a contemporary form of sentimental pastoral parallel those of Greg Garrard, who cautions against environmentalism that is nothing more than an extension of the apocalyptic rhetoric that has been part of the Judeo-Christian tradition for thousands of years. Although ecocritics must start from the recognition of an "unprecedented global environmental crisis,"[6] green literature that does nothing more than produce an unrelieved hopelessness about the future of the earth risks becoming a self-fulfilling prophecy.

The poet's best defense against damaging dogmatism, according to Michael Longley, is to describe the world in a meticulous way that inspires in readers reverence and wonder for nature.[7] Longley's contention that "a poet's mind should be like Noah's ark with lots of room for creatures" implies both the need for a deep appreciation of nature and a degree of sensitivity to the threats that it faces. Whereas postmodernism is inclined to treat all identity, even that of nature, as a construct, an ecological perspective insists that nature must ultimately be regarded as an autonomously existing system in which we all are "deeply implicated, inextricably bound."[8] Thus, the pastoral impulse to celebrate nature, to value it for its own sake in all its unique particularity, becomes all the more pressing, as does the need for a more scientific understanding of the environment that is more acutely aware of the threats to the pastoral retreat.

Indeed, Gifford writes, the final irony is that precisely because so many people sense the lack of a separation between urban and rural existence, our need for a literature that explores "our impulse toward retreat and return" becomes all the more pressing "for the very reasons that Barrell and Bull declared the pastoral dead in English poetry after Hardy."

Whereas many contemporary Irish poets—Caitriona O'Reilly, Eilean Ní Chuilleanain, Michael Hartnett, Noel Monahan, Richard Murphy, Mary O'Malley, Francis Harvey—exemplify the possible directions that post-pastoral poetry can take, Moya Cannon and Paula Meehan convey especially well the dual responsibilities of the form: the joyful celebration of nature's immanence is matched by attunement to environmental threats that serves to highlight the intrinsic value of pastoral retreat all the more.

Moya Cannon's poems are often set in the burren region of western Ireland to which Longley's "Ice-Cream Man" alludes. The seemingly barren plates of limestone that yield up to the careful observer hidden streams and lakes, beautiful and rare wildflowers that seem to appear magically from stone, are natural phenomenona that she recognizes as worthy of celebration quite apart from their religious significance for either Celts or Christians. Indeed, by consistently recognizing the miraculous in the world around her to be the ultimate grounds for worshipfulness for both Celt and Christian, Cannon leaves the reader with little choice but to value nature for its own sake, as in the poem "Holy Well," included in her first collection, *Oar:*

> Images of old fertilities
> testify to nothing more, perhaps,
> than the necessary miracle
> of water trapped and stored
> in a valley where water is fugitive.

Cannon refers in this poem to the importance of trapping and storing water to sustain life (even Ireland has experienced occasional droughts), the explanation for the well's mythic and symbolic significance. In Irish myth, wells and springs had sacred sources, and were regarded as entrances to the otherworld as well as the dwelling places of goddesses—Bóann or Sionann, or, famously in a Boland poem, Anna Liffey—embodied in the water's flow.9 In the Christian tradition, the sacrament of baptism is inextricably linked to water, and Christ is described as the water of life. More broadly, the western tradition has long associated water with artistic inspiration: Milton's "Lycidas" refers to muses as "the sisters of the sacred well" because of their association with the Pierian spring, regarded as a source of inspiration in Greek mythology.10

Cannon recognizes that the pagan and even the Christian significance of the well she visits are fading: Mary's trade dwindles, as gradually only old people make visits to the well for healing. While the poem registers its skepticism of such religious certitudes, her final stanza is a reminder that nature itself is ultimately their source:

> Yet sometimes,
> swimming out in waters
> that were blessed in the hill's labyrinthine heart,
> the eel flashes past.

By personifying the hill, imbuing it with a heart, by acknowledging that the water within was indeed blessed, and by describing, in present tense, the eel flashing past, Cannon suggests that there continues to be deeper spiritual significance in the holy well—the welling water that resulted in its construction, the tree that grows on and marks the site (in this case an ash) as well as the landscape on which it rests. Supernatural fish—salmon, trout, or eel—still appear in a well's depths to those seeking omens for the future. The fish motif is thought to derive from a belief that well goddesses could take the form of ish, as well as the belief that salmon possessed supernatural wisdom. Yet on our own visits to the well, Cannon explains that these so-called supernatural fish might be accounted for by the occasional blind, albino fish that manage to survive in an underground stream or a turlough—hidden lake—common in the burren region.

Despite these scientific explanations for the seemingly supernatural, despite the demise of the religions out of which grew supernatural explanations, Cannon's poem uses figurative language in such a way as to associate these occurrences with illumination and inspiration—the eel that flashes past—for which the landscape itself is the source, thereby conveying the mindfulness in nature. Ultimately, the poem itself serves as a testament to the fact that despite the demise of the religions and cultures that once revered these landmarks, the land remains a source of inspiration to the poet.

The opening poem in her collection "Eagle's Rock" describes another familiar site in the burren:

> There are green slashes down there,
> full of wells and cattle,
> and higher places, where limestone, fertile, catacombed,
> breaks into streams and gentians.

Cannon's pairing of "limestone" and "fertile" appears to be an oxymoron, and in another setting would be, but she is describing the burren, whose porous limestone does indeed conceal hidden lakes and streams that emerge with rainfall. Her description of streams emerging from limestone—that is, water from stone—is likewise a biblical allusion to Moses's striking of the rock in order to get water for the Israelites during their sojourn in the wilderness in flight from the Egyptians. Water, with all its obvious life-sustaining and cleansing properties, symbolizes hope in the midst of despair, and in biblical typology this symbolism is extended to God's incarnation as Christ, the water of salvation for a parched and perishing world.[11]

Cannon notes that the eagles that inspired the place's name, "Eagle's Rock," have all been shot; the poem's central irony is that the predators from whom the rock gets its name have been hunted, whereas the prey survives into perpetuity:

> The eagles are hunted, dead,
> but down among the scrub and under the hazels
> this summer's prey tumbles already
> out of perfect eggs.

New life emerges from what had been relegated as prey; water springs forth from rock; hope arises from an apparently desolate setting. Cannon's imagery echoes these ironic reversals—"feather arrogant against stone," referring to the predatory eagles who gave the rock its name, plays on the common association of stone with death, whether in gravestones or in the Celtic standing stones that dot the landscape she describes, reminding us that the predators themselves ultimately fell victims to death. Just as "Holy Well" concludes with life-affirming imagery, "Eagle's Rock," with life tumbling miraculously from the perfect eggs, invites the reader to conceive of the possibility of hope in the midst of despair.

In other poems, Cannon's subtle use of a common motif in Celtic literature —shape-shifting—likewise suggests the possibility of and hope for transformation. "Blossom Viewing in the Burren" features what appear to be cattle but are upon closer inspection thorn trees. In the midst of this barren landscape on which she notes there is no breeze and "life . . . is unredeemed," Cannon inserts a qualifier:

> *unless,* in bitter winter,
> a tree can know again in its still sap
> these weeks of blossoming, this perfect unfolding.

By imbuing a tree with the power of knowing and insinuating that life can be redeemed *only* through this knowledge, Cannon's multivalent personification brilliantly ascribes to a natural process the same kind of consciousness traditionally attributed to the divine intervention that resulted in the "perfect unfolding" of a plan for the salvation of humanity. Cannon's rendering of nature's own extraordinary power to "redeem" itself recalls the veneration for and worship of nature that existed in many ancient cultures. The many references to trees in early Celtic texts suggest that they were at one time worshipped. In Kuno Meyer's *Selections from Ancient Irish Poetry,* trees provide not only shelter and sustenance but also song (through the birds that shelter in them), poetic inspiration, and even support for the sky.[12] In the Anglo-Saxon tradition, too, "The Dream of the Rood" features the cross itself speaking as a wondrous tree that fought and died in a battle, ultimately rising again to ensure humanity's salvation. Although "The Dream of the Rood" sought to persuade its audience of the desirability of Christian salvation, its metaphor for the cross draws on an ancient pagan tradition in which the tree, symbolic of all nature, possesses remarkable shape-shifting and regenerative powers: alive, to produce flowers and fruit; as firewood, to provide heat and illumination; as a battering ram, to ensure victory in battle; and finally, through the seeds it has produced during life, to rise again.

In "Thirst in the Burren" the deceptively dry limestone hills yield water, signified by funnels and clefts from which "ferns arch their soft heads." In yet another oxymoron, Cannon describes

a headland full of water, dry as a bone,
with only thirst as a diviner,
thirst of the inscrutable fern
and the human thirst
that beats upon a stone.

Thirst is a "diviner," the term used to describe one who finds an underground source for water by means of a divining rod, but more broadly, anyone who tells the future by means of divining. With its root in the word "divine," it also implies one who has managed to intuit the source of the divine, giving the poem spiritual connotations. By drawing a connection between human thirst and that of the natural world, personifying the fern as "inscrutable," and by portraying seemingly dry stone miraculously responding to both thirsts, Cannon obliquely attributes to the landscape a consciousness that corresponds with that of humans.

The gesture of beating on a stone alludes to Moses's striking the rock to provide water for the Israelites. In Victorian typology, the stone might represent not only a type of Christ, who, when struck (crucified) produces waters of grace but also the stony heart of the believer,[13] which Yeats's "Easter 1916" echoes: "Too long a sacrifice / Can make a stone of the heart." Cannon's reference to beating upon a stone invites this comparison: it is a metaphor for a seemingly futile effort to satisfy a thirst—physical or spiritual—that ultimately proves rewarding.

Cannon's poem "Thalassa" takes its name from the Greek word for sea. "Thalassa" is the Greek personification of the sea, the mother of Aphrodite, and in some stories, the mother of us all. The poem describes the experience of momentary disorientation when getting up and deciding to go home, until

some echo under the stones
seduces our feet,
leads them down again
by the grey, agitated sea.

Her choice of a personifying name for the sea and the words "seduces" and "agitated" work together to imbue the seascape with a sort of consciousness, a design that corresponds to our own.

The title of the poem "Ultramontane" translates literally as "beyond the mountains" and can refer either to people living north of the Alps or, more specifically, to strong adherents of papal authority, originally concentrated in the region north of the Alps. The poet's origin in Donegal, a windswept, desolate, and harsh region in the northwest of Ireland (and because the west was further from the reach of British colonial authority, it became a stronghold first for the indigenous language and religion and later for Catholicism), would suggest that she chronicles the people's attempt to reconcile their surroundings with the biblical accounts presented via Irish Catholicism. The question they read in "the soft green book" (perhaps an oblique description of the softer Mediterranean climate from which Christian tales of origin arose), "Who made the world?" is answered as follows:

> We learnt to love a garden
> with trees full of soft fruit
> while, outside, the wind ripped at briars.
>
> And when spring came we cut rushes
> to weave crosses.

In this landscape, which more closely resembles a postlapsarian wilderness than any idealized Eden, one harshness (ripping at briars) demands another harshness (cutting rushes in order to create some comparable symbol of salvation from their harsh landscape). Crosses known as "Brigid's crosses" are traditionally woven on St. Brigid's feast day, which also marked the first day of spring (Imbolc) in the Celtic calendar, fixed at February 1 in the Gregorian calendar.[14]

Cannon's second collection, *The Parchment Boat,* occasionally returns to the burren, as well as to the site of the Holy Well. Observing in the poem "Introductions" that "some of what we love we stumble upon," Cannon writes,

> And more
> discloses itself to us—
> a well among green hazels,
> a nut thicket.

Surveys of well sites by researchers such as Walter and Mary Brenneman reveal that many sites comprise three elements: a water source such as a well or spring; a sacred tree, usually very old and large; and a protrusion such as a hill or standing stone.[15] In addition to the previously discussed associations of the well with the otherworld and thus with inspiration, the sacred tree— the axis mundi—was widely believed to unite earth to the otherworld. Yeats regarded the hazel tree as the Celtic axis mundi. Sacred water sources are often linked to the fruit of certain trees, particularly the hazelnut, as in this poem. Because the hazel was considered a fairy tree, its nuts a source of wisdom and its wood sacred to poets, used for wands and divining rods, it was a taboo fuel on any hearth.[16] Connla's Well, reputedly located under the sea, had hazels of wisdom that dropped into the water to be fed upon by salmon who thereby gained their supernatural wisdom.[17] Finally, stones—whether large stones with depressions in them ("beds" on which a woman could lie to ensure conception and birth), standing stones, or statues—were all associated with divine blessing.[18]

Thus the poem depicts a confluence of physical objects—well, hazel tree, nut thicket—that traditionally symbolize inspiration as well as the human connection with the divine. The final lines of the poem evoke the ritual of communion:

> And more
> comes to us, carried
> as carefully as a bright cup of water,
> as new bread.

Cannon's communion does not feature the standard ingredients of Christian communion—bread and wine—but bread and water, a familiar way of representing the most basic elements necessary for sustaining life. Yet she does not refer merely to physical sustenance: the gifts she refers to are carried *as carefully* as bread and water might be, thereby implying that their value is just as great, though it is spiritual rather than physical.

"Viola D'amore" relies on the same images:

> Sometimes love does die,
> but sometimes, a stream on porous rock,
> it slips down into the inner dark of a hill,
> joins with other hidden streams
> to travel blind as the white fish that live in it.
> It forsakes one underground streambed
> for the cave that runs under it.
> Unseen, it informs the hill,
> and, like the hidden strings of the *viola d'amore,*
> makes the hill reverberate,
> so that people who wander there
> wonder why the hill sings,
> wonder why they find wells.

The viola d'amore is "a distinctive kind of fiddle . . . strung with six gut strings of which the lower three are covered (that is, are wire-wound like most modern strings), while below the fingerboard are stretched six steel strings, which are neither plucked nor bowed but are there merely to duplicate and prolong the sound of the upper strings."[19] These hidden strings that resonate when the visible strings are plucked are known, in musical terminology, as "sympathetic," and are strung on an instrument that translates as "viola of love." Thus they provide a fitting analogy for the hidden streams of human emotion that Cannon implies have their sources in the visible, the tangible. Love is depicted as a stream on porous rock, joining other hidden streams, presumably also of love. The hidden streams of the burren have long had religious significance: many old churches contain a crypt or grotto that opens into a subterranean spring, considered to be the hidden holy center of the sacred enclosure.[20] Although Cannon does not allude to the streams' religious significance, her personification of water that "forsakes a streambed" and "informs a hill" imbues it with human-like volition. Indeed, the poem suggests that the natural processes that the stream undergoes make the hills reverberate in such a way as to reach the humans who walk the hills, making them wonder "why the hill sings . . . why they find wells." Those who behold them are left in a state of wonder because of those who have imbued nature with it in the first place—poets chief among them.

The epigraph with which Moya Cannon begins the title poem of *Carrying the Songs* (2008)—"Those in power write the history, those who suffer write the songs"—prepares the reader for a collection that chronicles the suffering that emigration and colonization have produced by means of the songs that have emerged from the suffering.

Referring to the songs of emigrants as the "soul's currency," Cannon explores the way these songs are carried, or, in other words, the way languages are spread. Thematically continuous with her first two collections, many of the new poems are about language, about words and how they are carried: Cannon's own deft wordplay illustrates how the process works. In "Timbre," for example, she explores the word that originally was interchangeable with "timbrel," a percussion instrument, but that now refers more generally to the character and quality of sound. Its resemblance to the word "timber" leads her to write, "After the timber has been sawn / rough rings release the song of the place"—the rings in the wood analogous to the ripples or waves of sound produced by singing. Songs reveal the history of a people just as the rings in a tree reveal its history.

Other poems explore how the meanings of Irish words were either lost or forever altered when the English language displaced Irish. In "Whin," the words introduced by the English, "furze" and "gorse," are never adequate to describe the flowering plant—nor, metonymically, is English culture an adequate replacement for the Irish culture it displaced. Words of great spiritual significance have been diminished or lost in the process of colonization, as in "Banny," in which the word for stroking a cat gently comes from the Irish *beannaigh*, "to bless," or in "Rún," in which the true sense of the Gaelic word meaning "secret" is captured most fully only through the enigma of the poem. Cannon also considers the haunting prospect of losing language entirely: in "Forgetting Tulips," a former schoolteacher stricken with Alzheimer's, who had once taught children parts of speech, finds that he is losing his grasp on language—"shedding the nouns first"—relinquishing not only the words but the world that the words represent.

The poignancy of "Forgetting Tulips" lies in part in Cannon's attunement to the natural world, an ecologically centered perspective content to value nature for its own sake. In "Aubade," Cannon's interest lies in the small black bird who draws her out of sleep with the rich note of his song, subtle ironic contrast to the traditional aubade, centered as it is on lovers who regret all signs of dawn's arrival because it means they must part. The opening poem, "Winter Birds," begins with an epigraph from Giraldus Cambrensis about barnacle geese. Because they were believed to hatch from barnacles, these birds were regarded as fish and therefore suitable for eating on Fridays. The migration of the geese becomes a reflection on human migratory patterns as the Irish children in her father's class leave for Scotland in search of work, leading him to dub them "winter-birds." In other poems, language mediates between nature and culture, but it is not depicted as exclusive to human beings: in "The Force," Earth itself has a language; in "Script," the "perfect, cursive script" is left by a seal's breaststroke; and in "First Poetry," the birds themselves are poems, migrating between two worlds, which requires "an instinct for form and its rhythms."

"Some things can't be caught in words," the poet assures us, but her powerful evocations of a living earth in poem after poem suggest otherwise. "Bright City," for example, follows morning light that has the power to transfigure everything in its path, including the reader:

> I follow the morning light down the canal path,
> across the road and on to the Claddagh.
> In light which has turned canal, river and estuary to mercury,
> Even the cars on the Long Walk are transfigured.
>
> Five swans beat their way in past the mud dock,
> heavy, sounding their own clarion,
> carrying the world's beauty
> in on their strong white backs this Saturday morning.

In "Stranger," Cannon returns to the motif of the well, which had served in her collection *Oar* as one of many symbols for the eternal human need for water to not only maintain the body but sustain the soul. Her need to be near a well leads her past Dungarvan, where she finds one, "well-minded, gravelled, full and quick." Here, "mind" is used to convey the immanence of nature: the mind, or design, inherent in nature rather than simply the individual mind of the poet. Cannon describes the well as "a worn stone cup" for which "the hill was a pitcher / tilted forever / to fill." The poems of *Carrying the Songs* bear the received wisdom and pathos of centuries of other songs—songs that, like water from a well, satisfy time-worn human needs.

Dublin poet Paula Meehan's "Death of a Field," which describes a Dublin field that becomes a building site for an estate, reminds the reader that urban environments are as deserving of ecological attention as rural ones.[21] Whereas cities have often been regarded as distinct from nature, recent trends in ecocriticism recognize the need to consider them an integral part of the total environment. *The Nature of Cities: Ecocriticism and Urban Environments* (1996), edited by Michael Bennett and David W. Teague, is a collection of essays that offers the ecological component often missing from cultural analyses of the city—yet as with much ecocriticism, its focus is on American settings. In their attention to Irish cityscapes, poets like Meehan expand the range of the relatively new field of ecocriticism. Notably, Meehan's poem elegizes not the Irish people, as had countless nationalist "group elegies" for centuries, but the field itself. Fields have been relied on nearly as often as women to allegorize Ireland (as in "four green fields"), and thus are popular literary symbols. In Joyce's "Eveline," and indeed throughout *Dubliners,* the field symbolizes Ireland and its dispossession, Ireland's conquest:

> One time there used to be a field there in which they used to play every evening with other people's children. Then a man from Belfast bought the field and built houses in it—not like their little brown houses but bright brick houses with shining roofs. The children of the avenue used to play together in that field—the Devines, the Waters, the Dunns, little Keogh the cripple, she and her brothers and sisters.

In other words, the man from Belfast, an outsider to the community, and presumably a Protestant, builds houses presumably intended for other outsiders, a process of gentrification that inevitably displaces the indigenous population. John B. Keane's "The Field" likewise builds on the allegorical representation of Ireland as a field to delve into complex and changing relationships between the people and the land in contemporary Ireland.

Significantly, Meehan's field is not depicted merely as an abstraction, as a literary symbol, but as an entity worthy of consideration in its own right. Furthermore, it is not usurped by outsiders but falls prey to an ever-expanding population and a host of global corporations that pollute it, destroying the flora and fauna that have great symbolic significance—herbs with healing properties, birds with magical powers, plants associated with the realm of fairies:

> The end of dandelion is the start of Flash
> The end of dock is the start of Pledge
> The end of teazel is the start of Ariel
> The end of primrose is the start of Brillo
> The end of thistle is the start of Bounce

The end of sloe is the start of Oxyaction
The end of herb robert is the start of Brasso
The end of eyebright is the start of Fairy

All are subsumed by the demands of multinational corporations that deceptively market their products with names that recall the vanquished world of the fairies: as in "Ariel" and "Fairy," produced, respectively, by Persil and by Proctor and Gamble. Fairy liquid has incidentally become a generic term for washing liquid throughout the U.K. Some readings of Shakespeare's *A Midsummer Night's Dream* suggest that its fairy world alludes to that of the Celts, displaced and marginalized in the course of Anglo-Saxon conquest. Luke Gibbons maintains that the visionary elements in literature and the popular imagination, with their persistent emphasis on the "undead" and their narratives of recurrence and return, provide one of the few means by which the legitimacy of colonial confiscations and conquests could be contested. In Meehan's poetry, as well as that of many contemporary Irish poets, the conquest of the environment is as deserving of both elegy and activism as British conquest had been.

Whereas my study of pastoral has been confined to contemporary poetry, the evocative imagery and culturally loaded symbolism associated with Ireland's four green fields have obviously inspired the pastoral impulse in other genres as well—and there is every sign that these proliferating versions of pastoral will continue to thrive. Nicholas Grene finds a common source for these manifestations of pastoral in the more predominantly rural west: "the imagined west was where we all came from: it was the truest, deepest Ireland, in its primal state pre-Anglicanization, precolonial, even pre-Christian. From Yeats's County Sligo to Heaney's County Derry or Friel's County Donegal . . . from Kavanagh's 'Great Hunger' to the bleak realism of John McGahern's fictions or the grimly unromantic scenes of Tom Murphy's plays."22

In drama as in poetry, the pastoral of the Irish literary revival yields quickly to anti-pastoral, from Synge's 1907 *Playboy of the Western World* to John B. Keane's 1965 play *The Field*. In a 1992 essay that examines traditions in Irish drama, Thomas Kilroy observes that often Ireland is represented as "a place apart, a place retaining some of the innocence of the pre-modern, a kind of literary environmentalism, a version of greenery."23 Just as Patrick Kavanagh was compelled to challenge these simplicities in poetry, Irish playwrights have been compelled to challenge them as pastoral nostalgia is qualified by contemporary realities. Rural settings in plays like Tom Murphy's *Bailegangaire* (1985) and Brian Friel's *Dancing at Lughnasa* (1990), balanced as they are between past and present, offer ironic commentaries on a rapidly changing postcolonial Ireland. Marie Jones's *Stones in His Pockets* (1996), set in a rural

County Kerry town, relies on the traditional rural/urban tension of pastoral for its primary conflict when a Hollywood crew arrives to film a movie and one of the local teenagers drowns himself with stones in his pockets after being insulted by one of the film stars. The implication is that the American pastoralization of the Irish landscape is ultimately destructive to the pastoral retreat. Conor McPherson's *The Weir* (1997), set in rural Ireland, draws out the complexities of Irish rural life by means of a conversation in a local pub between three westerners and a Dublin visitor.24 The play takes place when the actual rural landscape was disappearing at an unprecedented rate, with burgeoning construction brought about by the Celtic Tiger. Perhaps most famously, however, Martin McDonagh's recent *Leenane Trilogy*, which opened in Galway in 1996, offers the most thorough deconstruction of the Irish myth of nurturing mother and motherland from which pastoral originated.

In film, Kevin Rockett traces the privileging of pastoral in Irish film to mainstream Irish nationalism's representation of the countryside as the site of authentic Irishness. Martin McLoone likewise notes the symbolic significance of the rural west of Ireland. His *Irish Film: The Emergence of a Contemporary Cinema* (2000) discusses the way in which cultural nationalism defined Gaelic Irish identity as essentially rural in character: "If Britain at this time was the most urban and most industrial society in the world, it is hardly surprising that cultural nationalism should emphasize its own rural 'otherness.'"25 Landscape becomes the source of Irish self-image, and thus pastoral's fundamental conflict between urban and rural, as well as its exploration of the relationship between landscape and self, often finds expression in Irish film.

Most film critics trace Irish film's explorations of pastoral to John Ford's *The Quiet Man* (1952), set in rural western Ireland, and inextricably linking landscape and character. Luke Gibbons's study of *The Quiet Man* speaks of its "forty shades of pastoral": Technicolor enhances the film's idealization of Ireland's vivid green rural landscape, and the film's theme song "The Isle of Innisfree" further reinforces this portrayal, invoking Yeats's idealization in "The Lake Isle of Innisfree."

Films such as *Into the West* (1992) and *The Secret of Roan Inish* (1994) serve to "vindicate the authentic experience of the west at the expense of the alienating character of the city"26 in the manner of pastoral. *Into the West* juxtaposes an older, simpler version of Ireland with one that is modern, urbanized, and technologically advanced. As the main characters journey back through the heartland of Ireland, they recover their culture and themselves, eventually vowing never to return to the city again. All of the disorienting transformations in Irish society increase the longing for a pastoral retreat, located in a west that is clearly depicted as the country's spiritual and cultural wellspring.

Yet just as Irish poetry and drama attest to the need for an anti-pastoral that renders the landscape as the site of labor, and a more complex pastoral that acknowledges the threats to the pastoral retreat, Irish film does as well. Grene coins the term "black pastoral" to describe works of the 1990s such as Alan Parker's film version of Frank McCourt's *Angela's Ashes,* and Neil Jordan's film version of Patrick McCabe's *Butcher Boy.* He writes,

> It is not just that all of them turn the green idyll of Ireland into a black dystopia. Just as black comedy subverts earlier conventions of comedy, black pastoral involves a similar kind of travesty of the pastoral mode. In Irish pastoral, the west of Ireland or Ireland as a whole have been conceived as sites of origin, where we as readers/audience come from, but no longer are.[27]

Whereas pastoral takes the audience back to its origins, black pastoral mocks the impulse to return.

Jordan's film version of *The Butcher Boy* forces the viewer to witness the literal explosion of Ireland's pastoral landscape. One sequence, for example, opens with a panoramic view of Ireland's natural beauty—emerald hills and valleys and an azure-blue lake—a shot reminiscent of a postcard from a John Hinde collection, in which all flaws, all evidence of civilization, even the overcast skies so characteristic of Ireland, are carefully eliminated. This familiar image of a romanticized and stylized rural Ireland, which has dominated cinematic representations for decades, gives way to a strikingly different image "when the lake suddenly erupts in the atomic mushroom cloud of a nuclear explosion, shattering both nature (and its slightly exaggerated cultural representation)."[28] The explosion presages Francie Brady's own explosion into murderous violence and suggests the wider cultural and political forces that lead to Francie's, and indeed Ireland's, identity crisis. The story takes place in 1963, a year marked by not only the Cuban missile crisis but the inauguration of Ireland's national television service. It's also associated with the adoption of the American concept of modernity in Ireland. Television, observes Martin McLoone in his review of the film *The Butcher Boy,* "is something of a cultural Trojan Horse, leading modernity's assault on tradition and bringing into this sheltered world the powerful discourses of American popular culture."[29]

Yet McCabe's novel is infused with the pastoral nostalgia that provides the basis for the film version of pastoral. In the novel, Francie buys his mother a present in Dublin as an act of atonement for running away: "a slice of a tree cut out and a rhyme carved into the wood and decorated all around the edges with green shamrocks. At the bottom was an old woman in a red shawl rocking by the fireside." It reads, "A Mother's love's a blessing no matter where you roam," yet by the time Francie returns from roaming, his mother has committed suicide, effectively mocking the sentimentalization of both mother and motherland. Philip Nugent's music book, *Emerald Gems of Ireland,* features on its cover "the ass and cart on the front going off into misting green mountains"[30] and includes songs of "romantic Ireland" such as "The Halls of Tara," "The Kerry Dances," and "Beautiful Bundoran." When Francie searches for a comparable gift for his estranged friend Joe, a man in a music shop directs him to a "far better book" than *Emerald Gems: A Treasury of Irish Melodies.* Francie notes that on the cover of this more re-cent book, "There was no ass and cart on the front of it just an old woman in a shawl standing at a half-door staring at the sun going down behind the mountains,"[31] suggesting the way the nineteenth-century romantic view of Ireland has been qualified or diminished by the forces of modernity and, in particular, industrialization. When Francie attempts to present the book to Joe, hoping to restore their friendship, his gesture is rejected. By associating these artifacts with Francie's consistent failure to achieve any connections with contemporary Irish society, McCabe suggests that these idealized im-ages prove ineffectual and reductive in "real life."

Edna O'Brien's *Down by the River* features the same idyllic setting of her earlier *Country Girls* trilogy, with its tension between the rural world and modernity—but the lush green landscape described in the opening paragraph serves only to deceive the thirteen-year-old protagonist, Mary, as well as the reader, as to the true nature of reality: it is the setting for the incest that oc-curs with her father. "Out in the country things get very murky," says Mary, whose subsequent pregnancy, suicide attempt, and quest for an abortion force her into the center of a national debate over women's reproductive rights and certainly situate the novel within the tradition of complex pastoral. O'Brien has often written of "Mother Ireland," and in this novel, the conventional conflation of woman and land—"Mother Ireland" and the Irish state—is in-terrogated through the main character, Mary, whose plight has been ignored by her own mother and whose name is a reminder of the role of Mariology—so detrimental to the lives of real women—in Irish nationalist rhetoric.

Denis Donoghue's review of John McGahern's *All Will Be Well* recognizes in the clean, precise descriptions of Irish rural life "a version of pastoral"—one that characterizes McGahern's work, from *The Dark* to *That They May Face the Rising Sun.* Titled *By The Lake* for an American audience presum-ably less attuned to the traditions of pagan Ireland, the book renders the lake by which the main characters live, with its neighboring fields and meadows, as much a character as the characters themselves. McGahern occasionally uses of full-scale Homeric simile: "Patrick Ryan's reemergence into this slow mindlessness was like the eruptions of air which occur in the wheaten light of mown meadows in a heat wave. Dried grass and leaves, and even bits of sticks, are sent whirling high in a noisy spinning cylinder of dust and violent air, which then as quickly dies, to reappear like a mirage in another part of the meadow." The Homeric allusion in his description of a tough laborer under attack by a swarm of bees suggests that the Irish rural setting is as worthy of sustained attention as classical pastoral settings had been. In Mc-Gahern's fiction, we see the distinction upon which Patrick Kavanagh built his own version of pastoral—between "provincial" and "parochial" sensibili-ties. Whereas the former is always looking back to the capital for affirmation, the latter cherishes the local as the only true matter for art. He concludes his sonnet "Epic" having Homer speak these words: "I made the Iliad from such / A local row. Gods make their own importance."[32] In all genres, vari-ous versions of pastoral will continue to unearth the immanence in the local landscape.

NOTES

PREFACE

1. Anthony Bradley, "Pastoral in Modern Irish Poetry," 79.
2. Glen Love, "*Et in Arcadia Ego*: Pastoral Meets Ecocriticism," 6.
3. Terry Gifford, *Pastoral*, 80.
4. Gifford, *Pastoral*, 129.
5. Christine Cusick, *Out of the Earth: Ecocritical Readings of Irish Texts*, Cork University Press, 2010.

INTRODUCTION

1. Peter Marinelli, *Pastoral*, 46.
2. Anthony Verity, trans., *Theocritus: Idylls*, xv.
3. Verity, *Theocritus: Idylls*, xvi.
4. Humphrey Tonkin, *Spenser's Courteous Pastoral: Book 6 of the Faerie Queene*, 286.
5. Paul Alpers, *What Is Pastoral?*, 24.
6. Alpers, *What Is Pastoral?*, 113.
7. Alpers, *What Is Pastoral?*, xvii.
8. David Young, *The Heart's Forest: A Study of Shakespeare's Pastoral Plays*, 18.
9. Sukanta Chaudhuri, *Renaissance Pastoral and Its English Developments*, 1.
10. Tonkin, *Spenser's Courteous Pastoral*, 286.
11. Marinelli, *Pastoral*, 11.
12. Frank Kermode, *English Pastoral Poetry, from the Beginnings to Marvell*.
13. Nicholas Grene, "Black Pastoral: 1990s Images of Ireland," 67–75.
14. Luke Gibbons, *The Quiet Man*, 10.
15. Annabel Patterson, *Pastoral and Ideology*, 229.
16. John Barrell and John Bull, *The Penguin Book of English Pastoral Verse*, 115.
17. David Gardiner, "Unsentimental Prophecy: John Montague and *The Dolmen Miscellany* (1962)," 70.
18. John Montague, *The Figure in the Cave and Other Essays*, ed. Antoinette Quinn, 76.

19. Declan Kiberd, *Irish Classics*, 118.

20. Kiberd, *Irish Classics*, 277.

21. Patterson, *Pastoral and Ideology*, 229.

22. Jonathan Bate, *The Song of the Earth*. Bate describes how Whit Sunday customs associated with the spring at Eastwell were abandoned when the spring became private property, and how the Plough Monday holiday was abandoned with the drive toward more intensive productivity.

23. Barrell and Bull, *The Penguin Book*, 430.

24. John Clare, *"I Am": The Selected Poetry of John Clare*, ed. Jonathan Bate, 413.

25. Charles Martindale, "Green Politics: The Eclogues," in *The Cambridge Companion to Virgil*, 122.

26. Leo Marx, *The Machine in the Garden*, 9–10.

27. Barrell and Bull, *The Penguin Book*, 431.

28. Barrell and Bull, *The Penguin Book*, 432.

29. Martindale, "Green Politics," 122.

30. Sidney Burris, *The Poetry of Resistance: Seamus Heaney and the Pastoral Tradition*.

31. Terry Gifford, *Green Voices: Understanding Contemporary Nature Poetry*, 19.

32. Oona Frawley, *Irish Pastoral: Nostalgia and Twentieth-Century Irish Literature*, 5.

33. Frawley, *Irish Pastoral*, 15–20.

34. Kiberd, *Irish Classics*, 75.

35. Kiberd, *Irish Classics*, 76.

36. Kiberd, *Irish Classics*, 595.

37. Bradley, "Pastoral in Modern Irish Poetry," 79.

38. G. W. Watson, *Irish Identity and the Literary Revival: Synge, Yeats, Joyce, and O'Casey*, 97.

39. Bradley, "Pastoral in Modern Irish Poetry," 82–83.

40. Kiberd, *Irish Classics*, 421.

41. Declan Kiberd, *Inventing Ireland: The Literature of the Modern Nation*, 481.

42. Bradley, "Pastoral in Modern Irish Poetry," 79.

43. Anthony G. Bradley, *Contemporary Irish Poetry*, 2.

44. Kiberd, *Irish Classics*, 593.

45. Joe Cleary, *Outrageous Fortune: Capital and Culture in Modern Ireland*, 153.

46. Kiberd, *Irish Classics*, 594.

47. Cleary, *Outrageous Fortune*, 150.

48. Kiberd, *Irish Classics*, 629.

49. Terry Eagleton, *Heathcliff and the Great Hunger: Studies in Irish Culture*, 17.

50. Peter Fallon, trans., *The Georgics of Virgil*, 34–35.

51. C. Day Lewis, trans., *The Georgics of Virgil*.

52. Fallon, *The Georgics of Virgil*, 121.

53. Fallon, *The Georgics of Virgil*, 123.

54. Fallon, *The Georgics of Virgil*, 122–26.

55. Love, "Et in Arcadia: Pastoral Meets Ecocriticism," 69.

56. Gifford, *Pastoral*, 98.

57. Neil Corcoran, ed., *The Chosen Ground: Essays on Contemporary Poetry of Northern Ireland*, 23.

58. Antoinette Quinn, "'The Well-Beloved': Montague and the Muse," ed. Murray and Christopher, 28.

59. John Montague, *The Figure in the Cave and Other Essays*, ed. Antoinette Quinn, 65–66.

60. Montague, *The Figure in the Cave*, 74–75.

61. Montague, *The Figure in the Cave*, 74.

62. Seamus Heaney, *Preoccupations: Selected Prose, 1968–1978*, 180.

63. Patricia Haberstroh, *Women Creating Women: Contemporary Irish Women Poets*, 133.

64. Joseph Swann, "Family Resemblances: Shapes and Figures in Contemporary Irish Poetry," 33.

65. Gifford, *Pastoral*, 152.

66. Lawrence Buell, *The Environmental Imagination: Thoreau, Nature Writing, and the Formation of American Culture*, 7–8.

67. Carolyn Merchant, *The Death of Nature: Women, Ecology, and the Scientific Revolution*, 95.

68. Merchant, *The Death of Nature*, xvii.

69. Gifford, *Pastoral*, 3.

70. Lesley Wheeler, "Medbh McGuckian's *The Flower Master* as a Critique of Female Modernism," 8.

71. Gifford, *Pastoral*, 166.

72. Gloria Orenstein, "The Greening of Gaia: Ecofeminist Artists Revisit the Garden," 1.

73. Patricia Yeager, ed., *The Geography of Identity*, 432.

CHAPTER 1

A Lost Pastoral Rhythm: The Poetry of John Montague

1. Quinn, "The Well-Beloved," 28.

2. Montague, *The Figure in the Cave*, 65-66.

3. Gardiner, "Unsentimental Prophecy," 71.

4. Gardiner, "Unsentimental Prophecy," 74.

5. Kiberd, *Irish Classics*, 124–36.

6. Interview with the author, Galway City, Ireland, September 7, 2004.

7. Terence Brown, *Ireland: A Social and Cultural History*, 84.

8. Montague, *The Figure in the Cave*, 74–75.

9. S. J. Connolly, *The Oxford Companion to Irish History*, 265.

10. Connolly, *The Oxford Companion to Irish History*, 459.

11. R. F. Foster, *Modern Ireland 1600-1972*, 38–39.

12. James MacKillop, *Dictionary of Celtic Mythology*, 73. Subsequent citations will be made parenthetically in the text.

13. Gearóid Ó hAllmhuráin, "Dancing on the Hobs of Hell: Rural Communities in Clare and the Dance Halls Act of 1935," 12.

14. Quinn, "The Well-Beloved," 31.

15. John Montague, "Jawseyes," 159–60.

16. Quinn, "The Well-Beloved," 33.

17. St. Therese, http://littleflowerpilgrimages.com/sttherese.htm.

18. Liam Ó Dochartaigh, *"Ceol na mBréag:* Gaelic Themes in *The Rough Field*," 202.

19. Ó Dochartaigh, *"Ceol na mBréag,"* 203.

20. Dennis O'Driscoll, "An Interview with John Montague," 64–65.

21. Anne Ross, *Pagan Celtic Britain: Studies in Iconography and Tradition*, 163.

22. Anne Ross, *Pagan Celtic Britain*, 146-63.

23. Kiberd, *Inventing Ireland*, 617.

24. Montague, *The Figure in the Cave*, 51–56.

25. Anne Ross, *Pagan Celtic Britain*, 55.

26. Quinn, "The Well-Beloved," 27.

27. E. Estyn Evans, *Irish Folk Ways*, 162.

28. John Barry, foreword to Liam Leonard, *The Environmental Movement*, vi.

29. Denis O'Hearn, *Inside the Celtic Tiger: The Irish Economy and the Asian Model*, 51–54.

30. Reb Volley, "Earth Day," EcoLife NI, http://greensheenblogger.blogspot.com/search/label/Earth%20Day.

31. Colum McCann, *Ballygawley in the Twentieth Century*.

32. Montague, *The Figure in the Cave*, 44.

33. John Montague, "The Rough Field," in *Collected Poems*, 68.

34. Orenstein, "The Greening of Gaia," 1.

35. Gifford, *Pastoral*, 80.

36. Margaret Atwood, *Second Words: Selected Critical Prose*, 382.

37. Montague, *Collected Poems*, 52.

38. Douglas Sealy, "The Sound of a Wound: An Introduction to the Poetry of John Montague from 1958 to 1988," 20.

39. Deirdre and Laurence Flanagan, *Irish Place Names*, 57.

40. Linda Revie, "The Little Red Fox, Emblem of the Irish Peasant in Poems by Yeats, Tynan, and Ní Dhomhnaill," 113.

41. G. B. Corbet and Stephen Harris, *Handbook of British Mammals*.

42. Montague, *Collected Poems*, 83–124.

43. William D. Paden, "Pastourelle," 888.

44. Montague, *Collected Poems*, 125–85.

45. Montague, *Collected Poems*, 129.

46. Montague, *Collected Poems*, 133.

47. Montague, *Collected Poems*, 136.

48. Montague, *Collected Poems*, 222.

49. Montague, *Collected Poems*, 222.

50. Montague, *Collected Poems*, 272.

51. Montague, *Collected Poems*, 271.

52. O'Driscoll, "An Interview with John Montague," 64–65.

53. Montague, *The Figure in the Cave*, 118.

54. Montague, *The Figure in the Cave*, 40.

55. Montague, *The Figure in the Cave*, 40.

CHAPTER 2

"The God in the Tree":
Seamus Heaney and the Pastoral Tradition

1. Heaney, *Preoccupations*, 180.

2. Heaney, *Preoccupations*, 80.

3. Heaney, *Preoccupations*, 174.

4. Heaney, *Preoccupations*, 36.

5. Interview with the author, National University of Ireland Galway, November 17, 2004.

6. Burris, *The Poetry of Resistance,* 42.

7. Burris, *The Poetry of Resistance,* 12.

8. Ronald Schuchard, introduction to *The Place of Writing,* by Seamus Heaney, 6.

9. Theodor W. Adorno, "Lyric Poetry and Society," 157.

10. Burris, *The Poetry of Resistance,* 53.

11. Blake Morrison, *Seamus Heaney,* 17.

12. Robert Buttel, *Seamus Heaney,* 29.

13. Burris, *The Poetry of Resistance,* x.

14. Tyler Hoffman, *Robert Frost and the Politics of Poetry,* xii.

15. Rachel Buxton, *Robert Frost and Northern Irish Poetry,* 4.

16. Buxton, *Robert Frost and Northern Irish Poetry,* 66.

17. Robert Frost, "Introduction to *King Jasper,* by E. A. Robinson," vii.

18. John F. Lynen, *The Pastoral Art of Robert Frost.*

19. Burris, *The Poetry of Resistance,* 15.

20. Heaney, *Preoccupations,* 132.

21. Heaney, *Preoccupations,* 186.

22. Heaney, *Preoccupations,* 182.

23. Heaney, *Preoccupations,* 35–37.

24. Heaney, *Preoccupations,* 132.

25. Heaney, *Preoccupations,* 184.

26. Jonathan Allison, "Patrick Kavanagh and the Antipastoral," 73–74.

27. Heaney, *Preoccupations,* 83.

28. Heaney, *Preoccupations,* 176.

29. Fallon, trans., *The Georgics of Virgil,* 121.

30. Burris, *The Poetry of Resistance,* 11–12.

31. Burris, *The Poetry of Resistance,* 40.

32. George Puttenham, *The Arte of English Poesie,* 31.

33. "Ireland," Central Intelligence Agency, World Factbook, accessed July 7, 2011, https://www.cia.gov/library/publications/the-world-factbook/fields/2097.html.

34. "A Chronology of Key Events in Irish History 1800 to 1967," Cain Web Service, http://cain.ulst.ac.uk/othelem/chron/ch1800–1967.htm.

35. Evans, *Irish Folk Ways.*

36. Henry Hart, *Seamus Heaney: Poet of Contrary Progressions,* 13.

37. P. V. Glob, *The Bog People: Iron-Age Man Preserved.*

38. James Randall, "Interview with Seamus Heaney," 14.

39. Thomas Docherty, "Ana-: or Postmodernism, Landscape, Seamus Heaney," 208.

40. Morrison, *Seamus Heaney,* 57.

41. Burris, *The Poetry of Resistance,* 112–13.

42. Morrison, *Seamus Heaney,* 73.

43. Morrison, *Seamus Heaney,* 73.

44. Burris, *The Poetry of Resistance,* 42–43.

45. Margaret Burton, "A Consideration of Heaney's *The Strand at Lough Beg,*" 7.

46. Gifford, *Pastoral,* 101.

47. Thomas G. Rosenmeyer, *The Green Cabinet: Theocritus and European Pastoral Poetry,* 191.

48. Kermode, *English Pastoral Poetry,* 21.

49. Kermode, *English Pastoral Poetry,* 21.

50. Peter Sacks, *The English Elegy: Studies in the Genre from Spenser to Yeats,* 21.

51. Helena Feder, "Ecocritism, New Historicism, and Romantic Apostrophe," 43.

52. Josephine Miles, *Pathetic Fallacy in the Nineteenth Century: A Study of a Changing Relation between Object and Emotion*, i.

53. Feder, "Ecocritism, New Historicism, and Romantic Apostrophe," 53.

54. Sacks, *The English Elegy*, 22.

55. Alpers, *What Is Pastoral?* 238.

56. William Empson, *Some Versions of Pastoral*, 131.

57. Allison, "Patrick Kavanagh and the Antipastoral," 73–74.

58. Seamus Heaney, *Sweeney Astray: A Version from the Irish*, ii.

59. Hart, *Seamus Heaney*, 49.

60. Seamus Heaney, *Seeing Things*.

61. George Bernard Shaw, *Seven Plays by George Bernard Shaw*, 755.

62. Kuno Meyer, ed, *The Voyage of Bran*, 3.

63. Adrian Room, *A Dictionary of Irish Place-Names*, 66.

64. Heaney, *Preoccupations*, 182.

65. Hugh Kenner, *The Pound Era*, 100.

66. Seamus Heaney, *Electric Light*.

67. Meg Tyler, *A Singing Contest: Conventions of Sound in the Poetry of Seamus Heaney*, 3.

68. Tyler, *A Singing Contest*, 127.

69. Tyler, *A Singing Contest*, 12.

70. Tyler, *A Singing Contest*, 39.

71. Randall, "Interview with Seamus Heaney," *Ploughshares*, 18.

72. Gifford, *Pastoral*, 170.

73. Denis Donoghue, *We Irish: Essays on Irish Literature and Society*, 13.

Chapter 3

"Love Poems, Elegies: I am losing my place":
Michael Longley's Environmental Elegies

1. Fran Brearton, "Walking Forwards into the Past: An Interview with Michael Longley," 35–39.

2. John Lyon, "Michael Longley's Lists," 239.

3. Alan J. Peacock, "Prolegomena to Michael Longley's Peace Poem," 67.

4. Peter McDonald, "Lapsed Classics: Homer, Ovid, and Michael Longley's Poetry," 36.

5. Sacks, *The English Elegy*, 14.

6. Michael Longley, *The Ghost Orchid*.

7. Elmer Kennedy-Andrews, "Conflict, Violence, and the Fundamental Interrelatedness of All Things," 74–75.

8. Michael Longley, "Interview: Michael Longley and Jody Allen-Randolph," 305.

9. Longley, "Interview," 307.

10. Robyn Eckersley, *Environmentalism and Political Theory: Toward an Ecocentric Approach*, 49.

11. Bate, *The Song of the Earth*, 28.

12. Buell, *The Environmental Imagination: Thoreau, Nature Writing, and the Formation of American Culture*, 7–8.

13. Bate, *The Song of the Earth*, 182.

14. Glen Love, "Revaluing Nature," 234–36.

15. Bate, *The Song of the Earth*, 26.

16. Sacks, *The English Elegy*, 3.

17. Sacks, *The English Elegy*, 19.

18. Sacks, *The English Elegy*, 118–19.

19. Jahan Ramazani, *Poetry of Mourning: The Modern Elegy from Hardy to Heaney*, 23.

20. Eckersley, *Environmentalism and Political Theory*, 55.

21. Kennedy-Andrews, "Conflict," 55.

22. Brian John, "The Achievement of Michael Longley's *The Ghost Orchid*," 145.

23. Ruth Ling, "The Weather in Japan: Tact and Tension in Michael Longley's New Elegies," 286.

24. Christopher Caldwell, "Man Out of Time," http://slate.msn.com/id/2089950/.

25. Brearton, *The Great War in Irish Poetry*, 265.

26. Peter McDonald, "Michael Longley's Homes," 68.

27. Sacks, *The English Elegy*, 19–20.

28. Ruth Ling, "The Double Design of Michael Longley's Recent Elegies, *The Ghost Orchid*, and *Broken Dishes*," 39–50.

29. Kennedy-Andrews, "Conflict," 85.

30. Richard Rankin Russell, "Inscribing Cultural Corridors: Michael Longley's Contribution to Reconciliation in Northern Ireland," 227.

31. Ling, "The Weather in Japan," 287.

32. Kennedy-Andrews, "Conflict," 87.

33. Brearton, *The Great War in Irish Poetry*, 270.

34. "Peatlands," Northern Irish Environmental Agency, accessed July 7, 2011, http://www.peatlandsni.gov.uk/formation/nipeatlnds.htm.

35. Kennedy-Andrews, "Conflict," 88.

36. Ling, "The Weather in Japan," 287.

37. Lawrence J. Taylor, *Occasions of the Faith: An Anthropology of Irish Catholics*, 64.

38. Peacock, "Prolegomena," 64–65.

39. Peacock, "Prolegomena," 65.

40. Michael Longley, *Tuppenny Stung: Autobiographical Chapters*, 75.

41. Peacock, "Prolegomena," 73.

42. McDonald, "Lapsed Classics," 74.

43. Neil Everndon, *The Social Creation of Nature*.

44. Neil Corcoran, "My Botanical Studies: The Poetry of Natural History in Michael Longley," 117.

45. Sarah Broom, "Learning about Dying: Mutability and the Classics in the Poetry of Michael Longley," 94–97.

46. Broom, "Learning about Dying," 106.

47. Kennedy-Andrews, "Conflict," 90.

48. Kennedy-Andrews, "Conflict," 94–95.

49. Gifford, *Pastoral*, 151.

50. Longley, "Interview," 307.

51. Longley, "Interview," 305.

52. Broom, "Learning about Dying," 100.

53. Broom, "Learning about Dying," 100.

54. Lyon, "Michael Longley's Lists," 240.

55. Kennedy-Andrews, "Conflict," 91.

56. Lyon, "Michael Longley's Lists," 243.

57. Broom, "Learning about Dying," 99.

58. "The Burren Connect Project, accessed July 7, 2011, http://www.burrenconnect. ie/.

59. McDonald, "Lapsed Classics," 136.

60. Kennedy-Andrews, "Conflict," 93.

61. John, "The Achievement of Michael Longley's *The Ghost Orchid*," 147.

62. John, "The Achievement of Michael Longley's *The Ghost Orchid*," 148.

63. Alan J. Peacock and Kathleen Devine, *The Poetry of Michael Longley*, xiv.

64. MacKillop, *Dictionary of Celtic Mythology*, 126.

65. Michael Longley, *The Ghost Orchid*.

66. John, "The Achievement of Michael Longley's *The Ghost Orchid*," 150.

67. Broom, "Learning about Dying," 111–12.

68. Ling, "The Weather in Japan," 287.

69. Sacks, *The English Elegy*, 21.

70. Ling, "The Weather in Japan," 295.

71. Clive Wilmer, "Michael Longley in Conversation," 42.

72. Love, *"Et in Arcadia,"* 87.

73. Love, *"Et in Arcadia,"* 88.

74. Margaret Mills Harper, "An Interview with Michael Longley," 61.

75. Everndon, *The Social Creation of Nature*, 95.

CHAPTER 4

Learning the Lingua Franca of a Lost Land:
Eavan Boland's Suburban Pastoral

1. Eavan Boland, "An Un-Romantic American," 73.

2. Boland, "An Un-Romantic American," 79.

3. Mark Gregory Seidl, *Elizabeth Bishop and the Subject of Pastoral*, 3499-3500; Robert Don Adams, "Elizabeth Bishop and the Pastoral World," 3.

4. Feder, "Ecocritism," 43.

5. Boland, "An Un-Romantic American," 86.

6. Boland, "An Un-Romantic American," 76.

7. Boland, "An Un-Romantic American," 75.

8. Boland, "An Un-Romantic American," 76–77.

9. Boland, "An Un-Romantic American," 86.

10. Burris, *The Poetry of Resistance*, 18.

11. Harold Toliver, *Pastoral Forms and Attitudes*, 113.

12. Michael C. J. Putnam, *Virgil's Pastoral Art: Studies in the Eclogues*, 62.

13. Greg Garrard, *Ecocritism*, 21.

14. Putnam, *Virgil's Pastoral Art*, 289.

15. Putnam, *Virgil's Pastoral Art*, 289-90.

16. Andrew J. Auge, "Fracture and Wound: Eavan Boland's Poetry of Nationality," 139.

17. MacKillop, *Dictionary of Celtic Mythology*, 311.

18. Boland, "An Un-Romantic American," 73.

19. Boland, "An Un-Romantic American," 75.

20. Seidl, *Elizabeth Bishop and the Subject of Pastoral*, 46.

21. Seidl, *Elizabeth Bishop and the Subject of Pastoral*, 48.

22. Seidl, *Elizabeth Bishop and the Subject of Pastoral*, i.

23. Guy Rotella, *Reading and Writing Nature: The Poetry of Robert Frost, Wallace Stevens, Marianne Moore, and Elizabeth Bishop*, 189.

24. Rotella, *Reading and Writing Nature*, 218.

25. Jody Allen-Randolph, "Private Worlds, Public Realities: Eavan Boland's Poetry 1967-1990," 5–22, 124.

26. Allen-Randolph, "Private Worlds, Public Realities," 123.

27. Peter Kupillas, "Bringing It All Back Home: Unity and Meaning in Eavan Boland's Domestic Interior Sequence," 17.

28. Toliver, *Pastoral Forms and Attitudes*, 142.

29. Renato Poggioli, *The Oaten Flute. Essays on Pastoral Poetry and the Pastoral Ideal*, 22.

30. Seidl, *Elizabeth Bishop and the Subject of Pastoral*, 107.

31. Seidl, *Elizabeth Bishop and the Subject of Pastoral*, 109.

32. Seidl, *Elizabeth Bishop and the Subject of Pastoral*, 111–12.

33. Elizabeth Bishop, *The Complete Poems 1927-1979*.

34. Joanne Feit Diehl, *Women Poets and the American Sublime*, 37.

35. Allen-Randolph, "Private Worlds, Public Realities," 14.

36. Rictor Norton, *The Homosexual Pastoral Tradition*, 1.

37. Margaret Ferguson, Mary Jo Salter, and Jon Stallworthy, *The Norton Anthology of Poetry*, 140.

38. David Ferry, *The Odes of Horace*, 143.

39. Ferguson et al., *The Norton Anthology of Poetry*, 848.

40. Kupillas, "Bringing It All Back Home," 14.

41. "Delphi," http://www.britannica.com/eb/article.

42. Eavan Boland, *An Origin Like Water: Collected Poems 1967–1987*, 139.

43. Haberstroh, *Women Creating Women*, 71.

44. Homeric Hymns, http://sunsite.berkeley.edu/OMACL/Hesiod/hymns.html.

45. Burris, *The Poetry of Resistance*, 1.

46. Clair Wills, *Improprieties: Politics and Sexuality in Northern Irish Poetry*, 57.

47. Haberstroh, *Women Creating Women*, 71.

48. Kupillas, "Bringing It All Back Home," 18.

49. Alicia Ostriker, *Stealing the Language: The Emergence of Women's Poetry in America*, 108–10.

50. Eavan Boland, *Outside History*.

51. Eavan Boland, *In a Time of Violence*.

52. Eavan Boland, *The Lost Land: Poems*.

53. Boland, "An Un-Romantic American," 85.

54. "Trees," http://whom.co.uk/squelch/trees_britain.htm.

CHAPTER 5

"In My Handkerchief of a Garden":
Medbh McGuckian's Miniature Pastoral Retreats

1. Walter R. Davis and Richard A. Lanham, *A Map of Arcadia: Sidney's Romance in Its Tradition*, 38–39.

2. Toliver, "Pastoral Forms and Attitudes," 140.

3. Donald M. Friedman, *Marvell's Pastoral Art*, 12–13.

4. Interview with the author, Queen's University Belfast, May 13, 2005.

5. Wills, *Improprieties*, 42.

6. Wills, *Improprieties,* 68.

7. Interview with the author, Queen's University, 2005.

8. Joseph Lennon, *Irish Orientalism: A Literary and Intellectual History,* 281.

9. Lennon, *Irish Orientalism,* 302–3.

10. Lennon, *Irish Orientalism,* 286.

11. Lennon, *Irish Orientalism,* 247.

12. Lennon, *Irish Orientalism,* 254.

13. Lennon, *Irish Orientalism,* 262.

14. Stella Coe, *Ikebana: A Practical and Philosophical Guide to Japanese Flower Arrangement,* 23.

15. Wheeler, "Medbh McGuckian's *The Flower Master,*" 8.

16. Coe, *Ikebana,* 22.

17. Lesley Wheeler, "Both Flower and Flower Gardener: Medbh McGuckian's *The Flower Master* and H. D.'s *Sea Garden,*" 92.

18. Interview with the author, Queen's University Belfast, May 13, 2005.

19. Sacks, *The English Elegy,* 21.

20. Wheeler, "Medbh McGuckian's *The Flower Master,*" 7.

21. Wheeler, "Medbh McGuckian's *The Flower Master,*" 8.

22. Coe, *Ikebana,* 129.

23. Coe, *Ikebana,* 22–23.

24. Haberstroh, *Women Creating Women,* 129.

25. Toliver, *Pastoral Forms and Attitudes,* 142.

26. Norton, *The Homosexual Pastoral Tradition,* 1.

27. Wheeler, "Both Flower and Flower Gardener," 494–519.

28. Raymond Williams, *The Country and the City,* 251.

29. Personal letter to McCracken, February 11, 2001.

30. Wheeler, "Medbh McGuckian's *The Flower Master,*" 2.

31. Wheeler, "Medbh McGuckian's *The Flower Master,*" 3.

32. Interview with the author, Queen's University Belfast, May 13, 2005.

33. Thomas Docherty, "Initiations, Tempers, Seductions: Postmodern McGuckian," 193.

34. Sarah Fulford, *Gendered Spaces in Contemporary Irish Poetry,* 183.

35. Interview with Sean Fox, agricultural economics, Kansas State University, August 27, 2005.

36. Patrick Goodenough, "Deadly Australian Wildfires Fuel Debate about Controlled Burning.," CNS News. http://www.cnsnews.com/node/43320.

37. "St. Therese," http://littleflowerpilgrimages.com/sttherese.htm.

38. "Beatrix Potter," http://www.peterrabbit.co.uk/beatrixpotter/beatrixpotter3.cfm?territory=1&country=1.

39. Docherty, "Initiations, Tempers, Seductions," 198.

40. Garrard, *Ecocritism,* 26.

41. Haberstroh, *Women Creating Women,* 132.

42. Eileen Cahill, "Because I Never Garden: Medbh McGuckian's Solitary Way," 265.

43. Gifford, *Pastoral,* 28.

44. "Beatrix Potter," http://www.peterrabbit.co.uk/beatrixpotter/beatrixpotter3.cfm?territory=1&country=1.

45. "Five Marks of the Decay of the Gods," http://www.dharmabliss.org/Five%20 Marks%20of%20Decay.htm.

46. Gail Tsukiyama, *The Street of a Thousand Blossoms*, 98.

47. Celeste Heiter, "For the Love of Lychees: An Interview with Lychee Growers Bill Mee and Krystal Folino," http://www.thingsasian.com/goto_article/.

48. Docherty, "Initiations, Tempers, Seductions," 193.

49. "The RIC Good Wood Guide," http://www.rainforestinfo.org.au/good_wood/ ntox_trs.htm.

50. "Impudence," http://www2.dicom.se/fuchsias/impudence.html.

51. David Jordan, "Globalisation and Bird's Nest Soup."

52. "Rippleseed Plantain Herb," http://www.sinoherbking.com/sk3/46084.html.

53. Art Stone, "Chrysanthemum Stone," http://www.hgms.org/Articles/Chrysan-themumStone.html.

54. Richard Kerridge, ed., *Writing the Environment: Ecocriticism and Literature*, 7.

55. William Dwight Whitney and Benjamin Eli Smith, *The Century Dictionary and Cyclopedia: A Work of Universal Reference in All Departments of Knowledge with a New Atlas of the World*, 6862.

56. Docherty, "Initiations, Tempers, Seductions," 200.

57. Wheeler, "Medbh McGuckian's *The Flower Master*," 6–7.

58. "Orchids," http://www.orchids.co.in/generic-names/vernacular-nomenclature. shtm.

59. "Orchids," http://www.orchids.co.in/generic-names/vernacular-nomenclature. shtm.

60. Evans, *Irish Folk Ways*, 103.

61. Evans, *Irish Folk Ways*, 141–42.

62. Ross, *Pagan Celtic Britain*, 436–37.

63. David Ross, "English Gardens."

64. Veena Talwar Oldenburg, *Dowry Murder: The Imperial Origins of a Cultural Crime*, vii.

65. "Orangery," http://en.wikipedia.org/wiki/Orangery.

66. Micha Lindemans, "Juno," http://www.pantheon.org/articles/j/juno.html.

67. "Dill," http://botanical.com/botanical/mgmh/d/dill—13.html.

68. "Artemisia Abrotanum," http://www.ibiblio.org/pfaf/cgiin/arr_html?Artemisi a+abrotanum&CAN'LATIND.

69. MacKillop, *Dictionary of Celtic Mythology*, 318.

70. Patterson, *Pastoral and Ideology*, 49.

71. Patterson, *Pastoral and Ideology*, 53.

72. Wills, *Improprieties*, 71.

73. Fulford, *Gendered Spaces in Contemporary Irish Poetry*, 177.

74. Fulford, *Gendered Spaces in Contemporary Irish Poetry*, 175.

75. Fulford, *Gendered Spaces in Contemporary Irish Poetry*, 175.

76. Fulford, *Gendered Spaces in Contemporary Irish Poetry*, 176.

77. Kerridge, *Writing the Environment*, 6.

78. Garrard, *Ecocritism*, 23.

79. Molly Bendall, "Flower Logic: The Poems of Medbh McGuckian," 368.

80. Fulford, *Gendered Spaces in Contemporary Irish Poetry*, 187.

81. Love, *"Et in Arcadia,"* 231.

CHAPTER 6

"When Ireland Was Still under a Spell": Miraculous Transformations in the Poetry of Nuala Ní Dhomhnaill

1. Laura O'Connor, "Medbh McGuckian, and Nuala Ní Dhomhnaill, 'Comhra,'" 599.

2. Declan Kiberd, *Inventing Ireland*, 339.

3. Stephen Slemon, "Magic Realism as Postcolonial Discourse," 408.

4. Gifford, *Pastoral*, 106.

5. Gillian Rose, *Feminism and Geography: The Limits of Geographical Knowledge*, 116.

6. Rose, *Feminism and Geography*, 117.

7. Merchant, *The Death of Nature*, 204.

8. John Wilson Foster, *Nature in Ireland: A Scientific and Cultural History*, 31–32.

9. Foster, *Nature in Ireland*, 32.

10. Heaney, *Preoccupations*, 132.

11. Haberstroh, *Women Creating Women*, 133.

12. Heaney, *Preoccupations*, 131–32.

13. Yeager, ed., *The Geography of Identity*, 432.

14. Kenneth Jackson, *Studies in Early Celtic Nature Poetry*, 80.

15. Sean O'Sullivan, ed., trans., *Folktales of Ireland*, xv.

16. O'Sullivan, *Folktales of Ireland*, v.

17. MacKillop, *Dictionary of Celtic Mythology*, 92.

18. Robert Lloyd Praeger, *The Way That I Went*, 364–66.

19. Simon O'Faolain, "The Archaeology of the Dingle Peninsula," http://www.iol.ie/~rainbow/archaeology.html.

20. P. N. Wyse Jackson, "The Geology of Kerry," 32.

21. Nuala Ní Dhomhnaill, *Selected Poems: Rogha Dánta*, 85.

22. Glob, *The Bog People*, 74–75.

23. Glob, *The Bog People*, 113–19.

24. Merchant, *The Death of Nature*, 193.

25. O'Connor, "Medbh McGuckian," 604.

26. Deborah McWilliams Consalvo, "Adaptations and Transformations: An Interview with Nuala Ní Dhomhnaill," 318.

27. Deborah McWilliams Consalvo, "The Lingual Ideal in the Poetry of Nuala Ní Dhomhnaill," 158.

28. O'Faolain, "The Archaeology of the Dingle Peninsula."

29. MacKillop, *Dictionary of Celtic Mythology*, 317.

30. MacKillop, *Dictionary of Celtic Mythology*, 224.

31. Ross, *Pagan Celtic Britain*, 338.

32. Ross, *Pagan Celtic Britain*, 313–16.

33. Ross, *Pagan Celtic Britain*, 341.

34. Ross, *Pagan Celtic Britain*, 257.

35. MacKillop, *Dictionary of Celtic Mythology*, 317.

36. Ross, *Pagan Celtic Britain*, 351.

37. Ross, *Pagan Celtic Britain*, 321.

38. Rosalind Clark, *The Great Queens: Irish Goddesses from the Morrigan to Cathleen ni Houlihan*, 23–24.

39. Cleary, *Outrageous Fortune*, 183.

40. M. Louise Cannon, "The Extraordinary within the Ordinary: The Poetry of Eavan Boland and Nuala Ní Dhomhnaill," 34.

41. Gerry Smith, *Space and the Irish Cultural Imagination,* 117.

42. Rebecca Wilson, *Sleeping with Monsters: Conversations with Scottish and Irish Women Poets,* 154.

43. Consalvo, "The Lingual Ideal," 160.

44. Consalvo, "The Lingual Ideal," 148.

45. Nuala Ní Dhomhnaill, *Pharaoh's Daughter.*

46. Slemon, "Magic Realism as Postcolonial Discourse," 411.

47. Consalvo, "The Lingual Ideal," 148.

48. O'Connor, "Medbh McGuckian," 602.

49. MacKillop, *Dictionary of Celtic Mythology,* 317.

50. Ross, *Pagan Celtic Britain,* 55.

51. Bo Almqvist, "Of Mermaids and Marriages: Seamus Heaney's 'Maighdean Mara' and Nuala Ní Dhomhnaill's 'An Mhaighdean Mhara,'" 1.

52. Nuala Ní Dhomhnaill, "The Merfolk and the Written Word," 441–42.

53. Ní Dhomhnaill, *Selected Poems,* 53.

54. Lucy McDiarmid, "Heaney and the Politics of the Classroom," 119.

55. Ní Dhomhnaill, "The Merfolk and the Written Word," 441–42.

56. Clark, *The Great Queens,* 24.

57. MacKillop, *Dictionary of Celtic Mythology,* 30.

58. Nuala Ní Dhomhnaill, *The Astrakhan Cloak,* 71.

59. Nuala Ní Dhomhnaill, *The Water Horse,* 117.

60. Nuala Ní Dhomhnaill, "Mis and Dubh Ruis: A Parable of Psychic Transformation," 200.

61. Ní Dhomhnaill, *Selected Poems,* 9.

62. According to Ireland Forest Information and Data, deforestation ended at the close of the 1990s, since which there has been a gradual gain in forest cover.

63. Merchant, *The Death of Nature,* 148.

64. Merchant, *The Death of Nature,* 9.

65. Ní Dhomhnaill, *The Astrakhan Cloak.*

CONCLUSION

The Future of Pastoral

1. Love, "Revaluing Nature," 231–35.

2. Garrard, *Ecocritism,* 182.

3. Gifford, *Pastoral,* 171.

4. Eamonn Wall, *A Tour of Your Country,* 21.

5. Gifford, *Pastoral,* 172.

6. Kerridge, *Writing the Environment,* 5.

7. Harper, "An Interview with Michael Longley," 62.

8. Love, ed., *Practical Ecocriticism,* 26.

9. Anne Ross, *Pagan Celtic Britain,* 51–56.

10. Alex Preminger and T.V.F. Brogan, eds., "Muse," 802.

11. George P. Landow, "The Smitten Rock," in *Victorian Types, Victorian Shadows; Biblical Typology in Victorian Literature, Art, and Thought.*

12. Kuno Meyer, *Selections from Ancient Irish Poetry,* 47.

13. Landow, "The Smitten Rock."

14. MacKillop, *Dictionary of Celtic Mythology,* 52, 239–40.

15. Bridget Haggerty, "The Holy Wells of Ireland," accessed July 12, 2011, http://www.irishcultureandcustoms.com/alandmks/holywells.html·

16. MacKillop, *Dictionary of Celtic Mythology,* 235.

17. Anne Ross, *Pagan Celtic Britain,* 55.

18. Nicholson, "The Holy Wells of Ireland."

19. "Viola D'Amore," Hidden World of the Viola D'Amore, accessed July 12, 2011, http://www.violadamore.com/avd.asp.

20. Bridget Haggerty, "The Holy Wells of Ancient Ireland," accessed July 12, 2011, http://www.irishcultureandcustoms.com/ALandmks/HolyWells.html.

21. Michael Bennett and David W. Teague, eds., *The Nature of Cities: Ecocriticism and Urban Environments.*

22. Grene, "Black Pastoral," 68.

23. Thomas Kilroy, "A Generation of Playwrights," 141.

24. Eamonn Jordan, "Pastoral Exhibits: Narrating Authenticities in Conor McPherson's *The Weir,*" 351.

25. Martin McLoone, *Irish Film: The Emergence of a Contemporary Cinema,* 18.

26. McLoone, *Irish Film,* 20.

27. Grene, "Black Pastoral," 68.

28. McLoone, *Irish Film,* 32.

29. Martin McLoone, "The Abused Child of History: Neil Jordan's *The Butcher Boy,*" 34.

30. Patrick McCabe, *The Butcher Boy,* 116.

31. McCabe, *The Butcher Boy,* 184.

32. John B. Breslin, "Pastoral," 123.

BIBLIOGRAPHY

Adams, Robert Don. "Elizabeth Bishop and the Pastoral World." In *Worcester, Massachusetts: Essays on Elizabeth Bishop, from the 1997 Elizabeth Bishop Conference at WPI.* Edited by Laura Jehn Menides and Angela G. Dorenkamp. New York: Peter Lang, 1999.

Adorno, Theodor W. "Lyric Poetry and Society." In *Critical Theory and Society.* Edited by Stephen Eric Bronner and Douglas Mackay Kellner. New York: Routledge, 1989.

Allen-Randolph, Jody. "Private Worlds, Public Realities: Eavan Boland's Poetry 1967–1990." *Irish University Review* 23, no. 1 (Spring/Summer 1993): 5–22.

Allison, Jonathan. "Patrick Kavanagh and the Antipastoral." In *Cambridge Companion to Contemporary Irish Poetry.* Ed. Matthew Campbell. Cambridge: Cambridge University Press, 2003. http://cco.cambridge.org/extract?id=ccol0521813018_CCOL0521813018A004.

Almqvist, Bo. "Of Mermaids and Marriages: Seamus Heaney's 'Maighdean Mhara' and Nuala Ní Dhomhnaill's 'An Mhaighdean Mhara.'" *Bealoideas: The Journal of the Folklore of Ireland Society* 58 (1990): 1–74.

Alpers, Paul. *What Is Pastoral?* Chicago: University of Chicago Press, 1997.

"Artemisia Abrotanum." http://www.ibiblio.org/pfaf/cgiin/arr_html?Artemisia+abrotanum&CAN=LATIND.

Atwood, Margaret. *Second Words: Selected Critical Prose.* Toronto: Anansi, 1982.

Auge, Andrew J. "Fracture and Wound: Eavan Boland's Poetry of Nationality." *New Hibernia Review* 8, no. 2 (Summer 2004): 121–41.

Barrell, John, and John Bull. *The Penguin Book of English Pastoral Verse.* Harmondsworth, U.K.: Penguin, 1982.

Barry, John. Forward to Liam Leonard, *The Environmental Movement in Ireland*, vi. New York: Springer, 2007.

Bate, Jonathan. *The Song of the Earth*. Cambridge: Harvard, 2002.

"Beatrix Potter." http://www.peterrabbit.co.uk/beatrixpotter/beatrixpotter3.cfm?territory=1&country=1.

Bendall, Molly. "Flower Logic: The Poems of Medbh McGuckian." *Antioch Review* 48, no. 3 (Summer 1990): 367–71.

Bennett, Michael, and David W. Teague, eds. *The Nature of Cities: Ecocriticism and Urban Environments*. Tucson: University of Arizona Press, 1999.

Bishop, Elizabeth. *The Complete Poems 1927–1979*. New York: Noonday Press, 1979.

Boland, Eavan. *In a Time of Violence*. New York: Norton, 1994.

———. *The Lost Land: Poems*. New York: Norton, 1998.

———. *An Origin like Water: Collected Poems 1967–1987*. New York: Norton, 1996.

———. *Outside History*. New York: Norton, 1990.

———. "An Un-Romantic American." *Parnassus: Poetry in Review* 14, no. 2 (1988): 73–92.

Bradley, Anthony G. *Contemporary Irish Poetry*. Berkeley: University of California Press, 1988.

———. "Pastoral in Modern Irish Poetry." *Concerning Poetry* 14, no. 2 (1981): 79–96.

Brearton, Fran. *The Great War in Irish Poetry*. Oxford: Oxford University Press, 2000.

———. "Walking Forwards into the Past: An Interview with Michael Longley." *Irish Studies Review* 18 (Spring 1997): 35–39.

Breslin, John B. "Pastoral." Review of *By the Lake*. *Commonweal* (May 17, 2002): 123.

Broom, Sarah. "Learning about Dying: Mutability and the Classics in the Poetry of Michael Longley." *New Hibernia Review* 6, no. 1 (2002): 94–112.

Brown, Terence. *Ireland: A Social and Cultural History*. London: Fontana, 1985.

———. "John Montague: Circling to Return." In *Northern Voices: Poets from Ulster*, 149–70. Dublin: Gill and Macmillan, 1975.

Buell, Lawrence. *The Environmental Imagination: Thoreau, Nature Writing, and the Formation of American Culture*. Cambridge, Mass.: Belknap Press, 1995.

Burris, Sidney. *The Poetry of Resistance: Seamus Heaney and the Pastoral Tradition*. Athens: Ohio University Press, 1990.

Burton, Margaret. Unpublished paper. "A Consideration of Heaney's *The Strand at Lough Beg*." 2005.

Buttel, Robert. *Seamus Heaney*. Lewisburg: Bucknell University Press, 1975.

Buxton, Rachel. *Robert Frost and Northern Irish Poetry.* Oxford: Clarendon Press, 2004.

Cahill, Eileen. "Because I Never Garden: Medbh McGuckian's Solitary Way." *Irish University Review* 24, no. 2 (Autumn/Winter 1994): 264–71.

Caldwell, Christopher. "Man Out of Time," *Slate Magazine,* Oct. 17, 2003, http://slate.msn.com/id/2089950/.

Cannon, M. Louise. "The Extraordinary within the Ordinary: The Poetry of Eavan Boland and Nuala Ní Dhomhnaill." *South Atlantic Review* 60, no. 2 (May 1995): 31–46.

Chaudhuri, Sukanta. *Renaissance Pastoral and Its English Developments.* Oxford: Clarendon Press, 1989.

"A Chronology of Key Events in Irish History 1800 to 1967." Cain Web Service. http://cain.ulst.ac.uk/othelem/chron/ch1800–1967.htm.

Clare, John. *"I Am": The Selected Poetry of John Clare.* Ed. Jonathan Bate. New York: Farrar, Straus, and Giroux, 2003.

Clark, Rosalind. *The Great Queens: Irish Goddesses from the Morrigan to Cathleen ni Houlihan.* Gerrards Cross, U.K.: Colin Smythe, 1991.

Cleary, Joe. *Outrageous Fortune: Capital and Culture in Modern Ireland.* Notre Dame: Field Day Publications, 2007.

Coe, Stella. *Ikebana: A Practical and Philosophical Guide to Japanese Flower Arrangement.* Woodstock, N.Y.: Overlook Press, 1984.

Connolly, S. J. *The Oxford Companion to Irish History.* Oxford: Oxford University Press, 1998.

Consalvo, Deborah McWilliams. "Adaptations and Transformations: An Interview with Nuala Ni Dhomhnaill." *Studies: An Irish Quarterly Review* 83, no. 331 (Autumn 1994): 313–20.

———. "The Lingual Ideal in the Poetry of Nuala Ní Dhomhnaill." *Eire-Ireland* 30, no. 2 (1995): 148–61.

Corbet, G. B. and Stephen Harris. *Handbook of British Mammals.* Oxford: Blackwell, Science, 1991.

Corcoran, Neil. "My Botanical Studies: The Poetry of Natural History in Michael Longley." In *The Poetry of Michael Longley.* Ed. Alan J. Peacock and Kathleen Devine. Gerrards Cross, U.K.: Colin Smythe, 2001.

Corcoran, Neil, ed. *The Chosen Ground: Essays on Contemporary Poetry of Northern Ireland.* Chester Springs, Pa.: Dufour Editions, 1991.

Davis, Walter R., and Richard A. Lanham. *A Map of Arcadia: Sidney's Romance in Its Tradition.* New Haven: Yale University Press, 1965.

Diehl, Joanne Feit. *Women Poets and the American Sublime.* Bloomington: Indiana University Press, 1990.

"Dill." http://botanical.com/botanical/mgmh/d/dill—13.html.

Docherty, Thomas. "Ana-: or Postmodernism, Landscape." In *Seamus Heaney.* Ed. Michael Allen. New York: St. Martin's, 1997.

——. "Initiations, Tempers, Seductions: Postmodern McGuckian." In *The Chosen Ground: Essays on the Contemporary Poetry of Northern Ireland*. Ed. Neil Corcoran, 191–210. Chester Springs, Pa.: Dufour Editions, 1991.

Donoghue, Denis. *We Irish: Essays on Irish Literature and Society*. New York: Knopf, 1986.

Eagleton, Terry. *Heathcliff and the Great Hunger: Studies in Irish Culture*. New York: Verso, 1995.

Eckersley, Robyn. *Environmentalism and Political Theory: Toward an Ecocentric Approach*. Albany: SUNY Press, 1992.

Empson, William. *Some Versions of Pastoral*. Norfolk, Conn.: New Directions, 1950.

Evans, E. Estyn. *Irish Folk Ways*. New York: Devin-Adair, 1957.

Everndon, Neil. *The Social Creation of Nature*. Baltimore: Johns Hopkins University Press, 1992.

Fallon, Peter, trans. *The Georgics of Virgil*. Loughcrew: Gallery Press, 2004.

Feder, Helena. "Ecocritism, New Historicism, and Romantic Apostrophe." In *The Greening of Literary Scholarship*. Ed. Steven Rosendale. Iowa City: Iowa University Press, 2002.

Ferguson, Margaret, Mary Jo Salter, and Jon Stallworthy, eds. *The Norton Anthology of Poetry*, 4th ed. New York: W. W. Norton, 1996.

Ferry, David. *The Odes of Horace*. Oxford: Clarendon Press, 1998.

"Five Marks of the Decay of the Gods." Accessed July 13, 2011. http://www.dharmabliss.org/Five%20Marks%20of%20Decay.htm.

Flanagan, Deirdre, and Laurence Flanagan. *Irish Place Names*. Dublin: Gill and Macmillan, 1994.

Fontenrose, Joseph. *The Delphic Oracle: Its Responses and Operations, with a Catalogue of Responses*. Berkeley: University of California Press, 1978.

Foster, John Wilson. "The Landscape of Planter and Gael in the Poetry of John Montague." *Canadian Journal of Irish Studies* 1 (November 1975): 17–33.

——. *Nature in Ireland: A Scientific and Cultural History*. Montreal: McGill, 1997.

Foster, R. F. *Modern Ireland 1600–1972*. London: Allen Lane; New York: Viking/Penguin, 1998.

Frawley, Oona. *Irish Pastoral: Nostalgia and Twentieth-Century Irish Literature*. Dublin: Irish Academic Press, 2005.

Friedman, Donald M. *Marvell's Pastoral Art*. London: Routledge and Kegan Paul, 1970.

Frost, Robert. Introduction to *King Jasper*, by E. A. Robinson. New York: Modern Library, 1935.

Fulford, Sarah. *Gendered Spaces in Contemporary Irish Poetry*. Bern: Lang, 2002.

Gardiner, David. "Unsentimental Prophecy: John Montague and *The Dolmen Miscellany* (1962)." In *Well Dreams: Essays on John Montague*. Ed. Thomas Dillon Redshaw, 63–80. Omaha: Creighton University Press, 2004.

Garrard, Greg. *Ecocriticism*. London: Routledge, 2004.

Gibbons, Luke. *The Quiet Man*. Cork: Cork University Press, 2002.

Gifford, Terry. *Green Voices: Understanding Contemporary Nature Poetry*. Manchester: Manchester University Press, 1995.

———. *Pastoral*. London: Routledge, 1999.

Glob, P. V. *The Bog People: Iron-Age Man Preserved*. New York: Faber and Faber, 1969.

Gonzales, Alexander G., ed. *Contemporary Irish Women Poets: Some Male Perspectives*. Westport, Conn.: Greenwood Press, 1999.

Goodenough, Patrick. "Deadly Australian Wildfires Fuel Debate about Controlled Burning." CNS News. http://www.cnsnews.com/node/43320.

Gray, Cecile. "Mebh McGuckian: Imagery Wrought to Its Uttermost." In *Learning the Trade: Essays on W. B. Yeats and Contemporary Poetry*. Ed. Deborah Fleming, 113–33. West Cornwall, Conn.: Locust Hill Press, 1993.

Greg, W. W. *Pastoral Poetry and Pastoral Drama*. London: A. H. Bullen, 1906.

Grene, Nicholas. "Black Pastoral: 1990s Images of Ireland." *Litteraria Pragensia* 10, no. 20 (2000): 67–75.

Haberstroh, Patricia. *Women Creating Women: Contemporary Irish Women Poets*. Syracuse: Syracuse University Press, 1996.

Haggerty, Bridget. "The Holy Wells of Ancient Ireland." Irish Culture and Customs. http://www.irishcultureandcustoms.com/ALandmks/HolyWells.html.

Hall, Donald. "The Nation of Poets." *Parnassus* 6 (Fall-Winter 1977): 145–60.

Harper, Margaret Mills. "An Interview with Michael Longley." *Five Points: A Journal of Literature and Art* 8, no. 3 (2004): 56–71.

Hart, Henry. *Seamus Heaney: Poet of Contrary Progressions*. Syracuse: Syracuse University Press, 1992.

Haughton, Hugh. "Place and Displacement in Derek Mahon." In *The Chosen Ground: Essays on Contemporary Poetry of Northern Ireland*. Ed. Neil Corcoran. Chester Springs, Pa.: Dufour Editions, 1991.

Heaney, Seamus. *Electric Light*. New York: Farrar, Straus, and Giroux, 2001.

———. *Finders Keepers: Selected Prose, 1971–2001*. New York: Farrar, Straus, and Giroux, 2002.

———. "The Placeless Heaven: Another Look at Kavanagh." *The Government of the Tongue: Selected Prose, 1978–1987*. New York: Farrar, Straus, and Giroux, 1990.

———. *Preoccupations: Selected Prose, 1968–1978*. London: Faber and Faber, 1980.

———. *Seeing Things*. London: Faber and Faber, 1991.

———. "The Sense of Place." In his *Preoccupations: Selected Prose 1968–1978*, 131–49. London: Faber and Faber, 1980.

———. *Sweeney Astray: A Version from the Irish*. New York: Noonday Press, 1988.

———. "The Trade of an Irish Poet." *Guardian*, May 25, 1972, 17.

Heiter, Celeste. "For the Love of Lychees: An Interview with Lychee Growers Bill Mee and Krystal Folino." Things Asian. Accessed July 13, 2011. http://www.thingsasian.com/stories-photos/2662;jsessionid=EA85BD36FBE33 293D831C3C5120531B2.

Hoffman, Tyler. *Robert Frost and the Politics of Poetry*. Hanover, N.H.: University Press of New England, 2001.

"Homeric Hymns." Online Medieval and Classical Library. Accessed July 13, 2011. http://sunsite.berkeley.edu/OMACL/Hesiod/hymns.html.

"Impudence." Accessed July 13, 2011. http://www.aplantshome.com/encyclopedia/pda_c3df.html.

"Ireland." CIA World Fact Book. Accessed July 13, 2011. https://www.cia.gov/library/publications/the-world-factbook/geos/ei.html.

Jackson, Kenneth. *Studies in Early Celtic Nature Poetry*. Cambridge: Cambridge University Press, 1935.

John, Brian. "The Achievement of Michael Longley's *The Ghost Orchid*." *Irish University Review* 27, no. 1 (Spring 1997): 139–51.

Jordan, David. "Globalisation and Bird's Nest Soup." *Internation Development Planning Review* 26, no. 1 (2004): http://www.jordanresearch.co.uk/pubs.html.

Jordan, Eamonn. "Pastoral Exhibits: Narrating Authenticities in Conor McPherson's *The Weir*," *Irish University Review* 34, no. 2 (Autumn-Winter 2004): 351.

Kearney, Timothy. "Beyond the Planter and the Gael: An Interview with John Hewitt and John Montague." *Crane Bag* 4, no. 2 (1980): 85–92.

Kennedy-Andrews, Elmer. "Conflict, Violence, and the Fundamental Interrelatedness of All Things." In *The Poetry of Michael Longley*. Ed. Alan J. Peacock and Kathleen Devine. Gerrards Cross, Buckinghamshire: Colin Smythe, 2001.

Kenner, Hugh. *The Pound Era*. Berkeley: University of California Press, 1971.

Kermode, Frank. *English Pastoral Poetry, from the Beginnings to Marvell*. New York: Norton Library, 1972.

Kerridge, Richard, ed. Introduction to *Writing the Environment: Ecocriticism and Literature*. London: Zed, 1999.

Kersnowski, Frank. *John Montague*. Lewisburg, Pa.: Bucknell University Press, 1975.

Kiberd, Declan. *Inventing Ireland.* Harvard University Press, 1997.

———. *Irish Classics.* London: Granta, 2000.

Kiely, Benedict. "John Montague: Dancer in a Rough Field." *Hollins Critic* 15 (December 1978): 1–14.

Kilroy, Thomas. "A Generation of Playwrights." *Irish University Review* 22 (Spring-Summer 1992): 141.

Kupillas, Peter. "Bringing It All Back Home: Unity and Meaning in Eavan Boland's Domestic Interior Sequence." In *Contemporary Irish Women Poets: Some Male Perspectives.* Ed. Alexander G. Gonzales. Westport, Conn.: Greenwood Press, 1999.

Landow, George P. "The Smitten Rock." In *Victorian Types, Victorian Shadows: Biblical Typology in Victorian Literature, Art, and Thought.* Boston: Routledge and Kegan Paul, 1980.

Lennon, Joseph. *Irish Orientalism: A Literary and Intellectual History.* Syracuse: Syracuse University Press, 2004.

Lewis, C. Day, trans. *The Georgics of Virgil.* New York: Oxford University Press, 1947.

Lindemans, Micha F. "Juno." Encyclopedia Mythica. Accessed July 13, 2011. http://www.pantheon.org/articles/j/juno.html.

Ling, Ruth. "The Double Design of Michael Longley's Recent Elegies *The Ghost Orchid* and *Broken Dishes.*" *Irish Studies Review* 10, no. 1 (2002): 39–50.

———. "The Weather in Japan: Tact and Tension in Michael Longley's New Elegies." *Irish University Review: A Journal of Irish Studies* 32, no. 2 (Autumn-Winter 2002): 286–302.

Longley, Michael. *The Ghost Orchid.* Winston-Salem, N.C.: Wake Forest University Press, 1996.

———. "Interview: Michael Longley and Jody Allen-Randolph." *Colby Quarterly* 39, no. 3 (September 2003): 295–303.

———. *Tuppenny Stung: Autobiographical Chapters.* Belfast: Lagan Press, 1994.

Love, Glen A. "*Et in Arcadia Ego:* Pastoral Meets Ecocritism." In *Practical Ecocriticism: Literature, Biology, and the Environment.* Charlottesville: University of Virginia Press, 2003.

———. "Revaluing Nature: Toward an Ecological Criticism." In *The Ecocritical Reader: Landmarks in Literary Ecology.* Ed. Cheryll Glotfelty and Harold Fromm. Athens: University of Georgia Press, 1996.

Love, Glen, ed. *Practical Ecocriticism: Literature, Biology, and the Environment.* Charlottesville: University of Virginia Press, 2003.

Lynen, John F. *The Pastoral Art of Robert Frost.* New Haven: Yale University Press, 1960.

Lyon, John. "Michael Longley's Lists." *English* 45, no. 183 (1996): 228–46.

MacKillop, James. *Dictionary of Celtic Mythology*. Oxford: Oxford University Press, 1998.

Mahon, Derek. "Poetry in Northern Ireland." *Twentieth-Century Studies* 4 (November 1970): 89–93.

Marinelli, Peter. *Pastoral*. New York: Routledge, 1999.

Martin, B. K. "Medieval Irish Nature Poetry." *Parergon* 21 (1978): 19–32.

Martindale, Charles. "Green Politics: The Eclogues." In *The Cambridge Companion to Virgil*. Ed. Charles Martindale. Cambridge: Cambridge University Press, 1997.

Marx, Leo. *The Machine in the Garden*. New York: Oxford University Press, 1964, 2000.

McCabe, Patrick. *The Butcher Boy*. London: Picador, 1992.

McCann, Colum. *Ballygawley in the Twentieth Century*. Ballygawley: Ballygawley Local Hisory Group, 2000.

McDiarmid, Lucy. "Heaney and the Politics of the Classroom." In *Critical Essays on Seamus Heaney*. Ed. Robert F. Garratt. New York: G. K. Hall, 1995.

McDonald, Peter. "Lapsed Classics: Homer, Ovid, and Michael Longley's Poetry." In *The Poetry of Michael Longley*. Ed. Alan J. Peacock and Kathleen Devine. Gerrards Cross, Buckinghamshire: Colin Smythe, 2001.

——. "Michael Longley's Homes." In *The Chosen Ground*. Ed. Neil Corcoran, 65–81. Bridgend, Wales: Seren Books; Chester Springs, Pa.: Dufour, 1992.

——. *Mistaken Identities: Poetry and Northern Ireland*. Oxford: Clarendon Press, 1997.

McLoone, Martin. "The Abused Child of History: Neil Jordan's *The Butcher Boy*." *Cineaste*, September 1998, 32–36.

——. *Irish Film: The Emergence of a Contemporary Cinema*. London: British Film Institute, 2000.

Merchant, Carolyn. *The Death of Nature: Women, Ecology, and the Scientific Revolution*. New York: Harper and Row, 1980.

Meyer, Kuno, ed. *The Voyage of Bran*. London: David Nutt, 1895.

——. *Selections from Ancient Irish Poetry*. London: Constable, 1911.

Miles, Josephine. *Pathetic Fallacy in the Nineteenth Century: A Study of a Changing Relation between Object and Emotion*. London: Octagon, 1965.

"Ireland Forest Information and Data." Mongabay.com. Accessed July 13, 2011. http://rainforests.mongabay.com/deforestation/2000/Ireland.htm#18.

Montague, John. *Collected Poems*. Princeton: Princeton University Press, 1993.

——. *The Figure in the Cave and Other Essays*. Ed. Antoinette Quinn. Syracuse: Syracuse University Press, 1989.

——. "Global Regionalism: Interview with John Montague." Interviewed by Adrian Frazier. *Literary Review* 22 (Winter 1979): 153–74.

——. "An Interview with John Montague: Deaths in the Summer." By Stephen Arkin. *New England Review and Bread Loaf Quarterly* 5 (Autumn-Winter 1982): 214–41.

——. "Jawseyes." *The Crane Bag* 2 (1978): 159–60.

Morrison, Blake. *Seamus Heaney.* London: Methuen, 1982.

Ní Dhomhnaill, Nuala. *The Astrakhan Cloak.* Trans. Paul Muldoon. Winston-Salem, NC: Wake Forest University Press, 1993.

——. "The Merfolk and the Written Word." *Southern Review* 31 (Summer 1995): 441–42.

——. "Mis and Dubh Ruis: A Parable of Psychic Transformation." In *Irish Writers and Religion.* Edited by Robert Welch. Gerrards Cross, U.K.: Rowman and Littlefield, 1992.

——. *Pharaoh's Daughter.* Winston-Salem, NC: Wake Forest University Press, 1990.

——. Poems. *Southern Review* 31, no. 3 (July 1995): 432–43.

——. *Selected Poems: Rogha Dánta.* Trans. Michael Hartnett. Dublin: New Island Books, 1993.

——. *The Water Horse.* Winston-Salem, NC: Wake Forest University Press, 2000.

——. "Why I Choose to Write in Irish, the Corpse That Sits Up and Talks Back." In *Representing Ireland: Gender, Class, Nationality.* Ed. Susan Shaw Sailer. Gainesville: University Press of Florida, 1997.

Nicholson, Francine. "The Holy Wells of Ireland." Celtic Resource Center. http://www.univie.ac.at/keltologie/CRC/CRCWells.html.

Norton, Rictor. *The Homosexual Pastoral Tradition.* Accessed February 18, 2005. http://www.infopt.demon.co.uk/pastor07.htm.

O'Connor, Laura. "Medbh McGuckian, and Nuala Ní Dhomhnaill, 'Comhra.'" *Southern Review* 31, no. 3 (Summer 1995): 581–614.

Ó Dochartaigh, Liam. "*Ceol na mBréag:* Gaelic Themes in *The Rough Field.*" In *Well Dreams: Essays on John Montague* Edited by Thomas Dillon Redshaw. Omaha: Creighton University Press, 2004.

O'Driscoll, Dennis. "An Interview with John Montague." *Irish University Review* 19, no. 1 (Spring 1989): 58–72.

O'Faolain, Simon. "The Archaeology of the Dingle Peninsula." Retrieved September 15, 2003. http://www.iol.ie/~rainbow/archaeology.html.

Ó hAllmhuráin, Gearóid. "Dancing on the Hobs of Hell: Rural Communities in Clare and the Dance Halls Act of 1935." *New Hibernia Review* 9, no. 4 (2005): 918.

O'Hearn, Denis. *Inside the Celtic Tiger: The Irish Economy and the Asian Model.* London: Pluto, 1998.

O'Loughlin, Michael J. K. "Woods Worthy of a Consul: Pastoral and the Sense of History." *Literary Studies: Essays in Memory of Francis A. Drumm.*

Ed. John H. Dorenkamp. Worcester, Mass.: College of the Holy Cross, 1973.

O'Sullivan, Sean, ed., trans. *Folktales of Ireland*. Chicago: University of Chicago Press, 1966.

Oldenburg, Veena Talwar. *Dowry Murder: The Imperial Origins of a Cultural Crime*. Oxford: Oxford, 2002.

"Orangery." http://en.wikipedia.org/wiki/Orangery.

"Orchids." Accessed July 7, 2007. http://www.orchids.co.in/genericnames/vernacularnomenclature.shtm.

Orenstein, Gloria. "The Greening of Gaia: Ecofeminist Artists Revisit the Garden." In *Reweaving the World: The Emergence of Ecofeminism*. San Francisco: Sierra Club Books, 1990.

Ostriker, Alicia. *Stealing the Language: The Emergence of Women's Poetry in America*. Boston: Beacon Press, 1986.

Paden, William D. "Pastourelle." In *The New Princeton Encyclopedia of Poetry and Poetics*. Ed. Alex Preminger and T.V.F. Brogan. Princeton: Princeton University Press, 1993.

Patterson, Annabel. *Pastoral and Ideology*. Berkeley: University of California Press, 1987.

Peacock, Alan J. "Prolegomena to Michael Longley's Peace Poem." *Eire-Ireland* 23 (Spring 1988): 60–74.

Peacock, Alan J., and Kathleen Devine. *The Poetry of Michael Longley*. Gerrards Cross, Buckinghamshire: Colin Smythe, 2001.

Poggioli, Renato. *The Oaten Flute: Essays on Pastoral Poetry and the Pastoral Ideal*. Cambridge, Mass.: Harvard, 1975.

Praeger, Robert Lloyd. *The Way That I Went*. London: Collins, 1937.

Preminger, Alex, and T.V.F. Brogan. "Muse." In *The New Princeton Encyclopedia of Poetry and Poetics*. Ed. Alex Preminger and T.V.F. Brogan. Princeton: Princeton University Press, 1993.

Putnam, Michael C. J. *Virgil's Pastoral Art: Studies in the Eclogues*. Princeton, N.J.: Princeton University Press, 1970.

Puttenham, George. *Arte of English Poesie*. Qtd. in *A Book of English Pastoral Verse*. Edited by Barrell and Bull. New York: Oxford University Press, 1975.

Quinn, Antoinette. "'The Well-Beloved': Montague and the Muse." *Irish University Review: John Montague Issue* (ed. Christopher Murray) 19, no. 1 (Spring 1989): 27–43.

Ramazani, Jahan. *Poetry of Mourning: The Modern Elegy from Hardy to Heaney*. Chicago: University of Chicago Press, 1994.

———. *Yeats and the Poetry of Death*. New Haven, Conn.: Yale University Press, 1990.

Randall, James. "Interview with Seamus Heaney." *Ploughshares* 5 (1979): 173–88.

Redshaw, Thomas Dillon. *Well Dreams: Essays on John Montague*. Omaha: Creighton University Press, 2004.

Revie, Linda. "The Little Red Fox, Emblem of the Irish Peasant in Poems by Yeats, Tynan, and Ní Dhomhnaill." In *Learning the Trade: Essays on W. B. Yeats and Contemporary Poetry*. Ed. Deborah Fleming. West Cornwall, Conn.: Locust Hill Press, 1993.

RIC Good Wood Guide. http://www.rainforestinfo.org.au/good_wood/ntox_trs.htm.

"Rippleseed Plantain Herb." http://www.sinoherbking.com/sk3/46084.html

Room, Adrian. *A Dictionary of Irish Place-Names*. Belfast: Appletree Press, 1986.

Rose, Gillian. *Feminism and Geography: The Limits of Geographical Knowledge*. Minneapolis: University of Minnesota Press, 1993.

Rosenmeyer, Thomas G. *The Green Cabinet: Theocritus and European Pastoral Poetry*. London: Duckworth Publishing, 2004.

Ross, Anne. *Pagan Celtic Britain: Studies in Iconography and Tradition*. London: Routledge and K. Paul; New York: Columbia University Press, 1967.

Ross, David. "English Gardens." Britain Express. http://www.britainexpress.com/History/english-gardens.htm

Rotella, Guy. *Reading and Writing Nature: The Poetry of Robert Frost, Wallace Stevens, Marianne Moore, and Elizabeth Bishop*. Boston: Northeastern University Press, 1991.

Russell, Richard Rankin. "Inscribing Cultural Corridors: Michael Longley's Contribution to Reconciliation in Northern Ireland." *Colby Quarterly* 39, no. 3 (September 2003): 221–40.

Sacks, Peter. *The English Elegy: Studies in the Genre from Spenser to Yeats*. Baltimore: Johns Hopkins University Press, 1987.

"St. Therese." Little Flower Pilgrimages. Accessed July 13, 2011. http://www.littleflowerpilgrimages.com/littleflower-html/st_therese.htm.

Schrank, Bernice. "Brendan Behan's *Borstal Boy* as Ironic Pastoral." *Canadian Journal of Irish Studies* 18, no. 2 (December 1992): 68–74.

Scuchard, Ronald. Introduction to *The Place of Writing*, by Seamus Heaney. Atlanta: Emory University Press, 1989.

Sealy, Douglas. "The Sound of a Wound: An Introduction to the Poetry of John Montague from 1958 to 1988." In *Well Dreams*. Ed. Thomas Dillon Redshaw. Omaha: Creighton University Press, 2004.

Seidl, Mark Gregory. *Elizabeth Bishop and the Subject of Pastoral* 57, no. 8 DAIA (February 1997): 3499–3500.

Shaw, George Bernard. *Seven Plays by George Bernard Shaw*. New York: Dodd, Mead, 1951.

Slemon, Stephen. "Magic Realism as Postcolonial Discourse." In *Magical Realism: Theory, History, Community*. Ed. Louis Parkinson Zamora and Wendy B. Faris. Durham: Duke University Press, 1995.

Smith, Art. "Chrysanthemum Stone." http://www.hgms.org/Articles/ChrysanthemumStone.html.

Smith, Gerry. *Space and the Irish Cultural Imagination*. New York: Palgrave, 2001.

Starbuck, George. "The Work!: A Conversation with Elizabeth Bishop." In *Elizabeth Bishop and Her Art*. Edited by Lloyd Schwartz and Sybil Estess. Ann Arbor: University of Michigan Press, 1983.

Swann, Joseph. "Family Resemblances: Shapes and Figures in Contemporary Irish Poetry." *WTV Wissenschaftlicher Verlag* (ed. A. W. Ward and A. R. Waller) 52 (1994): 29–57.

Taylor, Lawrence J. *Occasions of the Faith: An Anthropology of Irish Catholics*. Dublin: Lilliput Press, 1997.

Toliver, Harold. *Pastoral Forms and Attitudes*. Berkeley: University of California Press, 1984.

Tonkin, Humphrey. *Spenser's Courteous Pastoral: Book 6 of the Faerie Queene*. Oxford: Claredon Press, 1972.

"Trees." Tree Council of Ireland. Accessed July 13, 2011. http://www.tree council.ie/irishtrees/irishtrees.html.

Tsukiyama, Gail. *The Street of a Thousand Blossoms*. New York: Macmillan, 2007.

Tyler, Meg. *A Singing Contest: Conventions of Sound in the Poetry of Seamus Heaney*. London: Routledge, 2005.

Verity, Anthony, trans. *Theocritus: Idylls*. New York: Oxford University Press, 2002.

"Viola D'Amore." http://www.violadamore.com/avd.asp.

Volley, Reb. "Earth Day," http://greensheenblogger.blogspot.com/search/label/Earth%20Day.

Wall, Eamonn. *A Tour of Your Country*. Cliffs of Moher, County Clare: Salmon, 2008.

Watson, G. W. *Irish Identity and the Literary Revival: Synge, Yeats, Joyce, and O'Casey*. Critical Studies in Irish Literature, vol. 4. Washington, D.C.: Catholic University of America Press, 1994.

Wheeler, Lesley. "Both Flower and Flower Gardener: Medbh McGuckian's *The Flower Master* and H.D.'s *Sea Garden*." *Twentieth-Century Literature* 49, no. 4 (Winter 2003): 494–519.

———. "Medbh McGuckian's *The Flower Master* as a Critique of Female Modernism." *How2* 1, no. 3 (February 2000). Accessed July 13, 2011. http://www.asu.edu/pipercwcenter/how2journal/archive/online_archive/v1_3_2000/current/readings/wheeler.html.

Whitney, William Dwight, and Benjamin Eli Smith. *The Century Dictionary and Cyclopedia: A Work of Universal Reference in All Departments of Knowledge with a New Atlas of the World.* New York: Century Co., 1911.

Williams, Raymond. *The Country and the City.* New York: Oxford University Press, 1973.

Wills, Clair. *Improprieties: Politics and Sexuality in Northern Irish Poetry.* Oxford: Clarendon Press, 1993.

Wilmer, Clive. "Michael Longley in Conversation." *PN Review* 20, no. 4 (1994): 42.

Wilson, Rebecca. *Sleeping with Monsters: Conversations with Scottish and Irish Women Poets.* Edinburgh: Polygon, 1990.

Wyse Jackson, P. N. "The Geology of Kerry." Department of Geology. Trinity College, Dublin, Kerry County Museum, Tralee and ENFO, Dublin, 1994.

Yeager, Patricia, ed. *The Geography of Identity.* Ann Arbor: University of Michigan Press, 1996.

Yeats, W. B., ed. *A Treasury of Irish Myth, Legend, and Folklore.* New York: Gramercy, 1988.

Young, David. *The Heart's Forest: A Study of Shakespeare's Pastoral Plays.* New Haven: Yale University Press, 1972.

INDEX